CW00762382

THE
BONES
FALL IN A
SPIRAL

A NECROMANTIC PRIMER

ABOUT THE AUTHOR

Mortellus is a lineaged Third Degree Gardnerian High Priestex of the Long Island Line. In addition to their role as High Priestex, Mortellus is a Mortician, and holds degrees in Design, Education, Fine Arts, and Mortuary Sciences. Their areas of expertise include necromancy, necrobotany, mediumship, and the funerary rites of minority faith groups. Currently residing in Western North Carolina on three acres that doubles as the Covenstead for the Coven of Leaves with their spouse, adult child, five year old twins, and dog; generally wishing there was more time in the day for hiding in the studio and playing with clay.

You can follow Mortellus and all their work by visiting their website at mortellus.com.

WRITE TO MORTELLUS

If you would like to contact the author, please write to Mortellus in care of Crossed Crow Books and we will forward your message. Crossed Crow cannot guarantee that all letters will be answered, but all will be forwarded. Please write to:

Mortellus
C/O Crossed Crow Books
6934 N Glenwood Ave, Suite C
Chicago, IL 60626

FOREWORD BY
MORGAN DAIMLER

THE
BONES
FALL IN A
SPIRAL

A NECROMANTIC PRIMER

MORTELLUS

CROSSED CROW BOOKS CHICAGO, ILLINOIS

The Bones Fall in a Spiral: A Necromantic Primer © 2023 by Mortellus. All rights reserved. No part of this book may be reproduced in any manner whatsoever without written permission from Crossed Crow Books, except in the case of brief quotations embodied in critical articles and reviews.

First Edition.
First Printing. 2023.

Paperback ISBN: 978-1-959883-08-1
Library of Congress Control Number on file.

Cover design by Mortellus.
Illustrations on pages 110 and 208 by Joe Amorello.
Other interior illustrations, icons, and graphic elements by Mortellus.
Typesetting by Gianna Rini.
Edited by Becca Fleming.

Disclaimer: Crossed Crow Books, LLC does not participate in, endorse, or have any authority or responsibility concerning private business transactions between our authors and the public. Any internet references contained in this work were found to be valid during the time of publication, however, the publisher cannot guarantee that a specific reference will continue to be maintained. This book's material is not intended to diagnose, treat, cure, or prevent any disease, disorder, ailment, or any physical or psychological condition. The author, publisher, and its associates shall not be held liable for the reader's choices when approaching this book's material. The views and opinions expressed within this book are those of the author alone and do not necessarily reflect the views and opinions of the publisher.

Published by:
Crossed Crow Books, LLC
6934 N Glenwood Ave, Suite C
Chicago, IL 60626
www.crossedcrowbooks.com

Printed in the United States of America.

OTHER BOOKS BY MORTELLUS

Do I Have to Wear Black? Rituals, Customs & Funerary Etiquette for Modern Pagans, Expanded and Revised (Forthcoming, Crossed Crow Books)

For the Dead that I have served,
and for the Lives that I have created:
Rhiannon, Luna, and Sorin

DISCLAIMER

The author and publisher of *The Bones Fall in a Spiral* assume no liability for any injury or harm experienced surrounding the reading of this work. Nothing here should replace the guidance of your local laws or the guidance of medical professionals as the author does not claim to offer medical or legal advice. Please be advised that use of materials such as essential oils, herbs, grave dirt—and the cremated remains, osteological specimens, and blood of humans or animals—et cetera, should be approached cautiously, ethically, and at your own risk. Further, laws and regulations surrounding death, burial, and possession of human and animal remains vary widely and change frequently. Therefore, it is critical that you consult current and local guidance on any matters.

ACKNOWLEDGEMENTS

The first time I sat down to write acknowledgements for a book—it came easy. All the love and appreciation I felt for those around me flowed out onto the pages without thought or concern; but this second time? There was a pause. A moment in which I wondered if anyone even reads these passages. Whether I forgot anyone the first time around. Do I thank those same individuals again, or should acknowledgements be unique from book to book? At what point do they become a form letter after a fashion? *To whom it may concern: thank you.* The lesson I found here, in writing these acknowledgements, was that insomuch as I must accept that I am changed into someone I was not the last time I said thank you—so too are the people that I once thanked and will go on to thank again.

The acknowledgements will never be the same, because we will never be.

To my Family: Who could've guessed that two essential workers trapped in quarantine with twin toddlers and a teenager while I finished one book and wrote a second would be a nightmare? If they made a film about it, it'd be like that lighthouse movie. **Joseph:** This will always be for you, and frankly, I just don't know why you tolerate me; it all seems pretty awful to put up with. I didn't forget that you bet me "amounts of money" that I wouldn't say that "this book is not a supplement for your early 90s goth tabletop game" and you promised bonus points for working in the phrase "grim dark." There. I did it. **My children:** I will always love you more than anything I'm doing. **Rhiannon:** I know this was a tough time to hit adulthood, and I'm so sorry for all that you've lost. **Luna and Sorin:** I cannot wait to meet the people you are becoming.

To The Coven of Leaves: I missed you all so much over the last year, and I look forward to a time when we're all safely back together. To those of you who spent this pandemic making very essential boxes, teaching our nation's children, providing guidance, digging graves, working in the service industry, providing information through radio shows and podcasts—or just *surviving*—I'm proud to have you as part of my murder.

To My Dearest Friends and Chosen Family: Where would I be without any of you? Probably getting more done. **To The Co-Writer of the Epilogue,** who preferred to remain anonymous, *thank you.* **To F.D. C. Willard,** my thanks for their useful contributions to the discussion of physics included within.

To Paizo and the TTRPG Community: I'm so honored by the gift of trust that was allowing me to draw a parallel between the magic of Golarion/Pathfinder RPG, and real-world practice. It's always an honor to be a part of the TTRPG community, and I hope that I can continue to leave a mark on not only the practice of necromancy in the real world, but the portrayal of death magic in play.

To all those who missed out on rites of passage during the COVID-19 pandemic: Happy Graduation, and Happy Birthday! Congratulations on your wedding, new job, the birth of your child, your coming out, your name change, your transition, initiation, elevation, and on that new coven you started! I hope all your holidays were merry, and I'm so proud of you all for the thing you said no to, and for the thing you took a chance on. To so many of you, I'm so deeply sorry for your losses, and I have grieved right alongside you. So many have made a tremendous impact during this time of incredible loss and tragedy, so for all that you have done for so many, even when it seemed impossible and even when your life was at risk—*thank you.*

For the Ghosts haunting these pages: Amongst the pages of any book, there will always be ghosts haunting the bylines. To those dead who have lent me their energy, their words, I offer not only my thanks, but a place on my altar. All authors—one day—will be ghosts among the pages. When the time comes that I too have joined those ranks, know that if I am needed, I will come when you call.

For the Dead, whom I serve: I hope I do you service here, in showing others a way to you. This book a gift that Mortellus gives to Mors, that Mors might give to the Forgotten Dead.

Merry meet, merry part—merry meet again.
Mortellus

CONTENTS

FOREWORD

Death is the one true equalizer of all living things and one of the inevitabilities that all living things share. To live, ultimately, is to die. And yet for many people death is something terrifying and the idea of working with or connecting to the dead equally frightening. It is ingrained in many of us growing up in Western cultures, especially outside a rural setting, that the dead are to be feared and there is a strong cultural taboo around death, dying, and the dead to the point that most of our colloquial terms for death are euphemisms—a person isn't dead they've "passed on," or "gone to a better place." We are taught to fear ghosts and many works of fiction and movies use spirits of the dead to frighten the audience, because we are supposed to fear what they represent and fear the inevitability of joining them. Life and death are two sides to a single concept but reject one entirely in favor of the other. We live out of balance.

Necromancy and the necromancer, like ghosts and death more generally, have become things that evoke fear, that we are conditioned to fear. If death is bad, something to be fought against, and the spirits of the dead are reminders of the fate that awaits all living things then those who willingly engage with death and the dead must also be bad, must exist outside the safety of daily life. We are told that the line between life and death is impermeable to the living and to transgress that is to transgress the right order of things. And there's comfort in believing that, there's comfort in looking away from the intractableness of death and dying, from the many unanswered questions about what comes next. And yet...we all wonder what lies across that chasm between life and death. Ghosts are used as a horror because they frighten us, but also because they intrigue us. Fearing ghosts may be a common thing, but it also offers its own strange comfort as we see hope in continuing on after death in the very idea of ghosts. Necromancy may be, for many, the ultimate transgressive act but it is also rooted in a belief that life isn't ended by death but merely transformed. Death finds us all, sooner or later, but rather than an impenetrable wall separating living and dead perhaps if we press those boundaries we will find something more like the surface of a river, seemingly solid and separate but actually very different in nature.

Throughout human existence people have always dared those cultural limits and prohibitions, have sought answers about what happens after death, and have reached a metaphoric hand across that chasm. From historic accounts of witches and magical workers invoking the dead to modern spiritualists seeking to communicate with them, from ancient descriptions of séances to contemporary teenagers playing with Ouija boards, the living seek the dead and seek answers about what happens after death. People today fear those who work with the dead and stigmatize attempts to communicate with the disembodied, yet embrace ideas around keeping the memory of these who have died alive and continuing to acknowledge and engage with them, whether that's through photographs or candles lit in their names. The term necromancy has a grim reputation but it exists just beneath the surface of almost all of our lives. We dream of our dead, we ask them for help and guidance, we tell their stories—we keep them alive with us even after their body has died.

Necromancy may, indeed, be the oldest magic.

What this book asks us all to do is step back and rethink who and what necromancers are and, indeed, what necromancy is. To see it all not as inherently bad, in any sense of that term, but as inherently human, a drive we all have to understand what is beyond physical existence and what can be connected to and worked with. It is bad or good only in that we ourselves are bad or good and bring that with us to what we do. Not everyone will choose to step into active work with the dead, and not everyone should do such work, but *The Bones Fall in a Spiral* offers guidelines to move forward in a respectful manner if you want to, and it asks us all to understand the depth and nuance to necromancy beyond the popular imagination and stereotypes. This book is an invitation into a deeper understanding of life, death, belief, personal responsibility, and power—if you are willing to step forward with an open mind and willing to see the beauty where others find fear.

Morgan Daimler,
Author of *Fairies* and *A New Dictionary of Fairies*

PROLOGUE

I confess there were times when I worried readers might pick up this book, see the word *Wicca* somewhere in my biography, and wonder to themselves if this was a *fluffy* book about necromancy. Othered amongst the other, we often relegate practitioners of necromancy to the shadowy corners of magical communities. It's a rather funny thought that I might be perceived as taking a soft approach to something so often portrayed as the very embodiment of dark magic.

Throughout history, notable dabblers in necromancy have worked very hard to portray themselves as having done something good. As opposed to the alternative, that variety of necromancy best left relegated to, well, the left. One such person was Éliphas Lévi, author of *Transcendental Magic, Its Doctrine and Ritual*. Lévi makes clear a belief that "there are two kinds of necromancy, that of light, and that of darkness, the evocation by prayer, pentacle, and perfumes, and the evocation by blood, imprecations, and sacrileges."[1] "We," Lévi says, "have only practiced the first, and advise no one to devote themselves to the second."[2]

Unlike Lévi, Dee, Kelley, and other notables from necromancy's history, I'm no dusty Catholic hoping to justify my magical practices. I do not need to couch them in what might be deemed acceptable by polite society and will not debate whether necromancy is light or dark, as Lévi proposed. Death simply is and I believe that all magic, at its core, is neither good nor bad, but a force of energy comparable to electricity. Outcomes can be benevolent or malevolent, dependent entirely upon the practitioner themselves, and nothing else. In as much

---

1   Éliphas Lévi, *Transcendental Magic* (Red Wheel Weiser, 1968), 283.

2   Ibid.

as I am unwilling to water down necromantic practice, neither am I inclined to water down my magical perspective.

As someone who practices Traditional Witchcraft/Wicca, my writings will naturally have that lean (and indeed, my focus is on European necromantic practices). Throughout, you'll find that I have used the language and structural framework of that practice as a foundation for the work. Somewhere along the way, I hope I'm able to make the case that *Wicca itself* is fundamentally necromantic. That without death magic, we would not have Wicca or the Neopagan movement as we know it. It's my goal to challenge readers to reconsider preconceived notions of what necromancy, death—and perhaps even *Wicca*—are and are not. Whatever I have to say, it will never be *fluffy*.

There are some things that I would like to clarify from the start that this book is not and does not do. First, I would like to express that I always attempt to be thorough in my research and present a balanced view of any topic; but this work will contain much of my personal practice. You will encounter a great deal of *unverified personal gnosis*, or UPG, throughout, as well as materials I have created for my personal practice. I will attempt to make clear what is, and what is not, founded in historical precedent. Second, in my research, I encountered time and time again language that ostensibly regarded those seeking to learn death magic as though they were impossibly ignorant of magic—as though the majority of readers could never hope to have anything beyond an intellectual understanding of necromantic practice.[3] You won't find that here. I won't be asking that you stop to sign pages in blood, or to seek a teacher; I won't be treating the subject as though I'm letting you in on a secret that is mine and mine alone.[4] Let's all just establish a baseline of my having faith that you've brought to the table a basic understanding of magical principles. But if that isn't the case? I won't suggest that you won't understand what's written here, that you'll make grave errors, that your home will become irreparably haunted, or any other such thing. Perhaps, simply, that you won't be as effective as you might've liked to have been in your early attempts.

---

3   Martin Coleman, *Communing with the Spirits: The Magical Practice of Necromancy Simply and Lucidly Explained, with Full Instructions for the Practice of That Ancient Art* (Philadelphia, PA: Xlibris, 2005), 11.

4   Sorceress Cagliastro, *Blood Sorcery Bible* (Tempe, AZ: Original Falcon Press, 2011).

Necromancy is a magical specialization, and I recognize it isn't for everyone. Not everyone will be adept, or even comfortable, with what they read here; but I hope to impress upon you my sincere belief that death magic is fundamental. Each of us, in our own time, will confront and know death. In some form or another, we will all join the throngs of the Underworld who aid those we choose, or to those who've called to us, here on this Material Plane. So, learn this magic while you live, or learn it in death—but learn it you will. If you believe that work with the dead is your calling, you will succeed. I have faith in you and your ability to accomplish any of the things you set your mind to.

HOW THIS BOOK WORKS

I wanted to clarify upfront a little bit of language, particularly why I utilize the word *eidōlon* where many would use the word *ghost*, and *instrument* where others would use *tool*. *Ghost* is defined as the apparition of a deceased human, and since not every incorporeal being you encounter will be a *deceased* human, or even human at all, ghost does not suit our needs very well. According to *Haunted Greece and Rome: Ghost Stories from Classical Antiquity* by D. Felton, "Greek has several all-purpose words for apparition or ghost, including εἴδωλον (eidōlon)," and I'm rather fond of this particular term because it is purposeful in a way that *ghost* is not.[5] Most importantly, because it is inclusive of not only the dead but of the *living*—which is relevant to some of the topics included in this book.

In regard to instruments, it is historically common to utilize phrases such as tool, working tools, ritual tools, and so on when referring to certain objects that many commonly use in magical practice. While a student of mortuary sciences, it was commonly stated in the lab "these are *instruments*, not tools." An instrument, in a lab setting, is an object assigned a specific and delicate type of work—a hammer is a *tool*, a scalpel is an *instrument*. This came to be a feature of my own practice in that I am aligning the objects I use for necromantic practice to, well,

---

5   Debbie Felton, *Haunted Greece and Rome: Ghost Stories from Classical Antiquity*, 1st ed. (Austin: University of Texas Press, 1999), 24.

specific and delicate work. In that way, my athame becomes an instrument rather than simply a tool.

Throughout, I speak on the use of blood as an offering or spell component and would like to make clear that I do not believe you ever need more than three drops of your own blood safely collected from a fingertip and do offer an alternative. When collecting blood for such use, you will want to have on hand alcohol prep pads, a medical lancing device, bandages, and perhaps most importantly, a sharps container for proper disposal of biohazardous materials. Should you have a communicable illness or bleeding disorder, there may be extra considerations for you to account for. I ask that you not consider any of this to be medical advice, and strongly encourage you to seek out the opinion of a professional regarding the best methods for you.

Lastly, while *esoteric* might be defined as something understood by only a few, I'd like to assure that accessing the knowledge is not. Therefore, throughout this book, I've placed the symbols outlined below which act as practical roadmaps to some of the content within in hopes that it helps connect the threads of practice to my train of thought in the early parts of the work.

CONSULT YOUR BOOK OF SHADES
This symbol indicates that there are pathworkings, rituals, spells, and recipes contained in the Book of Shades that coordinate with the section you are reading.

BACK TO BASICS
This symbol indicates that the item being specified is a basic component utilized in many of the spells, recipes, rituals, and so on contained herein—and if relevant, where to find it.

——— PART ONE ———
NECROMANCY
WITHOUT A LICENSE

"To the dead we owe only the truth."
—Voltaire

1

NECROMANCY, ALIVE AND WELL

"If anyone stops us, as long as we mumble something pretentious about the glory of death, we should be fine."
— Derek Landy, *Death Bringer*

In *The Magus*, Francis Barrett notes that necromancy "has its name because it works on the bodies of the dead, and gives answers by the (eidōlon) and apparitions of the dead, and subterraneous spirits, alluring them into the carcasses of the dead by certain hellish charms, infernal invocations, deadly sacrifices, and wicked oblations."[6] The necromancer is at their core an evocotor, a caller of souls, and the one thing most seem to agree on is that necromancy is a sort of specialty that any practitioner might perform. From the storied Witch of Endor to Thomas Edison and their attempts at perfecting the Necrophone, we have always had a fascination with contacting those who have moved beyond the veil.[7]

Despite this recurring historical theme, when thinking of necromantic magic, most would imagine a famous grimoire written in a time when most believed that necromancers ate corpses, spent their time by moonlight in burial places, or walking backward after

---

6   Francis Barrett and Harry Price, *The Magus*, vol. 2 (London: Printed for Lackington, Allen, and Co, 1801), 69.

7   Alessandra Serrano, "Edison's Necrophone," Seiður: University of Tromsø, October 31, 2017, http://www.radio-science.net/2017/10/edisons-necrophone.html.

tossing bones into Catholic mass. For much of that time forward, and even still today, it is illegal in many places to practice the art of necromancy. Sometimes, however, it simply requires a license, such as in the city of San Francisco, which notes in the municipal code that "necromancy [...] or [...] any such similar thing or act" is something one might acquire a permit for.[8]

SO, WHAT IS NECROMANCY, ANYWAY?

Many would be quick to answer that question by noting that necromancy is *divination* that utilizes the *dead*—and just as many would be quick to inform you that the proper term should be *sciomancy*, divination through consultation with the *incorporeal* dead. In actuality, these sorts of corrections assume that neither I, nor anyone practicing necromantic magic today, works with human remains—which would be a bold, but incorrect assumption. Another fly in the ointment is that neither of these descriptions is correct on a practical level. As Daniel Ogden notes in *Greek and Roman Necromancy*, divination by the dead (necromancy proper) wasn't always easily separated from other magic involving the dead, and therefore, has been used somewhat colloquially throughout history.[9]

As we go forward, my working definition of the word *necromancy* will be any magic involving the dead, physical remains of deceased humans or animals, (skeletal or otherwise), and a necromancer, as a person who *specializes* in that sort of magic.

NECROMANCY'S EVIL REPUTATION

As I mentioned in the prologue, Éliphas Lévi insists in Chapter 13 of *Transcendental Magic: Its Doctrine and Ritual* that "there are two kinds of necromancy," the good kind and the bad kind. Lévi assures us, of course, that they have "only practiced the first, and advise no one to

---

8   "Article17.1: Regulations for Fortunetelling; Permit and License Provisions," American Legal Publishing Corporation, 2020, https://codelibrary. amlegal.com/codes/san _francisco/latest/sf_police/0-0-0-5579.

9   Daniel Ogden, *Greek and Roman Necromancy* (Princeton, NJ: Princeton University Press, 2005), xviii–xix.

devote themselves to the second."[10] Do I believe that there is "light" and "dark" necromancy? No, I do not. Do I believe that one process is inherently "good" and another "bad?" No, I do not. What I assert is that there is no form of magic at all that a modern practitioner of the occult arts might practice that would not be sacrilegious to *someone*, perhaps even other practitioners, and who among us has not dabbled in imprecations? A further, and not insignificant aside, what is wrong with using blood in your magic? Clearly our friend Mr. Lévi, who spent their early life in pursuit of the Catholic priesthood, had a few hang-ups, which really gets to the root of the issue.[11]

So many of our modern-day perceptions surrounding necromancy come from the words of Catholics drawing boundaries around what they thought was right and wrong. For most of history necromancy was as common as any other sort of magic, but with the rise of Catholicism came the vilifying of Pagan practice we are all too familiar with. No longer were we speaking to the dead, seeking comfort and the knowledge of the unknown, but evoking *demons*; rather than helpful practitioners, necromancers were now cavorting with the Devil—a reputation that persists into the modern day.[12] Equally true is that, like so many Pagan things, necromancy was just fine so long as it was not Pagans practicing it. It was often those same Catholics vilifying the practice that were writing the grimoire and texts we are so familiar with today—loudly practicing what they deemed evil for others to take part in.

IS NECROMANCY THE FOUNDATION OF NEOPAGANISM?

We are all familiar with the *Witchfather*, Gerald B. Gardner, the founder of what we know today as Gardnerian Wicca, but are we all familiar with the story of *how* Gardner came to be a part of it all in the first place? In *Gerald Gardner, Witch*, Jack Bracelin describes Gardner's

---

10   Lévi, *Transcendental Magic*, 283.

11   Éliphas Lévi, *The Doctrine and Ritual of High Magic: A New Translation*, trans. John Michael Greer and Mark Anthony Mikituk (New York: TarcherPerigee, 2017), X.

12   Richard Kieckhefer, *Forbidden Rites: A Necromancer's Manual of the Fifteenth Century* (Stroud: Sutton, 1997), 10–17.

experiences with spirit communication in 1927—the forty-third year of their life—as the "watershed moment," propelling Gardner down the path toward what later became Wicca.[13]

So much of Neopaganism is rooted in death. Take, for example, the libation of cakes and wine. A common declaration during this ritual act is the phrase "there is no part of us that is not of the gods." This quote is often attributed to Aleister Crowley, via *Liber XV*, the Gnostic Mass—but that is not its origin.[14] Its origins lie instead in the Egyptian *Book of the Dead*, where Chapter 42 notes, *"En aat am-a shu-t em neter"* or, "there is no member of mine devoid of a God."[15] A moment where so many pause to consider that we too are divine, my mind wanders instead to an ancient Sem Priest, face shrouded behind a black mask in honor of Anubis—the jackal-headed god of embalming and mummification—lovingly naming the deities associated with each individual part of the body as they prepare the dead.

As Éliphas Lévi stated, "death is a phantom of ignorance; it does not exist; everything in nature is living, and it is because it is alive that everything is in motion and undergoes an incessant change of form. Old age is the beginning of regeneration, it is the labour of renewing life, and the ancients represented the mystery we term death by the Fountain of Youth, which was entered in decrepitude and left in new childhood. The body is a garment of the soul."[16] In *Greek and Roman Necromancy*, Daniel Ogden states that "the pressing question at the broad psycho-sociological level" isn't "why did the *ancients* practice necromancy?" It's, "why don't *we* practice it?"[17] It's high time we gave necromancy a chance to become something accessible, and a generation growing more death positive should demand it. We need to strip away the stereotypes that have been unfairly applied to not only the practice

---

13   Jack Bracelin, *Gerald Gardner: Witch* (Octavo, 1960), 133.

14   Aleister Crowley, et al., *Magick: Liber ABA, Book Four, Parts I–IV* (York Beach, Maine: S. Weiser, 1994), 585.

15   John H. Taylor, *Ancient Egyptian Book of the Dead: Journey through the Afterlife*; [Exhibition at the British Museum from 4 November 2010 to 6 March 2011] (London: British Museum Press, 2010), 162–63.

16   Lévi, *Transcendental Magic*, 280.

17   Ogden, *Greek and Roman Necromancy*, XVI.

and those who choose it, but the dead, and take a hard look at what can be a meaningful part of every magical practitioner's toolbox.

ETHICAL CONSIDERATIONS

Necromancy can be a topic that many are uncomfortable with. While I believe that necromancy is, like death itself, neutral, that doesn't mean that most don't observe it to be *evil* in some measure. It's probably pretty important, for that reason, to know where I'm coming from ethically on the topic. Underneath the Pagan umbrella there are lots of ethical frameworks that we might choose to apply, such as the Rule of Three, the Wiccan Rede, Declaration 127, the upholding of Ma'at, and many, many more; but for me, magical ethics are all about establishing a personal code.

As an avid player of role-playing games such as *Dungeons & Dragons*, *Pathfinder*, and more, I've found that it can be fun to imagine what sort of character your real-world self would be if you were a character in a book or game setting. I'd like to think I would be a wizard type, all dusty leather-bound tomes, and purple robes covered in stars like the Cookie Crisp wizard; but friends are quick to set me straight, telling me that no, I would be a paladin. In role-playing games, paladins are holy fighters devoted to their deities or ideals, always ready to slay whatever evil is in front of them and are almost universally reviled by everyone for being a stick-in-the-mud.

In order to keep abilities granted them by their aforementioned deities, paladins must abide by a strict code. Perhaps it is a personal code, the laws of the land, or the laws of the deity they follow—but it must be followed to the letter. Other players often refer to them as "lawful stupid" because strictly following their code can, and often does, conflict with the surrounding characters. Ideally, these are characters (and players) that the paladin, and the individual portraying them, loves and wishes to cooperate with. But if something oversteps the boundaries of that code? They must react. A personal code is always going to be the sum total of who we are, and where we have been; our values, beliefs, and ethics, all rolled up in a big ol' morality burrito. Within this book, I'll talk a lot about what *I* believe is right, but I want you to remember that when someone puts forth *belief* as a foundation for *correctness*, that *belief* is just an *opinion*—even if the beliefs in question are my own.

As for necromantic practice itself, in *Greek and Roman Necromancy*, Daniel Ogden states "that necromancy was correspondingly wicked when practiced by someone wicked, even though the person might practice it in effectively the same way as a benign necromancer."[18] In effect, necromancy is as good or as bad as the person practicing it.[19] I think about this often as I stumble upon things like the spell "To Overcome a Girl" in *The Graveyard Wanderers* by Dr. Tom Johnson, which is a necromantic spell which ostensibly serves the purpose of assisting the practitioner in raping another human being. Or, for example, spells in *The Blood Sorcery Bible*, such as "To Cause Fertility (non-consensual)" as well as ritual instructions noting "gay couples" must have hetero-normative sexual intercourse to complete necromantic spell work, as it "has nothing to do with love."[20] It wouldn't be difficult for me to find dozens more examples for you of things that wouldn't fit within my personal code. Does that make them wrong? For me, yes, but ethics are debatable and shaped by cultural norms as well as religious influence, so you must make those choices for yourself.

Some would absolutely call into question whether we are interfering with the agency of the dead, or causing them disruption, in practicing necromancy—but history has shown us that the dead have nonchalant attitudes about being the subject of death magic.[21] Rather than being a disruption to their rest, it offered an opportunity to interact for a short amount of time with life, and with the living, as well as allowing the restless dead an avenue to achieve rest.[22] But at the end of the day, spells like those I've rattled off for you are not about necromancy.

18 Ogden, *Greek and Roman Necromancy*, 264.
19 Ibid.
20 Sorceress Cagliastro, *Blood Sorcery Bible. Volume 1: Rituals in Necromancy: A Treatment on the Science of Blood & Magnetics as They Pertain to Blood Sorcery and Necromancy* (Tempe, AZ: Original Falcon Press, 2011) 71, 81.
21 Ogden, *Greek and Roman Necromancy*, 264.
22 Ibid.

Those spells are instead about the people choosing to cast them, the people who wrote them—their magic, and who they are. Just like in any other magical practice, there will always be some who are drawn to the *stereotypes themselves*, and not the practice of necromancy in truth.

As for the rest of us, we must be the best that we can be, within the confines of our own practice, and our own moral and ethical code. And in so doing, we might break through those barriers built on a foundation of stereotypes and reclaim necromantic practice for what it has always been—a collaboration between the living and the dead for the betterment of all.

EXERCISE: CRAFTING A PERSONAL CODE

TIME AND PLACE: Any
SUPPLIES: Pen and Paper
PURPOSE: Establishing a moral and ethical baseline.

Simple though it may sound, I encourage you to take a moment to consider what your personal ethical code might look like. Write it down. Create boundaries around what you are comfortable with.

What does my own code look like?

- **I believe that magic is neither good nor bad, but a force of energy comparable to electricity.** Outcomes are benevolent or malevolent, depending entirely upon the practitioner.

- **I believe that my magic, my craft, and my tradition, not only can but should be inclusive.** Inclusive of all ages, races, sexual orientations, identities, and backgrounds.

- **I believe that cursing is *sometimes* necessary.** By *necessary*, I mean an action that is vital to accomplish the task at hand or fulfilling a need. I would only undertake it with a goal of protecting others from harm, or creating boundaries, and never with a goal of revenge, nor from a place of anger.

@ **I believe that tradition is just peer pressure from dead people.** As such, I adhere to the teachings of the tradition of which I am a part *insomuch as it doesn't cause harm.* When I look back on the founders of my tradition, Gardnerian Wicca, I see people who were willing to change the rules when necessary.

@ **I don't do magic of any kind for myself.** I've long held the measure of a witch is in what they do for others. It should not be about what we might gain, but about what we can *give.*

@ **I believe it is wrong to do magic that interferes with someone's autonomy, or that causes an effect that the subject would not otherwise have consented to.** I recognize that this is a murky area, and that maybe magic isn't fully compatible with consent, but I do my best to try.

@ **I adhere to stanza 127 of the Havamal;** when I see misdeeds, I speak out against them, consider the perpetrators my enemy, and make no truces or treaties with foes. I practice British Traditional Wicca but have a lot of Norse Heathen influence in my personal practice and figure that if you're going to borrow anything to appreciate from other cultures, it ought to be ethics.

@ **Lastly, I hold myself true to the geas I've sworn.** A *geas* is a type of magical prohibition that you agree to as part of a vow. In my case, these are vows/oaths I have made to certain deities, which include: not doing magic for myself, not wearing shoes in cemeteries unless *necessary*, and carrying a blade with me wherever I go.

Nobody else must follow or even like my personal magical code, and it's always going to be evolving and changing, because I'm committed to learning and becoming a better practitioner every single day. I hope that this gives you a picture of who I am underneath the window dressing and has inspired you to think about what your own personal magical code might look like. I think we learn a lot about ourselves by sitting with our boundaries, and death magic deals in boundaries above all else.

LAST WORDS

By making clear your own lines in the sand on certain topics, it will prepare you to define your position on the necromantic magic that you choose to do and your comfort level with certain practices. Perhaps your own code will look quite different from mine, and that's okay! What matters is that you yourself will know where you stand.

2

THE MAKING OF A NECROMANCER

"Some people experience a life-changing sensation that transforms how they see the world after a near-death experience, but we're all dying—nay, we're all dead—and it is up to us to be our own self-necromancers to find some form of life and spirit to reanimate the corpse of a life spent wanting."
— A. J. Darkholme, *Rise of the Morningstar*

So, necromancy still exists today, is worth reclaiming, and isn't what we all thought. What about the necromancer themselves? Who decides that this is going to be the specialization for them, and what makes that sort of person tick, so to speak? Despite being a practitioner of necromancy and having claimed the term *necromancer* for myself for quite a long time, I confess I struggled a bit to define who I feel a necromancer is as a person and wouldn't have included anything on this topic at all if every other modern book you could pull off a shelf didn't take the time to let us know who belongs, and who doesn't. Well, the short answer is that I believe that everyone who wants to be here belongs.

In a lot of ways, the biggest concern for the would-be necromancer to wrangle with is *belief*. While magical practices may not rely on a belief in deities, necromancy at the least demands a belief in the *dead*; that they can have some existence beyond life. It is for this reason that I believe that those who have touched death themselves through their own near-death experiences make the most effective practitioners of necromancy. They have seen the other side, felt that space, and can confidently navigate it without need for reassurance. This doesn't mean that if you yourself haven't experienced near death, you won't be able to practice this magic successfully. It just means that it may require something more akin to a leap of faith.

I don't always do well with leaning into the more "have a little faith" side of things. Sometimes it's easier to talk about magic as though it's an intellectual or scholarly experiment in psychological archetypes and visualizations, but death magic, the dead, and the Underworld are one area where I must let go. For those of you reading, I'm just going to trust that you're along for the ride, and if it isn't for you, it just won't be, and that's okay. I know that isn't everyone's experience, but as someone who experienced near death, or more accurately, the Lazarus Effect (spontaneously reviving after having been declared dead), I feel I can say that the Underworld is real. I've seen it, touched it, felt it—this is a place I've been. When I talk about the Underworld, I remember what it smelled like.

While I'm willing to suspend belief and say that these are all the experiences of a dying brain on the other side of a coma, they are my experiences. When I talk about death, I remember my heart slowing and stopping. When I talk about the dead, I'm seeing them before my very eyes. So, what does that mean for me as a necromancer? It means that I don't have to wonder if what I'm doing/feeling/attempting is real, and that is such a gift. I know that for a lot of you your work with the dead will go on faith of a sort, trusting in your experiences as you grow these new muscles and forge these new pathways, forming new and specialized neurons with which to manage this input. It may be hard, but you can do this. The first act of necromancy is always going to be raising yourself from the dead, because we can't have mastery over death if we don't know how to *live*.

TROPES, STEREOTYPES, AND GENERAL NONSENSE

When we see necromancers in media, they are often serving the role of *somethingmancer* which is a sort of media trope that involves, well, any specialized magic and a particular naming convention. It doesn't mean that it is indeed necromancy that we're looking at—though if you subscribe to the broad view that any magic plus death equals necromancy, perhaps it is. But of all the somethingmancers of fiction, necromancers stand alone, because death magic in fiction is never benevolent. The necromancer in media is evil incarnate, those who disturb the dead, twisting them to do their dark bidding using *black magic* to raise an army of the damned. It's noted that "any […] (who practice) necromancy (are) guaranteed to fall hard onto the far side of the evil scale, and any […] who dares dabble in it can kiss (their) position on the good side goodbye."[23]

The general wisdom, according to Neil Zawacki, author of *How to Be a Villain*, is that necromancer is the perfect career choice for an "evil-doer" who isn't a "people person," noting that "good career entry points" for becoming a necromancer include "occultists, dabblers in Voodoo, grave diggers, morticians (oh no, I'm starting to see their point) […] and inheritors of scary books wrapped in human flesh."[24] Well, I suppose I fit a lot of that criteria. I'm certainly not a "people person" in the classic sense.

We did not always regard necromancy in this light. It wasn't until the fourteenth to sixteenth centuries that it became equated with demonology, earning its terrible reputation. And from there, to the Spiritualist movement and its not-insignificant association with fraud, indelibly associating it with trickery, falsehood, and the Devil—leaving death magic regarded as either a pretender's art or evil. And which is worse? To be branded a worker of something vile and dark? Or to be viewed as one might a prime-time reality star, cold reading strangers and plying them with vagaries that they hope hit home?

But for all the stereotypes surrounding the necromancer, few are worse, and more bewildering, than the heteronormative and often misogynistic viewpoints that so many modern works on necromancy are rife with. Who would have thought that a topic like death magic would need an inclusivity statement? And yet, here I am, with overwhelming evidence that the vast majority of modern materials (necromantic or otherwise) available are rife with hetero-normative standards. These works often relying on a binary of information that implies—if not outright states—that only *men* or *women* can practice magic, and materials addressing necromantic practice are no different, often going a step further to suggest that *men* are more suited to the work.

---

23 tvtropes.org, "Necromancer," TV Tropes, 2021.

24 Neil Zawacki and James Dignan, *How to Be a Villain: Evil Laughs, Secret Lairs, Master Plans, and More!!!* (San Francisco: Chronical Books, 2003).

In *Communing With The Spirits* Martin Coleman states that "female" practitioners of necromancy will lack "physical modesty," and have sexual dreams "so vivid that you (awaken) as a result of […] orgasm," and live "close to the edge of social acceptability." [25] "These women," Coleman states, "are found at the extreme ranges of dress and sexual behavior."[26] "Men" who practice necromancy fare no better in the text, being described as "commanding and dominating," and won't be from the "Casper Milquetoast school of masculinity."[27] For multiple pages, droning on about what a binary of "men" and "women" must be if they are to be necromancers.[28] These, Coleman says, are the "personal characteristics of a necromancer," after all.[29]

In the *Blood Sorcery Bible*, we're treated to the opinion that PIV sex rituals are required for the practice of necromancy, making clear that anything outside of the author's heteronormative sexual scripting just won't do. In fact, it states that "gay couples should consider […] close sorcery associates" for the acts described as required, noting that it "has nothing to do with love." All this after having described a PIV sex act to be performed by "a man and a menstruating woman" in enough detail to confirm exactly how those genders are being defined.[30] Why am I telling you all this when we ought to be talking about death magic? Because these heteronormative foundations of practice and sexist stereotypes cause harm, and above all, because *everyone* dies, and therefore, *everyone* can practice necromancy.

WHAT MAKES A NECROMANCER? HOW DO I KNOW IF THAT'S WHAT I AM?

So, you can see spirits and sometimes talk to them. Perhaps you even have dreams of the dead. But what does that mean, and what does it mean to be a necromancer? I often get these sorts of

---

25 Coleman, *Communing with the Spirits*, 42.

26 Ibid.

27 Ibid.

28 Coleman, *Communing with the Spirits*, 39–49.

29 Ibid.

30 Cagliastro, *Blood Sorcery Bible*, 80–81.

questions and want to be clear that the only thing that defines a necromancer is, well, *practicing* necromancy—which as I've stated already is an area of magical specialization. Since it often comes up, I'll say in contrast that mediumship is a *psychic ability*, and while psychics (those with extrasensory perception) aren't necessarily *mediums* (one who can perceive and communicate with the dead), all mediums are psychics. Mediumship *could* be reasonably defined as necromancy, circumstantially, and I don't think that mediumship *isn't* necromancy. But I *would* define necromancy primarily as a magical *practice* that involves working with the dead—both corporeal and incorporeal—to accomplish magical goals in addition to receiving information and insight. And a *necromancer*? Simply as someone who practices it.

Mediumship can be a very handy skill for a necromancer to have, but isn't necessarily...well, *necessary*, to get the job done, to do the work. But to the question, *what does it mean* to be a necromancer (or a medium, for that matter)? It may surprise you to find that most of the work is with the *living*. The dead don't generally need (or want) our help, as a general rule. Instead, they're here to give it, and we deathworkers live in service to them. A voice with which to speak, hands that might hold, arms that might lift up; that through us, those around us might occupy a world with a little less sorrow. For most of history necromancers served their community, and I believe that is what we should strive for today, to be *service-oriented* in our necromantic practice. The true work of a necromancer is not in what the dead can do for you, but in what you can do for the dead.

CONSULT YOUR BOOK OF SHADES
If you're considering experimenting with a necromantic practice, the sigil spell *Acquiring Knowledge of the Grave* on page 160 of the Skills and Attributes section of the Book of Shades is a good place to start.

LAST WORDS

Working with the dead for many involves overcoming fears, and when confronting fears that surround the *incorporeal* dead—in particular—I often caution individual practitioners to exercise rational skepticism. It's always good to always start with a baseline of questioning yourself. Being really honest with yourself as a magical thinker makes magical experiences all the more powerful through a willingness to reject what feels inauthentic. In *Current Biology's* Neurological and Robot-Controlled Induction of an Apparition, researchers share that while studying participants who had seen apparitions, those apparitions were often found to be "an illusory own-body perception with well-defined characteristics that is associated with sensorimotor loss and caused by lesions in three distinct brain regions: temporoparietal, insular, and especially frontoparietal cortex."[31] Basically, the apparition seen was, well, the person seeing it.

Do I think that makes the fear any less real? Nope. Do I think that makes the vision any less real? Nope. Do I think that makes it any less magical? Quite the opposite. What if instead of some unknown spirit appearing in the dark, it was you? Not in the neurological sense of having lost differentiation between ourselves and an external entity (like the psychological misperception noted in the study), but rather some piece of your own soul, traveling outside the boundaries of your own body? Something worth considering when you're feeling nervous about the incorporeal beings in your own space.

---

31 Olaf Blanke et al., "Neurological and Robot-Controlled Induction of an Apparition," *Current Biology* 24, no. 22 (November 2014): 2681–86, https://doi.org/ 10.1016/j.isci.2020.101955.

3

DOMAINS IN THE DARKNESS

"You should never attack a necromancer in a cemetery; it's like chasing Rambo into a building full of loaded guns. Some people seem to help you kill them."

— Laurell K. Hamilton, Dead Ice

Authors of books such as these have set before them what at times seems an impossible task. Do we rely solely on past works and myths—though they may be limited, or apply our own experiences, a new perspective? While these new perspectives may be useful, profound, or relevant—they are vulnerable; and perhaps that is the gift. Not in the practice, or scholarship, but in sharing a truth that is wounding—and here's mine: I died. What I experienced between living, dying, and returning to this life (a life that I now feel was given to me by the very gods I serve) forever changed how I interact with the world of the living.

Anyone who read my first book, *Do I Have to Wear Black*, knows I've long had a love affair with the zero-point field theorized in quantum theory. An electromagnetic field that exists as a background to all things, a "disordered ocean of energy;" acting as a foundation upon which the universe is built.[32] It is something I've long held as what I believe the Underworld is, and where it might be found. It is in *Do I Have to Wear Black* that I write:

"When it comes to an afterlife, the underworld as it were, or the many halls of the deities that we hear tell of in so many legends, myths, and

---

32 Joachim Keppler, "The Role of the Brain in Conscious Processes: A New Way of Looking at the Neural Correlates of Consciousness," *Frontiers in Psychology* 9 (August 3, 2018), https://doi.org/10.3389/fpsyg.2018.01346.

cultures, that is string theory to me; a thousand worlds that we can feel, but cannot touch. Past lives? Memories of other places and times? A well of creation from which all things might derive? Well, that's a little harder to explain, but I'll try. For those of you who are not familiar with the Akashic record, it's an idea espoused by some that there is a nonphysical plane of existence upon which all of human existence has been recorded. All our thoughts, feelings, words, actions, and so on—marked there for all of eternity. I'm not quite certain I believe that, but I'm also not certain that it's entirely wrong. Nobel Peace Prize winner, philosopher, integral theorist, and, if it means anything to you—classical pianist—Dr. Ervin László preferred to conflate the idea of the Akashic Record with that of the Zero-Point Field theorized in quantum physics—a known force that remains unproved outside of theory. Essentially, there is, at the bottom of all things that we know of as reality, a flat plane from which all things come, and to which all things must return. Dr. László referred to this hive of energy as 'the original source of all things,' the birthplace of all things, the great cosmic mirror of existence, a churning cauldron of eternity, the womb of time, a sea of energy giving birth to the very stars."[33]

It is Joachim Keppler of the Department of Consciousness Research who takes it a step further in *The Role of the Brain in Conscious Processes: A New Way of Looking at the Neural Correlates of Consciousness* when they state that the zero-point field has the dual task of carrying not only energy, but consciousness, noting that "every (zero-point field) information state is associated with a conscious state," suggesting that the zero-point field is "an information-preserving medium," if the information we're talking about, is human consciousness, no longer bound to a living body.[34] This "disordered ocean of energy" they call it, repeatedly referring to this unknowable place as a sea, the depth of which we could not comprehend, at last concluding that "all conceivable shades of […] awareness are woven into the fabric of the (zero-point field)" rendering it not simply a sea of energy—but "a formless sea of consciousness."[35]

---

33 Mortellus, *Do I Have to Wear Black? Rituals, Customs & Funerary Etiquette for Modern Pagans* (Woodbury, MN: Llewellyn Publications 2021), 10–13.

34 Keppler, "The Role of the Brain in Conscious Processes."

35 Ibid.

And so, it is there at the bottom of the universe, within this churning cauldron of energy and dark matter, that the dead reside—in which thoughts become reality. It is there that we begin to understand how the mind might manifest change in the physical world, and there, that we see that the dead themselves are the very threads holding together the fabric of the universe. For if that zero-point field is, as is theorized, a sea of dark matter—and that sea is made up of consciousness—then the very dark matter holding together the universe must then be the dead; all those minds no longer confined to the physical realm by their corporeal form.[36] It goes without saying that I'm a bit of a nerd and that often colors my magical experience. I use the *Dark Souls* video game franchise as a metaphor for reincarnation, use tabletop role-playing games as a teaching tool, use polyhedral dice for divination, and within these very pages you'll find references to Pharasma, a (fictional) deity of death in Paizo's *Pathfinder Roleplaying Game*.

But here, as we delve deeper into the realms of the dead, I'd like to take you on a journey through the world of a comic book called *The Amory Wars*. The plot surrounds a fictional conflict taking place in "Heaven's Fence," a group of worlds tied together by an energy called the *Keywork*. I could probably fill a book writing about the mythos of this world, but today, I simply want to talk about the Keywork itself, because it's just such an elegant analogy for the magical realms and their interconnectedness.

While Heaven's Fence, within the fictional universe of *The Amory Wars*, is made up of many worlds, and many stars, it is the Keywork that binds them together.[37] A beam of light—made up of the souls of deceased individuals who once occupied a physical form on one of those many fictional physical planets. Within this mythos, there are those who have become enlightened, able to let go of their emotional connections to their lives lived, who move on to a utopia of a

---

36 Bo Lehnert, "Zero Point Energy as Origin of Dark Energy and Dark Matter," *Joint ITER-IAEA-ICTP Advanced Workshop on Fusion and Plasma Physics: AIP Conference Proceedings* 1445 (2012), https://doi.org/ 10.1063/ v1445.frontmatter

37 Claudio Sanchez and Chondra Echert, *The Amory War Series* (Los Angeles, CA: BOOM! Studios, 2012).

kind—but for the others, they remain the fuel that holds together the fabric of reality. They are consciousness. They are thought given form. And for us, here, now, whether you call it spiritual, magical, scientific, or theoretical—there is one inarguable constant—we are all a part of the fabric that is reality. And so, it is there, in the universe's all-pervading, all-knowing, electromagnetic background with its "unique power (and) spectral density," that we, a collection of thermodynamic miracles, become one among the fence.[38]

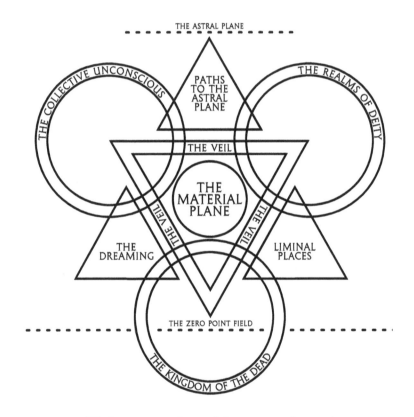

The interconnectedness of the unseen realms, and the navigable pathways between all their ordered chaos.

---

38 Keppler, "The Role of the Brain in Conscious Processes."

TRAVERSING THE UNSEEN REALMS

It has never been useful to me to think "Underworld, down there somewhere," "Celestial Plane, up there probably," and other similarly vague suggestions of where the realms of "other" might be. I'm a map kind of person. It's useful to me to visualize where I'm coming from, and where I'm going; this is why in the illustration on the previous page that I've tried to accomplish just that—mapping these unseen realms. A few things, certainly based on my personal experience, informed this map. First, taking a broad leap into just accepting quantum theory for the purposes of the zero-point field, we can determine it is the baseline—the "bottom"—and at that bottom, is the Underworld. The Kingdom of the Dead. That churning sea of consciousness, free of the constraints of a living body. Central, of course, would be the *Material Plane*, reality, the place we are currently occupying, and above that—the Astral Plane. Celestial, bound to thought and air, we might establish it as a kind of *above* to all that which is *below*. Bottom, middle, top—Underworld, Physical Plane, Astral. And while this serves our purposes pretty well, those are not the only realms worth considering.

Adjacent to the Astral/Celestial Plane—bound to mind, consciousness, and *higher vibrations*—we have both the Collective Unconscious, and Realms of Deity. Adjacent the Underworld, the Kingdom of the Dead, are the Dreaming and Liminal Spaces; but it isn't quite that simple. If, like me, you're a fan of string theory, you can account for all those other unseen and unnamed places (the realms of Fairy, and so on) by imagining infinite Material Planes shattering outward endlessly, close enough to sense and, possibly, interact with. While I don't plan on touching on the Astral Plane, the Realms of Deity, or the Collective Unconscious (they're slightly extraneous to our topic), I want to touch on the interconnected nature of these places and how we might meaningfully move between them. Certainly, the Astral Plane is an excellent pathway by which to access the Realms of Deity, and the Collective Unconscious, but not such a good path for traveling to the Underworld. Liminal Spaces and the Dreaming, on the other hand, are clear-cut paths to the Kingdom of the Dead—but not such a great path for traveling to the Astral Plane—and so on. Consider these a series of shortcuts through and around that veil, that shrouds us from not just the dead, but other planes and the beings that occupy them.

BACK TO BASICS

While experimenting with travel between Liminal Spaces *The Skeleton Key* talisman will be crucial to your work. This talisman will help you travel more easily granting you access to specific places within the cosmology beyond the veil and can be found on page 32 of this chapter.

THE LIMINAL SPACES

We get the word *liminal* from the Latin *līminālis* for threshold—a beginning—an entrance. A place between, in which we wait, in which we stand between the known and unknown. Richard Rohr, an author and Franciscan friar, describes Liminal Space as "sacred space," where "transformation takes place," calling it a "threshold [...] where we are betwixt and between [...] the old world is left behind (and) we're not sure of the new one."[39] Here, they say, is "the realm where God can best get at us because we are out of the way. In sacred space the old world is able to fall apart, and the new world can be revealed."[40] Inevitable spaces—varied, and holy from which we might move betwixt and between.

---

39 Richard Rohr, *Everything Belongs: The Gift of Contemplative Prayer* (New York: Crossroad Publishing, 2003), 159.
40 Ibid.

BURIAL PLACES

Cemeteries are an unusual place, necromantically. Not necessarily haunted or frequented by the dead in the way most might think (after all, why would they want to be there?), though they certainly have a hexicology all their own.[41] I quite like to think of them as a bit of a way station, as busy as any train platform with all manner of beings coming and going, traveling by way of bone. It's a useful (if silly) visualization to think of each burial plot as a tube at the bank drive-through, ferrying eidōlon to and fro as they go about their business, and you too might use this space in that way as you travel ethereally. Of course, any burial place will have guardians particular to it, such as the Ankou, the last person buried there in a given year, whose responsibility it is to reap the dead who will be buried there.[42]

Another example would be the first individual interred in any burial place, who you might consider a mayor of sorts. Show care to befriend them, as it is their job to keep the dead in and the living out. They will always have a vested interest in caretaking those within and without as they are eternally bound to the space, and gifts should always (and regularly) be made to this individual when working in a cemetery. I don't like to feel as though I have an economic relationship with the dead, if I'm walking into a space, taking what I need, and tossing some coins over my shoulder—that doesn't feel right to me.

I wouldn't, for example, leave cash on my partner's nightstand every time we sleep together and that's because we have a partnership, we know one another intimately and are invested in one another's needs. These are the kinds of relationships I build with the burial spaces in which I work. I know that I'm there as often as possible, cleaning, archiving, speaking to the dead as a friend and ally. Sure, I leave gifts for the beings occupying the spaces in which I work, but much like you would for any friend, I take them things they love because I care about them.

---

41 Danielle Dionne, *Magickal Mediumship: Partnering with the Ancestors for Healing and Spiritual Development* (Woodbury, MN: Llewellyn Publications, 2020), 191.

42 Ellen Badone, "Death Omens in a Breton Memorate," *Folklore* 98, no. 1 (January 1987): 99–104, https://doi.org/ 10.1080/0015587X.1987.9716401.

Some materials, such as *The Gospel of the Ghouls* by Baron and Baronessa Araignee, offer advice such as "When leaving the Cemetery, some necromancers burn incense at the threshold, while others thank the Chief of the Dead for admittance. Others do both, however, they even go to the extent of sweeping away their footprints as a sign of respect and reverence. Once you exit, never look back, as this is a universal signal for unfinished business and for the Dead to follow you home uninvited."[43]

Do I believe that? Not necessarily, but plenty do. I do have gestures of respect that I perform in those spaces, such as not wearing shoes in burial places (unless I am required to), but I don't go so far as to believe that we must prevent unwanted tag alongs. I am, after all, there to make friends.

GHOST STORY: BONAVENTURE CEMETERY,
SAVANNAH GEORGIA
Bonaventure Cemetery is best known for the haunting statue of a small child which graced the cover of *Midnight in the Garden of Good and Evil*. The locals know that child still wanders Bonaventure to this day. Having lost their life to pneumonia at age six, Gracie Watson is the face of that well-known piece of sculpture. If you leave coins at the feet of the statue, Gracie is known to let you have a glimpse of them darting through the headstones, and for those who stood too close? Tears of blood stream down the statue's lovely face.

HAUNTED PLACES

It's odd to me how we hold "haunted" places to a different standard. When someone says a place is haunted, we take that at face value and don't critically analyze the statement. Nobody wants to be the one to walk into Eastern State Penitentiary and say, hmm... actually, I'm not really feeling it here. So, our imagination fills in the blanks, a sort of self-fulfilling prophecy. If we wish for it to be haunted, then it will be, so it's important to keep this in mind and

---

43 Baron Araignee and Baronessa Araignee, *The Gospel of the Ghouls* (The Arcane Press, 2016), 146.

ask yourself what you believe. Between you and me, I'm likely to be very skeptical of *haunted* locations, and for a few reasons.

First off, *skepticism is really healthy*. It's *important* to be skeptical. If we're not, we aren't addressing our confirmation biases, and we need to challenge our ideas about things. Always. About everything. Second, people are mostly full of...well—they're full of something. Funny how hauntings always happen to be in interesting places that make for great tourist destinations. It's never somewhere completely boring like the box store near my hometown that is sitting on top of a cemetery that was bulldozed for a parking lot. How about the pretty ordinary houses all over the world that nobody ever died in, but just *attract* things? Sometimes truly haunted places are seemingly boring and full of life—and sometimes, interesting places just aren't haunted. But truly haunted places? They are holy, liminal, a doorway between worlds. Why would you ever want to ruin it by closing that door? And really, could you? Could anyone? Or will those doors always try to open somewhere in the world?

Ghost Story: The Winchester Mansion, San Jose, California

Sarah Winchester spent a life haunted by those who lost their lives to firearms manufactured by Winchester. To appease those vengeful apparitions, Sarah elected to build them a house and never stop building it. From the time they began, to the time of their own death in 1922, Sarah added nine kitchens, forty-seven fireplaces, thirteen bathrooms, forty staircases, two thousand doors, and over ten thousand windows. Some maddeningly sprawling into nothingness.

BRIDGES

Bridges have always served a specific purpose: connecting two disparate places. For this reason, bridges cannot escape their symbolic attachment to the crossing between life and death. A common motif in myths throughout the world is a spectral bridge by which the dead find their way to their final destinations within the Kingdom of the Dead. These bridges serve as pathways, and for that reason, mundane bridges here on the Material Plane act as a similarly Liminal Space—neither here nor there, suspended above whatever chasm might lie below.

Ghost Story: County Road 625 East, Avon, Indiana

Built for Big Four Railroad in 1906, the bridge that spans County Road 625 East in Avon, Indiana, has a presence of its own. So known it is for the cries of the dead, that those crossing it loudly honk their horns as they pass beneath it to drown out their wails. Locals know that a young parent crossed the bridge on foot while holding their sick infant, attempting to get them to a doctor, but they slipped and fell to their deaths. Today, the infant can be heard screaming as it falls, and the parent screaming as they search for them.

CROSSROADS

Widely regarded throughout the world as being associated with magic and the unknown, places where two roads meet—intersections between the material, and the other—have always been haunted places. Frequented by eidōlon, these in-between places, neither one road, nor the other, have been used throughout history as places where one might command the dead to appear. Much of the folklore surrounding crossroads suggests they are frequented—or *haunted* if you prefer—by various supernatural entities. Fairies, demons, ignis fatuus, even *witches*—if you'd like to count us among the supernatural. The dead, it would seem, have a lot of competition at the very crowded crossroads. Not without contradiction, some lore suggests that crossroads cannot be crossed by the dead, and so, if pursued by a malevolent eidōlon (if there truly is such a thing), one should head to the crossroads, leaving them safely on the other side.

Ghost Story: Devil's Crossroads, Clarksdale, Mississippi

The intersection of Highway 61 and Highway 49 in Clarksdale, Mississippi is likely the most well-known crossroads in all the world. Marked today with three big guitars, the Devil's Crossroads is supposedly the location at which Robert Johnson sold their soul to the Devil in exchange for musical mastery. (There are some who believe the true crossroad is the nearby intersection of Highway 8 and 1, Rosedale, and you'll have to decide for yourself.)

DOORS AND OTHER PASSAGEWAYS

From the myriad pieces of lore surrounding the use of doors as a means for warding the home against entry by the dead, to the folk belief that the newly dead always be carried out the back door, doors have long had a connection with death. Passing through a doorway is nothing short of abandoning one's current place and entering another—a ritual so mundane that it goes forgotten, a ritual in which we come and go.[44] It is from doors themselves that we derive the word liminal—the Latin *limina* meaning "threshold." A door adjusts our way of seeing and moving; suggesting a within and a without, a place that is not a place, a boundary that defines us as insiders—or outsiders. Doors provide a kind of context for possibility, a liminality that can be seen or unseen, real or imagined. You, even now, stand on a threshold of a kind. As you consider a new perspective, new magic, a new way of imagining things, a door is open to you—the welcome mat prominently displayed—but do you open it? Do you dare walk through?

GHOST STORY: VIKING AGE SCANDINAVIA,
AND DOORS FOR THE DEAD

History tells us that Viking Age people built free standing "doors to the dead," put doorways in burial places, and sometimes, buried the dead in doorways. These "ritualized doors functioned in three ways: they created connections between the dead and the living; they made up boundaries and thresholds that could be controlled; and they formed between-spaces, expressing liminality and, conceivably, deviance."[45] These were boundaries they could control, a Liminal Space that one could choose to open—and certainly, choose to close.

---

44 Marianne Hem Eriksen, "Doors to the Dead: The Power of Doorways and Thresholds in Viking Age Scandinavia," *Archaeological Dialogues* 20, no. 2 (November 8, 2013): 187–214, https://doi.org/ 10.1017/ S1380203813000238.

45 Ibid.

CONSULT YOUR BOOK OF SHADES
Building the Nekromanteion on page 197 of the Acts and Devotions section of the Book of Shades walks you through the process of navigating the liminal pathway that is a fundamental center of my own practice.

THE DREAMING

I say often that if you were meeting up with a new friend and neither knew how to get to the other's house, you might meet up at (for example) the Waffle House in Atlanta, Georgia. You've both been there. You know what it looks like, and how to get there. That is what the Dreaming is to the living and the dead. Both know how to effectively get there and navigate the space. This makes it often easier than communicating directly between the Material Plane and the Underworld. In *The Path of Shadows*, Gwendolyn Taunton writes that "The Land of the Dead, and the Land of Dreams are so close that the boundaries between the two [...] can even be crossed."[46] Indeed, according to these directions, the Dreaming is located adjacent Hades/the Underworld, "past the White Rock and the Sun's Western Gates and past the Land of Dreams (*demos oneiron*) [...] (are) the fields of Asphodel where the dead, the burnt-out wraiths of mortals, make their home."[47]

It is for this reason that I say that anyone interested in necromantic practice should master lucid dreaming. Rarely do magic and observable science overlap, but this is one area in which they do. Whether we believe these experiences to be literal or metaphorical, one can provably lucidly dream, and one can provably interact with the dead in dreams.

---

46 Gwendolyn Taunton, *The Path of Shadows: Chthonic Gods, Oneiromancy & Necromancy in Ancient Greece* (Colac, Victoria: Manticore Press, 2018), 135.
47 Kelly Bulkeley, *Dreaming in the World's Religions: A Comparative History* (New York: New York University Press, 2008), 142.

If you could speak to a deceased person, face-to-face, touch and hold them, and interact meaningfully like you could any living person, why would you not make that a reality? This is what the Dreaming can be for your practice. Once you've learned this skill, it can be used in many magical applications, particularly in communicating visually, verbally, and meaningfully, with the dead.

EXERCISE: LUCID DREAMING

Time and Place: Any
Supplies: A small toy, coin, or similar object
Purpose: Lucid dream training.

The Dreaming is a place where we might enhance our practice to include consistently aware experiences with the dead, and lucid dreaming, (the process by which one maintains awareness while dreaming and gains control over the dream environment) is how we can accomplish that.

It's one of few places and ways in which you can measurably meet and interact with the dead, with full visual and auditory input. To begin lucid dreaming, there are quite a few methods and exercises that you can employ, the first of which is the reality testing method.[48] In this method, all you need to do is ask yourself throughout the day whether you are asleep or awake while performing an activity that tests the environment.

A good example of this method comes from the movie *Inception*, in which a top is spun to see if it falls, or continues spinning, and other examples include finding your reflection in a mirror to look for distortions, holding your breath and trying to breathe through your nose, and so on. Doing this repetitiously means you're likely to repeat the reality testing method in your dreams as well, and when

---

48 Kristoffer Appel, Gordon Pipa, and Martin Dresler, "Investigating Consciousness in the Sleep Laboratory—an Interdisciplinary Perspective on Lucid Dreaming," *Interdisciplinary Science Reviews* 43, no. 2 (November 12, 2017): 192–207, https://doi.org/ 10.1080/03080188.2017.1380468.

reality fails the check, you'll have encountered a lucid moment. The second preferred method is a combination of the "wake back to bed," or WBTB, technique, combined with the "mnemonic induction lucid dream," or MILD, technique.[49] Here, you repeat a mantra you've chosen that clarifies that you'd like to know that you are dreaming (the MILD technique), combining this with setting alarms for a couple of hours before you normally wake, then after a few moments going right back to sleep (The WBTB technique), will assist you in developing lucid dreaming skills.

THE KINGDOM OF THE DEAD

Many realms exist in the Underworld. In these realms, at the bottom of a churning sea of consciousness and dark matter at the bottom of the universe, there are domains of particular death deities, lavish gardens, utopian islands, war-torn battlefields, and places of quiet reflection—each bearing a unique character and set of rules. In fact, I believe all Underworlds exist in this place—in much the same way that Australia shares space with Alaska on this big blue world we call home. But how do we get there? In *The Crooked Path: An Introduction to Traditional Witchcraft*, Kelden states that "The Underworld is accessed by traveling down the axis Mundi, which may involve climbing down the roots of a tree, entering an underground cave, or descending a staircase or ladder."[50] Me? I prefer to simply *fall*.

REALMS

The Underworld is called many names, and has as many appearances, rulers, and inhabitants, as there are stars in the sky—but some things remain constant. A lower realm, overseen by the gods of death and liminality, inhabited by the dead. In my descent into darkness, the

---

49 Ibid.

50 Kelden, *The Crooked Path: An Introduction to Traditional Witchcraft* (Woodbury, MN: Llewellyn Publications, 2020), 119–138.

depths of the Underworld as a child was a great expanse at the bottom of a dense, dark sea, and all the things I came to know of the Underworld as an adult existed within this expanse. This sampling of archetypical realms is largely reflective of Hades, the Underworld of the Greek myth, though the terminology reflects my own practice.

The neutral zone of the Underworld, **The Grey**, is where the broader population of the dead is to be found. Why define it with the word grey? Because it is a safe, and neutral place like the Greek Asphodel Meadows: for those who lived ordinary, mundane lives, without particular note. Though this may seem a harsh descriptor for a life, we must remember that *ordinary* simply is the counterpoint to *extraordinary*—each life is rich and impactful, some simply more so than others. For those who instead wasted their lives, there is **The Isle of Sorrows**. In the *Aeneid*, Virgil tells us that there is a field in which those who've wasted their lives (Virgil specifies on "ruthless love") might forever wander paths known only to their feet.[51] Unable to forget grief or loss—even in death—these inhabitants of the sorrowful places of the Underworld weep eternally.

The truly vile, however, inhabit **The Depths**. Zeus, in describing Tartarus in the *Iliad*, states that it is "as far beneath Hades as heaven is above earth," describing it as the "deepest gulf beneath the earth."[52] A gate of iron, a threshold made of bronze, a place where deities themselves hold those who disrupt divine order. But there is a contrast. Shangri-La, the Elysian Fields, Utopia, the Garden of Eden, Paradise. **The Pleasure Garden**, an elusive and much sought-after place representing dreams of peace—a hidden paradise outside the realms and concerns of the living or the dead. Within Hades, Elysium and/or the Isles of the Blessed exist as a place where only the most extraordinary of humans might reside in death. These places of sunlight and beauty, free of further service, toil, and of pain—an idealized afterlife for many. I like to imagine these are the places where Persephone might keep a garden and, perhaps, it's the reason the Underworld is rife with agricultural tools such as scythes and pitchforks.

---

51 Virgil, *Virgil: Eclogues-Georgics-Aeneid I–VI Vol. 1*, trans. H. Rushton Fairclough (William Heinemann. G.P. Putnam's Sons, 1916).

52 Homer, *The Iliad*, trans. A.T. Murray (London: Harvard University Press, 1924), 8.17.

WATERWAYS

If there's one thing the Underworld is not lacking, it's water. In addition to notable rivers and lakes, in any description of the Underworld, you might find—including my own death experience and descriptive text of the zero-point field—there is a sea. Many of these bodies of water hold a great deal of significance for not only the living and the dead, but for deities as well. Hades, in Greek myth, is encircled by five rivers, with the river Styx coiling around the realms of the dead seven times. Styx, *The River of Oaths*, a place where even deities made their promises, possessed waters that caused those who swam in them to become invulnerable. The river that must be crossed after death on one's journey to the Underworld, its banks lined with those who have no coin to pay the Conductor's fare. *The River of Forgetfulness*, of oblivion, Lethe is a place where the dead might leave their lives behind and prepare for reincarnation. To drink from the waters of Lethe is to wash the slate clean and leave your memories behind.

Acheron, *The River of Sorrow*, black and deep; endless sorrow flowing forth for eternity. Described as a place of healing, not punishment, the banks of the river Acheron are lined with those who were neutral in life. Those who never took a side. Deeper still in the depths of the Underworld lies *The River of Wailing*, the Cocytus. Its banks, lined with those who mourn—even in death—their tears feeding Cocytus, and those tears of sorrow flowing into Acheron. And lastly, *The River of Fire*. Filled with those who committed acts in life deserving of retribution, the Phlegethon is a coiling river of flame and torment, its banks guarded by guardians armed with arrows to fire at those who would attempt escape.

EXERCISE: CRAFTING A SKELETON KEY ☠

TIME AND PLACE: Between midnight and 3 a.m. In prepared ritual space
SUPPLIES: Basic necromantic ritual supplies, Human bone
OPTIONAL SUPPLIES: Pin vice, Cord
PURPOSE: To open that which is closed to the living, and to close that which is open.

The purpose of the skeleton key is to create an instrument that will assist you in moving through ethereal space and navigate the Underworld more effectively. With the addition of the *Locate* sigil, you can create a powerful instrument to guide your work with the dead. The first step, of course, is to find the bone that is right for your project. You'll want a bone that is strong and dense enough for carving and able to hold up to frequent use. You might consider a metacarpal, which is dense enough to make it ideal for carving and inscribing, in addition to having a satisfyingly key-like length.

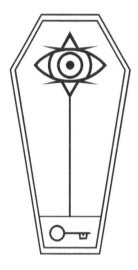

To Find That Which Is Lost

You may wish to add a cord so that it might be worn as a pendant or easily carried. Bones are naturally hollow, and so it isn't difficult to make an opening through it with a pin vice. I recommend not making a hole large enough for your cord, but rather passing a bit of wire through to create a makeshift jump ring. At this point, you may move on to finishing your key in any way you prefer (you could leave it plain, give it a protective coating, etch it with patterns, or stain it with inks or other stains), as well as inscribing it with the sigil above. End by consecrating your new key as a necromantic instrument.

Back to Basics

To begin, you'll want to set up your ritual according to the *Necromantic Ritual Outline* on page 119. When you've finished making it, you'll want to consecrate it using the *Consecration of Ritual Instruments for Necromantic Practice* ritual located on page 123 of the Rites and Rituals section of the Book of Shades.

Consult Your Book of Shades:

To gain a better understanding of the Underworld, refer to *Pathworking the Underworld* on page 143 of the Book of Shades, which will help you learn to navigate that space in a controlled manner. If you'd like to remain unnoticed by the dead while you explore, the *Invisibility* sigil spell on page 158 of the Skills and Attributes section will help you accomplish just that.

LAST WORDS

Perhaps the dead, these other realms, and magical experiences themselves, are all just science we don't have words for, which presents far more interesting questions than "are ghosts real." What are these places in the depths, to us, the living? A sea of darkness dotted with infinite lights, a vastness between and worlds surrounding each, unknown to us until we reach them. Here on this Material Plane, we are blinded to the fullness of the Underworld, and remain so for so long as a beating heart resides in our chest. The dark depths, the realms of the dead, where we move between people and places like flitting dreams—a place in which it is we who are ghosts.

4

THE NATURE OF
A SOUL

"Monsters are real, ghosts are real too. They live inside us, and sometimes, they win."
— Stephen King, *The Shining*

To begin a necromantic practice is, ostensibly, to work with the dead, and so, the question then becomes: who are they? It is an important part of this work to define what type of incorporeal being you are interacting with, where they reside, what they can and cannot do, and what knowledge they possess. To an extent, to answer those questions, we must determine the very structure of the soul. What do these things mean for one's afterlife, reincarnation, and beliefs? I believe that it's reasonably impossible to start down the path of necromantic specialization without considering these questions and answering them for yourself. Perhaps, at the end of it all, you'll have come to very different conclusions than I did, and that's just fine. In a universe of infinite possibility, all underworlds are possible, and yours does not have to look like my own. So it is, for these reasons, that a discussion of the dead must begin with a discussion of the soul.

For time immemorial, humanity has had a culture of veneration of the dead in some form or another, coupled with ideas of where the dead might or might not reside, what tasks they might perform, and so on. These ideas don't all play nicely together, particularly for a family with mixed cultural and religious backgrounds. How might you resolve a loved one being simultaneously in an afterlife such as Heaven, Valhalla, or Duat; are they reincarnated, haunting you, or acting as a guide? How does one reconcile seeing the eidōlon of someone living, or even themselves? How do we reconcile a person haunting two different people, or places?

Before the Christian idea of the singular soul overtook the public perception, cultures had a variety of unique positions on what made up the soul, many believing it not to be a singular entity, but existing in many parts. The Norse *fylgja*, *hugr*, and *hamr*, for example, show a system outside the singular "norm."[53] Plato hypothesized as well that the soul existed in multiple parts, consisting of the logos, thymus, and eros.[54] Many of today's Neopagan traditions have a practice of both reincarnation, and of magical ancestors (such as the Mighty Dead) who might take part in our goings on—and how can these co-exist?[55] The simple answer is that the soul is not singular.

Within the framework of a multifaceted soul, it might not just be possible, but is likely, that the deceased exists in many places at once and, in many forms. The question then becomes what part of the individual deceased is with you, what part of you yourself is haunting some part of the world as we speak, how do you reintegrate those parts with yourself and should you, and what do these things mean for broader haunting phenomena?

It's a reasonable question to ask what working with the dead means for those of us who are coming from a belief system that expresses a singular soul's journey or the soul as a singular entity. It's important to confront the existential and ontological questions and paradoxes that might arise now, so that we can walk into our rituals firm in our understanding of things. For me, I don't think that reincarnation, afterlives, hauntings, summoning, and so on are mutually exclusive and that viewpoint is not unique to me. My own beliefs were born in part from the ancient Egyptian/Kemetic concept of the soul, even if I diverge a bit from there.

---

53 Claude Lecouteux, *The Return of the Dead* (Rochester, VT: Inner Traditions, 2009), 163–70.

54 David Jones, Jason M. Wirth, and Michael Schwartz, *The Gift of Logos: Essays in Continental Philosophy* (Newcastle: Cambridge Scholars, 2010), 33–35.

55 Gerald Brosseau Gardner, *Witchcraft Today* (Secaucus, NJ: Citadel Press, 2004), 140.

THE PARTS OF A SOUL

I mentioned early on that throughout this book you would find some of my own UPG, as well as bits of my practice. As I talk about the soul, the dead, and the Underworld, that will be an area with a heavy injection of my own personal practice. Like any good fan of tabletop role-playing games, I took a *homebrew* approach (defined as following pre-established rules, but using your own names, places, and designations) to defining the soul, the occupants of the Underworld, and indeed, the Underworld itself. This approach was the only way that I could wrap all my thoughts and experiences up in a neat little bow. As such, this group of archetypes for the faceted soul is largely reflective of the complex beliefs ancient Egyptians/Kemets held about the soul, in which the soul is comprised of nine parts, each uniquely interacting with their life and afterlife. This came to be my structural framework for a variety of phenomena, though the terminology reflects my own practice.

THE ETHEREAL FORM

If the funerary rites of the dead are properly observed and the deities of death deemed the deceased worthy, the Ethereal body might go on to an afterlife, reincarnated, or conjoined through funerary ritual with other portions of the soul to form a powerful and intelligent working spirit. This enlightened and whole form of the Ethereal dead is likely to seek opportunities in death to assist the living by working as a control spirit, functioning as the Mighty Dead, or, returning to the lands of the living as an avenging spirit seeking to right wrongs.

A letter from Middle Kingdom Egypt from a living person to their deceased spouse, whom we might reasonably assume was haunting them, states:

> *"What wicked thing have I done to thee that I should have come to this evil pass? [...] But what thou hast done to me is to have laid hands on me, although I had nothing wicked to thee. [...] When thou didst sicken of the illness which thou hadst, I caused a master-physician to be fetched [...] I spent eight months without*

eating and drinking (properly). I wept exceedingly together with my household in front of my street-quarter. I gave linen clothes to wrap thee and left no benefit undone that had to be performed for thee. [...] I have spent three years alone without entering into a house, though it is not right that one like me should have to do it. This have I done for thy sake. But, behold, thou dost not know good from bad."[56]

This marks an excellent example of the reincarnated Ethereal body as an avenging spirit, though the letter shows little of what might be troubling the spirit. This portion of yourself might move around the world freely when you are in an altered state of consciousness, such as sleep or purposeful projection outside the body in pathworking.

CORRESPONDENCE: West, Hallows Eve
OPPOSED BY: The Carnal form
WHAT IS THE ETHEREAL FORM'S PURPOSE? In life, to interact with the incorporeal and liminal; in death, to interact with the living.
CAN THE ETHEREAL FORM BECOME SEPARATED FROM THE LIVING? The Ethereal form separates from your Carnal form to facilitate Ethereal travel.
CAN THE ETHEREAL FORM BE SUMMONED? The living might summon the Ethereal form (of potentially the living or the dead), though this form of the deceased might be ascended beyond the issues afflicting the living and therefore show disinterest in topics that they no longer feel are worthwhile.
DOES THE ETHEREAL FORM HAUNT? The Ethereal form may frequent an area, person, or group as an avenger, protector, or as a guide.
CAN THE ETHEREAL FORM BE BANISHED? The Ethereal form may be banished, exorcised, relocated, re-birthed, or reincarnated.
CAN THE ETHEREAL FORM BE DESTROYED? The Ethereal form cannot be destroyed.

---

56 Don Nardo, *Living in Ancient Egypt* (San Diego, CA: Greenhaven Press, 2004), 39.

VERDURE

One's life force after death is something that one can lose, thus suffering a second death. It is that living vital force that the dead might feed with offerings, that they might build up to remain strong. Verdure represents and reflects the power, energy, and currency the deceased possesses in the kingdoms of the dead. A similar concept would be the ancient Egyptian concept of Sekhem, or form, which is a concept defining one's life after death.[57]

CORRESPONDENCE: Northwest, Winter Solstice

OPPOSED BY: Vitality

WHAT IS VERDURE'S PURPOSE? Verdure is the breath of un-life possessed by the inhabitants of the Underworld and fed by offerings and remembrances. Opposite and equivalent to Vitality.

CAN VERDURE BECOME SEPARATED FROM THE LIVING? The living do not possess Verdure.

CAN VERDURE BE SUMMONED? Verdure can be summoned and contained through limited ritual means. This breath of un-life has no intelligence.

DOES VERDURE HAUNT? No. As it is a "life" force opposite and equivalent to Vitality, Verdure possesses no consciousness.

CAN VERDURE BE BANISHED? As it is a "life" force opposite and equivalent to Vitality, Verdure cannot be banished.

CAN VERDURE BE DESTROYED? When the dead are forgotten and receive no offerings, they have lost their Verdure and will fade from the Kingdoms of the Dead.

THE CEASELESS ONE

During funerary rites, the Character and Intellect are reunited, creating the immortal self or double. Without funerary rites, one's Character remains bound to the physical body, leaving them unable to maintain their memories or cross away from the Physical Plane. The Ceaseless One (the Ancient Egyptian *Akh*), is a living entity,

---

57 Rosalie David, *Religion and Magic in Ancient Egypt* (New York: Penguin Books, 2002), 58, 117–18, 142–45, 158–59.

able to interact intelligently as they choose in death. Many texts in funerary literature were intended to warn the dead how to behave in the afterlife, to prevent them from dying a second death.

In some ancient texts, the intellect is known as "the magically effective one," one's living sentient magical self, one's intellect, affecting the afterlife.[58] It is only through proper funerary rites that the deceased might be transformed into the Ceaseless One, which might exist so long as they are remembered, offered to, and so on. They might affect living loved ones by afflicting them with illness and bad luck if they do not make proper offerings, or keep up their burial site, or could bless them in an equal measure for gifts given.

CORRESPONDENCE: North, Autumnal Equinox

OPPOSED BY: The Witness

WHAT IS THE CEASELESS ONE'S PURPOSE? To join the incorporeal to the corporeal, in life or in death.

CAN THE CEASELESS ONE BECOME SEPARATED FROM THE LIVING? While the living do not possess a Ceaseless One, they do possess a component: the Intellect, which separates from your Carnal form to facilitate Astral travel.

CAN THE CEASELESS ONE BE SUMMONED? The Ceaseless One could be called upon by the living to aid in matters concerning the gods, and is a useful, summonable, intelligent version of the deceased in full possession of the life's memories of their living self. This form of the deceased might be ascended beyond the issues afflicting the living and therefore show disinterest in topics that they no longer feel are worthwhile.

DOES THE CEASELESS ONE HAUNT? Without proper funerary rites to become the Ceaseless One, the Intellect will become a roaming intelligence, dead or undead, capable of doing harm equivalent to poltergeist, revenants, et cetera.

CAN THE CEASELESS ONE BE BANISHED? The Ceaseless One, and its component, Intellect, may be banished or moved from one location to another.

---

58 James P. Allen, *Middle Egyptian: An Introduction to the Language and Culture of Hieroglyphs* (New York: Cambridge University Press, 2000).

Can the Ceaseless One be destroyed? The Ceaseless One, and its component, Intellect, cannot be destroyed, but may fade away if forgotten.

THE CHARACTER

That which makes you uniquely you: the Character. In this way, even objects might have a Character if they are indeed one of a kind. Pieces of art or sculpture, a handmade piece of furniture, a hand-sewn dress—these are all items that possess a Character. In many cultures, this part of the self (referred to by ancient Egyptians as the *Ba*) is represented as a bird after death.[59] The Character stands alone from other parts of the soul because it functions as the intelligent, complete form of the individual, which may choose to interact with the world after death as they might always have. This portion of yourself might move around the world freely when you are in an altered state of consciousness, such as during sleep or purposeful projection outside the body.

Correspondence: Northeast, August Eve

Opposed By: The Umbra

What is the Character's purpose? To join the incorporeal to the corporeal, in life or in death.

Can the Character become separated from the living? Through disassociation, yes. In moments of disassociation, we dispossess portions of the self from our Carnal form, which might include the Character, the Sobriquet, or the Umbra.

Can the Character be summoned? Summoning the Character can be quite useful for survivors seeking closure as they will behave in a manner that is in keeping with their behaviors in life and possess the memories of the living in entirety. The Character is, however, unintelligent, and likely to haunt a location familiar to them, playing out memories like a recording.

Does the Character haunt? As a haunting, the Character is likely to seek out people and places that were familiar to them in life.

---

59   David, *Religion and Magic in Ancient Egypt*, 58, 117–18, 142–45, 158–59.

Can the Character be banished? Yes, the Character can be banished or removed to a new location.

Can the Character be destroyed? When forgotten, the Character may begin to fade away until it ceases to be.

THE CARNAL FORM

An important part of the soul, the Carnal form—your physical body—is what joins the spiritual, the incorporeal—the soul—to the Material Plane of existence. In *The Return of the Dead*, Lecouteux posits that "the soul remained connected to the body as long as the body had not been destroyed."[60] It is an interesting thought that over many cultures, some part of the soul remains attached to their physical remains, no matter how small and unlikely the piece, leaving plenty of room for consideration of embalming of the dead as a purely magical choice in some instances. Lecouteux goes on to say that "it was sufficient for a little of the body's ash to be ingested by an animal for the soul to move into another body," which itself springs to mind many uses for human or animal remains in terms of channeling and shapeshifting.[61] The Carnal form might reasonably be occupied by multiple entities aside from the general components of one's own soul.

Correspondence: East, Beltane

Opposed By: The Ethereal form

What is the Carnal form's purpose? To create a bridge between the incorporeal to the corporeal, in life or in death.

Can the Carnal form become separated from the living? Only in the limited capacity of amputation, surgical removal of organs, et cetera, which may contain the essence of the person from whom they were removed.

Can the Carnal form be summoned? Insomuch as you can request a living person's presence, the Carnal form can be summoned.

Does the Carnal form haunt? As a revenant or other returned dead/undead, yes, or, like any number of people in my

---

60 Lecouteux, *The Return of the Dead*, 180.

61 Ibid.

life, they might haunt the couch, binging streaming media and potato chips.

Can the Carnal form be banished? Insomuch as you can request a living person to leave a given place, yes.

Can the Carnal form be destroyed? Yes, through acts such as cremation, aquamation, resomation, decomposition, et cetera.

VITALITY

Vitality distinguishes the dead from the living. The breath of life, the vital spark—it is not only living beings who have Vitality but also sustenance such as food and drink, blood, and physical activities such as manual labor, cooking, exercise, sex, and so on. When we offer these things to incorporeal beings such as the gods, or the dead, it is Vitality that they take from those offerings, leaving behind something lifeless. Spent. For the dead, gifts of Vitality offer them energy and strength, and feed their Verdure. That first breath and last breath are the dividing line of one's Vitality, and it is sustained through the consumption of food and drink. It is for this reason that these gifts are important for the dead, that they might sustain the deceased in the realms of the dead.

Correspondence: Southeast, Midsummer

Opposed By: Verdure

What is Vitality's purpose? To distinguish the living from the dead, to provide the spark of vigor and passion to life.

Can it become separated from the living? Only in the limited capacity of Vitality taken from offerings by incorporeal beings.

Can Vitality be summoned? The Vital Force can be summoned and contained through limited ritual means. This breath of life has no intelligence.

Does Vitality haunt? Vitality cannot haunt through any circumstance.

Can Vitality be banished? Not without causing the death of a living person.

Can Vitality be destroyed? Vitality is destroyed at the moment of physical death.

THE WITNESS

Formed from the sacred well of all things, your physical and metaphorical heart is your literal key to the afterlife, the Underworld, and the realms of the gods. Living or dead, if you are to pass through these Liminal Spaces, the heart bears witness and offers evidence for or against its bearer. This Witness is neutral, measured against the qualities of the gods, and may be hostile against you, depending on the life you have lived. In death, the heart must be carefully preserved so that it might bear witness for you, though in ancient Egypt, talismans might have been placed above the heart to prevent it from telling its tales. As we all know, to greet death with a heavy heart is a terrible thing, dooming one to an eternity of restlessness.

CORRESPONDENCE: South, Vernal Equinox

OPPOSED BY: The Ceaseless One

WHAT IS THE WITNESS'S PURPOSE? To bear witness to the life of its bearer.

CAN THE WITNESS BECOME SEPARATED FROM THE LIVING? Only in the limited capacity of a heart transplant. In this instance, it should be preserved for the time of your death, so be certain to acquire it post-operatively.

CAN THE WITNESS BE SUMMONED? The Witness cannot be summoned by any means.

DOES THE WITNESS HAUNT? Much as Mr. Poe was happy to report in The Tell-Tale Heart, one's Witness might become restless if unhappy with the current state of your life—and let you know as much.

CAN THE WITNESS BE BANISHED? Not without causing the death of a living person.

CAN THE WITNESS BE DESTROYED? Yes, through acts such as cremation, aquamation, resomation, decomposition, et cetera.

THE UMBRA

Containing a summarization of a person's true self, their behavior, and their characteristics, the Umbra is the impact an individual has had on the world. Any representation of an individual (photographs, statues, et cetera) contains a portion of one's shadow. An agent of death itself, working hand-in-hand with the gods of the dead, the Umbra has a life entirely of its own. The darkness that exists in the presence of light, the Umbra is one's deepest subconscious (while being distinct from the Jungian concept of the shadow, and therefore, "shadow work"), the well of one's darkness, the repository of one's dread memory and the paths we fear to tread.

CORRESPONDENCE: Southwest, Feast of Torches

OPPOSED BY: The Character

WHAT IS THE UMBRA'S PURPOSE? To act as a protector and mirror for good through the depth of dark possibility.

CAN THE UMBRA BECOME SEPARATED FROM THE LIVING? Through trauma, the Umbra might become separated from the Carnal form, temporarily or permanently. The Umbra may behave as an Avenger, haunting those who have wronged their living self or others.

CAN THE UMBRA BE SUMMONED? Umbra may be summoned and are intelligent summons with full knowledge of the life lived, as well as their experiences beyond the Carnal form.

DOES THE UMBRA HAUNT? With the possibility of becoming a powerful poltergeist, the Umbra is one of the most potentially dangerous intelligent hauntings.

CAN THE UMBRA BE BANISHED? The Umbra may be banished by reintegration with the Carnal form (if living) or, through proper funerary rites, be relocated to the Underworld.

CAN THE UMBRA BE DESTROYED? The Umbra cannot be destroyed.

THE SOBRIQUET

A vital and often overlooked part of the "soul," one's name is an entity that lives alongside you until your death. So long as the Sobriquet is read or spoken, it provides Verdure for the many parts of the soul. But if a name is forgotten? Killed? Put aside? Replaced with a new name? It ceases to be. The name stands out as unique because it is so variable, and there could be so many. That is why, in my work, I do not represent it as one of the points in the circle, but rather as the altar within it, as that connection where West meets West, a picture of all, and none.

Correspondence: Each Sobriquet may have correspondences with any of the cardinal directions and sabbats, and therefore, it is best represented by the center point of your circle.

Opposed By: Each Sobriquet may have oppositions with any number of the remaining eight.

What is the Sobriquet's purpose? Like the many sides of a die, the Sobriquet(s) act as representative(s) of the various selves we have been in life.

Can the Sobriquet become separated from the living? The Sobriquet might have a life in un-life of its own beyond you if spoken into being by others.

Can the Sobriquet be summoned? Sobriquets may be summoned but will only possess the memories and characteristics relevant to that name, and those that knew them.

Can the Sobriquet haunt? The Sobriquet may haunt in myriad complex ways.

Can the Sobriquet be banished? Yes, the Sobriquet can be banished or removed to a new location.

Can the Sobriquet be destroyed? When forgotten, put aside, or through physical death, the Sobriquet may die, even if the Carnal Form is still living. Examples of this might be near-death experiences, the Lazarus Effect, unused nicknames, or dead names in some contexts.

Back to Basics

For elemental correspondences and oppositions, refer to the illustration in Laying out and preparing your circle on page 107 of Chapter 7: The Necromantic Ritual. You'll notice that the Sobriquet is not included within that illustration and the reason for that is simple: various names might be associated with any number of quarters or opposed by any number of parts of the soul.

THE SOULS JOURNEY AFTER DEATH

Devin Hunter notes in *The Witches Book of Spirits* that they prefer to give the recently deceased ninety days for this process, which Hunter refers to as "reorientation."[62] Whether or not I agree with the timeframe or naming convention, it is good advice. I would be remiss if I did not say that on the mundane side of things, it's crucial that the living take the time to grieve in a mundane way before seeking out any magical experience with those they've lost. Otherwise, you risk creating a codependent bond between the living and the dead in which neither can truly move on, and that just isn't healthy for anyone.

Over a period of days, weeks, months, the newly deceased must make the journey—in all their fractured forms—across the lands of the dead, to settle their accounts. Perhaps a funny way to put it, but it is not without first having met judgment, and accounting for the life that they have lived, that the dead might venture forward on their path. This is one of many reasons why it is so very crucial that we not disturb the recently deceased. Along this journey the dead encounter a variety of archetypal entities, which might present as any number of beings depending on the beliefs and practice of the deceased.

FIRST ON THE JOURNEY: THE PSYCHOPOMP

From the Greek *psychopompós*, meaning "guide of souls," psychopomps have always been a beloved companion of any person inclined to work with the dead.[63] Incorporeal beings tasked with guiding the newly dead through their postmortem journey and to their final places of work or rest, the psychopomp is there for all, a neutral being with no cause to judge. Three days after death, at the conclusion of funerary rites, the facets of the soul begin their journey by meeting with a psychopomp at the entrances to the Kingdom of the Dead, where a

---

62 Devin Hunter, *The Witch's Book of Spirits* (Woodbury, MN: Llewellyn Publications, 2017), 202

63 Diodorus Siculus, Immanel Bekker, and Ludwig Dindorf, *Diodori Bibliotheca Historica, Vol 1–2: Vol. 1* (Leipzig: In Aedibus B. G. Teubneri, 1888), Chapter 96.

conductor waits to assist them across the river. What psychopomp greets them will depend on their beliefs in life, any oaths or geas they're subject to, practitioners who may have sent guides on their behalf, and so on. The same is true for the entrance and method of crossing the veil that they might find; these will vary depending on the individual's experiences.

That's the Spirit!

The shapeshifting Ankou of Breton, Cornish, Norman French, and Welsh folklore might appear with any number of faces; a tall, thin person wearing a hat, a skeletal "grim reaper" in robes and wielding a scythe, occasionally simply as an Umbral form. The Ankou comes by carriage led by black horses, the graveyard watcher, protector of the graveyard, and guide of the souls who die on the land to which they are bound. This figure is unique in that they are a bit of a career option for the dead, and are typically the first person to die in a given year, buried in a particular space. Each burial place has its own unique Ankou, which changes every year.[64]

SECOND ON THE JOURNEY: THE CONDUCTOR

Charon at the oars, Urshanabi and their ferry, or the Ankou with their carriage. The Conductor takes the souls who are permitted to make the journey across the river, the crossroads, the veil, those borderlands between us and the dead. These dread conductors are neutral beings who are bound to a set of rules, however, and often, those rules include payment for passage. In many instances, only those who met their final rest with coins under the tongue or placed upon the eyes had payment for the fare, reason enough not to neglect grave goods for your loved one. As for those unable to pay the fare? Often left stranded between the land of the living and the land of the dead to wander until their fare has been paid.

---

64 Ernest L. Abel, *Death Gods: An Encyclopedia of the Rulers, Evil Spirits, and Geographies of the Dead* (Westport, CT: Greenwood Press, 2009), 20.

THAT'S THE SPIRIT!

Conductor of souls, Charon stands ready to lead those who have found their way to the shore across the rivers of Hades. Though a psychopomp they may be, Charon is unique in that the services they offer do not come freely. One must have a coin to present to Charon, or eternally wander the banks of the rivers.

THIRD ON THE JOURNEY: THE GUARDIAN AT THE GATES

After being transported into the Kingdom of the Dead, those newly deceased pass through the gates, which are guarded by any number of figures. Many-headed Cerberus. Garmr, bloody and growling. The demoness Ammit, at once hippopotamus, lion, and crocodile. Aker, the great lion with mouth open wide. Regardless of the guardian, the message is clear: all may enter, none may leave.

THAT'S THE SPIRIT!

Few can resist the guard dog of the Underworld: Cerberus. The "Hound of Hades" is best known for their capture by Hercules, though I am very fond of the myth that we received aconite from them. It is said that when Hercules pulled Cerberus into the sunlight to which they were unaccustomed, they vomited bile from which sprung aconite. Underworld dog vomit plants… way less glamorous and spooky than wolfsbane is generally made out to be.

FOURTH ON THE JOURNEY: THE JUDGE

Once received into the Kingdom of the Dead, the newly deceased appears before the Judge. Like all things, the beliefs and oaths of the deceased play a role in whom they must appear before. Will it be Rhadamanthus, Minos, and Aeacus? Or will you stand before the assessors of Ma'at, the forty-two gods of Ancient Egypt, who observe as you give confession? Perhaps instead it will be Yama, Hindu deity of death and justice, who will judge you in accordance with Karma. These judges determine one's worth based on the life they have lived.

These judgements will determine what part of the Kingdom of the Dead portions of your soul will occupy—if any at all. Many will take up residence in neutral areas, some returning to the land of the living as working spirits, and some, singled out for other realms.

THAT'S THE SPIRIT!

Not only a judge of the dead, but a symbol of un-life, Osiris waits with the assessors of Ma'at to judge those brought before them by Anubis. Those brought before this ancient judge knew they would become one with Osiris, receiving immortality through their existence in the afterlife, and through their living families on the Material Plane.

CAN WE ASSIST THE DEAD ON THIS JOURNEY?

By providing Vitality through offerings and acts of service, we may ensure that the dead have energy and are well-fed to make the trip. Providing grave goods for the deceased is hugely important to those who won't be caretaken by their loved ones, broadly. Imagine being forced to relocate to a new place with nothing but the clothes on your back—it would be a struggle. We can aid these dead (and indeed, gain their good graces for future workings) by gifting them things to make the journey easier. Consider packing a small bag with any number of things that one might wish to have in the Underworld and adding in something that links it to that person, such as a bit of earth from their grave along with three drops of blood from your left ring finger, before burying or burning it. This remands that gift to them and eases the journey. Last, you might consider more per-manent gifts for either individuals that you wish to ensure are taken care of forever, or for yourself. Create a marker or memorial with text declaring your gift to a deity of your choosing, worded: *This (marker) a gift that (your name) gives to (deity), that (deity) might give to (deceased).* Here, in assuring that the deity's name is read—that they are remembered—we have given to the deity, and in turn, they will give to the dead on our behalf.

BACK TO BASICS

There is more on the use of blood in spell work in both the Prologue on page xxii, and under Necromantic Instruments and Materials on page 77. For an alternative to blood, see *Granting the Qualities of Blood* on page 157 of the Skills and Attributes section of the Book of Shades. If you'd like to try a divination to determine what facet of the soul you've been communicating with, see *Identifying Parts of the Soul in Contact* on page 170 of the Correspondence and Congruence section.

CONSULT YOUR BOOK OF SHADES:

To get a better understanding of the facets of the soul, refer to *Pathworking the Parts of the Soul* on page 147 of the Rites and Rituals section of the Book of Shades. For a look at what spell work with disincarnate faces of the soul might look like, see *Summoning the Speaker for the Silence* on page 202 in the Acts and Devotions section.

LAST WORDS

I encourage you to sit and ponder what a faceted soul might mean for actions like banishing, exorcism, and so on. When asked to "clear" a home, perhaps it is a living person, someone who belongs there, ponder their agency in the situation. Is that incorporeal being haunting you a part of your own soul? If you banish the Umbra, perhaps you are giving up your righteous passions and anger. Your balance. An avenging warrior. What if instead, it is your magical name that you've sensed; to banish them, are you taking away part of your own magical power? In the context of a faceted soul, is "house clearing," "banishment," or "exorcism" even the right choice? Or do these entities instead deserve conversation, contemplation, and investigation to determine their origin, purpose, and intentions? Perhaps that angry eidōlon doesn't truly mean harm. They've simply lost sight of their purpose. Do they have no one living left to avenge? Should we then instead work with them to become an ally, an agent in justice-seeking? Could we instead point them in a useful direction? These are all questions we should ask ourselves every day when we work with the dead.

5

DENIZENS OF
THE DEEPS

"Life is pleasant. Death is peaceful. It's the transition that's troublesome."
—Isaac Asimov

It's important when talking about, or working with, the dead to ensure that we're on the same page regarding terminology. Up to a point, I truly don't like the word *ghost* because it's fairly well void of meaning. What is a ghost...specifically? A deceased person? Okay. What part? What kind? Not every incorporeal being you encounter will be a deceased human, and I don't per se buy into the idea that every deceased human who's still here is *lost, wandering, restless,* or trapped in some unfortunate unfinished business trauma loop. They were once and still are human. They have agency. Purpose.

They can choose.

There are certainly reasons why some might stay earthbound or return to the Material Plane, such as to protect someone, to seek vengeance, to bring a warning or message, or to request proper funerary rituals—which makes up a lot of my work with the deceased; providing funerary rites and mourning them that they might find peace and wholeness. But ghost isn't a word that serves our needs very well. As I noted in the prologue, there are quite a few historically appropriate all-purpose words for the dead, and my preference is εἴδωλον (eidōlon) since we are working here, within these pages, with a set of ideas that includes the disincarnate facets of living humans.

St. Augustine, however, would choose a different word altogether, positing in *City of God* that the "souls of men are demons" while later contradicting themselves by stating that should they have been good men, they become lares, lemure or larvae if bad, or manes if neither.[65] While that may be an oversimplification to say so, it is certainly useful to note that you have some working categories of dead, be it in how they came to be in their current state, what realms they occupy, and their living disposition. If St. Augustine is to be believed, death makes those who enjoyed "inflicting injury" all the worse, as larvae are demons made of wicked men who will require sacrifices for their invocation, finding pleasure in the cruelties.[66] While it is true that during the medieval period, necromantic magic became twisted to suit Catholic ideals and the dead were always demons, come to trick the unwitting necromancer, but what an interesting thought that perhaps the cruel among us become demons in death.

THE CORPOREAL AND INCORPOREAL DEAD

Though most of our magic will center on incorporeal eidōlon, it's important that we recognize other sorts of beings, and talk about the language. Corporeal, of course, refers to things with physical presence—in simple terms, something you could pinch; incorporeal is the opposite—something that, were you to toss a pie at it, it would fly right through. Along that same vein, we have the animate (able to move) and inanimate (not able to move at all), though those terms tend to refer to corporeal beings—it's not too often that you see an incorporeal, *inanimate* being—but it's not outside the realm of possibility.

Additionally, there are the incarnate (eidōlon occupying bodies), the disincarnate (those without bodies), which might refer to the various eidōlon occupying your corporeal form as we speak, or perhaps, the eidōlon of a deceased person, occupying some other body. Though much of what we'll discuss here for the purposes of our magic is the incorporeal, disincarnate eidōlon of deceased human beings, as well as inanimate human remains, there is also the

---

65 Marcus Dods and Aurelius Augustinus, *The City of God Vol. 1* (Edinburgh: T & T Clark, 1888), 365.

66 Ibid.

corporeal dead with which to contend. I know what you're thinking. But Mortellus, are you about to seriously argue for vampires? Zombies? Yes. Yes, I am. What is living and what is dead is not such a straightforward thing. We've talked about the soul and its various parts; what happens if enough pieces of you are banished or die? How many facets must be lost before you become a zombie?

THE INANIMATE CORPOREAL DEAD

I joked above that I would argue for zombies, and that's only partially true, but I will make an argument for the walking dead. Many would disagree with me, but I believe that working with necromantic magic means (at times) working with physical remains, and what better example of the reanimating power of necromancy, of death magic, of working with the human body than organ donors? Life from death, a gift of resurrection, the inanimate corporeal dead.

THAT'S THE SPIRIT!
Living donors are honored with a ritual called an "Honor Walk" which consists of family, hospital staff, deathcare workers, and clergy, lining the walk from their ICU room to the operating suite where their organs are to be harvested.[67] These *inanimate* (no longer animated) *incarnate* (still occupying a physical body) *dead* are held in a liminal state between life and death, assisted by life support as we transport them to facilities for organ harvesting. What may seem a grim end to a life, is truly a necromantic miracle: building new life from death.

THE ANIMATE CORPOREAL DEAD

The *undead*…encompassing such creatures as zombies, vampires, and the like, revenants are simply: the *returned*. Living creatures who have been deceased, and through some means have been imbued with a sort of un-life. Does that make those individuals the same as zombies or vampires in the movies? Probably not, but we can all pretend that's true on Halloween. Something closer to the truth is more akin

---

67 LifeSource, "Honor Walk Resources," LifeSource, n.d.

to those who've lost hold of a piece of themselves, and as a result, become liminal beings who live among us every day without notice. What is a revenant, but the returned? Those who, like myself, once were dead, and, through some act of god or magic, have been returned to a state of un-life?

THAT'S THE SPIRIT!
One of my favorite examples of the returned, *animate* (animated) *corporeal* (occupying a physical form) *dead* are the often-overlooked cicadas. In *Phaedrus*, Socrates tells us that when the muses were born, humans were so drunk on inspiration that they sang until they died.[68] Heartbroken, the muses resurrected them from their bodies as cicada so that they might sing forever. They need no food or water, only to sing. Revenants resting in the earth, and clawing free of their graves to resurrect themselves from the shell of their bodies, undying, singing, until it is time to return once again to their rest in the darkness.

MANIFESTED EIDŌLON OF THE DECEASED

As we have, up to this point, utilized the term *eidōlon* (which is inclusive of the living and the dead), a distinction is necessary here. *Incorporeal* (no physical form) *manifestations* (something clearly seen) of the *deceased* are, above all, the classically familiar *ghost*.

THAT'S THE SPIRIT!
I can't think of many eidōlon more well-known, more prevalent, and more reported by reliable witnesses than that of the sixteenth President of the United States: Abraham Lincoln. For more than 150 years, presidents, vice presidents, diplomats, foreign dignitaries, and all manner of individuals coming and going into the White House have reported seeing (or feeling) Lincoln's ghost. But few are more dramatic than that of Queen Wilhelmina, who, while visiting the White House in 1942, and having heard a knock at their door, opened it only to

---

68 Plato and R. Hackforth, *Plato's Phaedrus: A Dialogue* (Cambridge, UK: Cambridge University Press, 1952).

find themselves face-to-face with Lincoln themselves—and promptly responded by fainting.[69]

MANIFESTED EIDŌLON OF THE LIVING

Poltergeist, translated as "noisy ghost," is an eidōlon associated with dramatic—if not malicious—behavior. Throwing objects, rearranging the home, attacking individuals, levitating objects, speaking, and knocking on doors. Generally associated with a singular location, or sometimes, person, poltergeist reign supreme as the ultimate example of the effects that eidōlon might have on the Material Plane. Many are of the mind, myself included, that most poltergeist activity is attributable to the living. While most would state that this would be caused by psychokinesis, I believe it to be disembodied manifestations of living individuals—in my opinion, the Umbra or the Character, disassociated or dispossessed (or in some cases, self-possessing) from the living as a result of trauma, to wreak havoc on a world they otherwise have no control over.

THAT'S THE SPIRIT!

Tina Resch had a troubled life. Abandoned at ten months old by their birth parent, Tina was adopted by abusive foster parents who made a career of taking in hundreds of children. Tina occupied a world that offered them little by way of protection, autonomy, or self-expression, and things were seemingly always difficult. As a child, Tina was blamed for several disturbances at school—erasers and other objects flying through the air—despite no one having seen them do it. As a result, Tina was heavily medicated, and, in addition to abuse at home, was now being bullied at school. Eventually, Tina was removed and made full-time caretaker to the other children in their home. Around this time, things started to change. Tina's adoptive parents reported clock hands spinning out of control, electronics turning on and off, even people being thrown about—both the poltergeist and Tina—receiving widespread media attention.

---

69   Jeff Belanger, *The World's Most Haunted Places: From the Secret Files of Ghost-village.com* (Pompton Plains, NJ: New Page Books, 2011).

Eventually, the world lost interest in Tina, and the story ended in tragedy after tragedy.

INHUMAN INCORPOREAL ENTITIES

It goes without saying that not every incorporeal being that you encounter will be an eidōlon. All manner of creatures exist in the veil to be encountered, from deities to elemental creatures to house spirits to even portions of your own soul disincarnate from your body. It isn't common, per se, for those who can perceive the dead to also perceive these types of incorporeal beings. Though admittedly, I have myself—on one occasion—seen a guardian in the south, an elemental of fire. This leads me to believe it is possible, if not likely.

THAT'S THE SPIRIT!
A form of deified progenitor, the Domovoy in Slavic faith practices, is a founder of a family, an ancient ancestor, who appears as a grey-haired elder human, an animal, or even taking the form of a more familiar ancestor. While a given home might have any number of "house spirits," they tend to derive from the primary Domovoy. House spirits are entities often mentioned and very little considered. Protective (if capricious), these spirits work for, guide, and warn members of their household. Often fiercely protective of children in the home, their role is to see you survive and further their family name.

EARTHBOUND SPIRITS

A colloquialism that I am none too fond of, "earthbound spirit" seems to refer to a deceased human person, who, for whatever reason, is trapped here on the Material Plane. I'm bothered by it for a few reasons, not the least of which is how little agency it implies the dead have, and the fact that it suggests that they *don't belong here*. There's also the little problem of them still not, well, being *here*. The veil is, of course, a place. The Ethereal Plane is occupied by all manner of beings who absolutely belong there, and plenty of dead not only choose to be there but have *work* that they do there. But for our purposes here, I'm going to use "earthbound spirits" to mean specifically the incorporeal dead who might otherwise reincarnate or move on to an afterlife, who, for specific reasons beyond their control, remain bound to the Material Plane—unable to cross over to any afterlife, underworld, or reincarnation. This may mean for a particular set amount of time, until they fulfill a specific need, or forever. To come back to the words of Devin Hunter, those who simply cannot cross over properly may be rare indeed, but they tend to have an objective source for that failing.[70] Breaking those down into categories of their own, you'll find three primary themes among them, and though there are exceptions, they tend toward hostility.[71] In this classification, I present the immature, the unburied, and the unlamented.

THE IMMATURE DEATH

Known to the ancient Greeks as the *immaturata*, these are, by my estimation, some of the more heartbreaking dead you might work with. These unfortunate *immature* dead, *taken* before their intended day of death, "did not die their own deaths," or died "before their time."[72] Their ranks will include victims of tragic accidents, violent crimes such as murder, or other such needless death and remain earthbound until their intended date of death is reached—be it an hour, or a lifetime. You may choose to give comfort and sanctuary to the young, work to calm and give peace to the angry, or utilize those restless and seeking justice in work inclined toward their cause of death.

> THAT'S THE SPIRIT!
> Folklore holds that a child in the Scottish village of Whittinghame was haunted for a time by a child who'd been murdered by a parent.[73] The story notes that while the child was often seen, they were avoided out of superstition, and the local mood

---

70 Hunter, *Witch's Book of Spirits*, 203.

71 Éva Pócs, *Body, Soul, Spirits, and Supernatural Communication* (Newcastle Upon Tyne: Cambridge Scholars Publishing, 2019), 132.

72 Ibid.

73 Robert Chambers, *The Popular Rhymes of Scotland, with Illustrations, Collected from Tradition* (Edinburgh: James Duncan; London: William Hunter; C. Smith & Co, 1826), 9–11.

was that they'd never be rid of the spectral child. Until one night, a drunken local spotted the little one, and being too inebriated for sense, called out "How's a' wi' ye this morning, Short-Hoggers?"[74] Which had the effect of delighting the child who declared "Oh weel's me noo, I've gotten a name; They ca' me Short-Hoggers o' Whittinghame!"[75] The child was never seen again after this night, suggesting that they spent their naturally allotted years, or more simply, just wanted someone to care enough to give them a name.

THE UNBURIED

Known also as the *Insepulti*, the unburied are those for whom there is no burial place. The missing in action, the drowned, the lost—those for whom there is no tomb, no burial, no rites that enable their movement toward the realms of the dead.[76] These souls remain bound to earth until given a cenotaph of remembrance, and be they larvae, lares, or manes, are quite easy to put to rest by doing so.

THAT'S THE SPIRIT!

Throughout the United States, there are scores of Revolutionary and Civil War battlefields rife with the unburied—and often unlamented—dead. One such story concerns an area called Little Round Top, a hill overlooking Gettysburg, Pennsylvania, upon which several extras were resting during the filming of the 1993 film *Gettysburg*. They later claimed to have been visited by a grizzled old character in Union uniform, whom they assumed was part of the production crew. The figure struck up a conversation about the battle, and before going on their way, gave several of them some extra rounds of ammunition which they assumed were blanks. It was later discovered that these were live musket rounds which dated to the Civil War and were in pristine condition.

---

74   Robert Chambers, *The Popular Rhymes of Scotland, with Illustrations, Collected from Tradition* (Edinburgh: James Duncan; London: William Hunter; C. Smith & Co, 1826), 9–11.

75   Ibid.

76   Pócs, *Body, Soul, Spirits and Supernatural Communication*, 132.

THE UNLAMENTED

The Unlamented or *Indeplorati* are those for whom none have wept. Of the three, I find this the toughest category of earthbound spirit. These are individuals that nobody mourned or wept for when they died.[77] And I know what you're thinking: that's very sad. Sure, it is, but there are often very good reasons for it. Take, for instance, an abuser, leaving behind a world full of people glad to see them go, or someone who died with no next of kin—no family remaining to mourn them. Be it innocent or purposeful, these spirits often wander angrily, forgotten by all. It is noteworthy that it was generally believed that those who died with no living family remaining would, by default, become "larvae," and it has been my experience that this is untrue. Many of those without surviving family become protectors of their ancestral home or powerful allies for the unhoused, having a soft spot for those with no place to call their own.

THAT'S THE SPIRIT!

It was during the eighteenth dynasty of Ancient Egypt and the New Kingdom period when the tenth ruler of that dynasty, Akhenaten, became Pharaoh. Having big dreams and not enough self-awareness to read the room, Akhenaten abolished the worship of the Kemetic gods and started a new faith: Atenism. Atenism was ostensibly monotheistic, and centered on worship of the sun disk Aten, already a popular form of worship albeit in the presence of polytheistic practices.[78] Both the people, and (presumably) gods, of Egypt did not take well to this dramatic change, least of all to their defacing of temples and inscriptions. And so it was that after their death, the people of Egypt made certain that Akhenaten paid a price for those choices. Statues destroyed, monuments dismantled, their name excluded from lists of pharaohs, Akhenaten was all but lost to history.[79] To this very day, it is said that the wandering Akhenaten haunts the Farafra

---

77 Pócs, *Body, Soul, Spirits and Supernatural Communication*, 132.

78 Erik Hornung, *Akhenaten and the Religion of Light* (Ithaca: Cornell University Press, 1999), 55, 84.

79 Lise Manniche, *The Akhenaten Colossi of Karnak* (American University in Cairo Press 2010), ix.

Desert, denied funerary rituals, and cursed by the priests of the gods Akhenaten denied worship to wander the deserts forever.[80]

WORKING SPIRITS

When it comes to the dead, it isn't as simple as getting to where you are supposed to be going. The dead have agency and are bound to very different rules than us. In many cases, the dead choose to work with the living in very particular ways, and these are only a few examples.

CONTROL SPIRITS

I often say that control spirits are simply "reverse mediums." Choosing to work with the living on behalf of the dead, they intercede with us, just as mediums intercede with them. We may seek these eidōlon as agents in our work or they might seek us.

THAT'S THE SPIRIT!
Reverend William Stainton Moses, a trance medium known for their work with the Society for Psychical Research, was known for working with several control spirits referred to as The Imperator Band. These spirits were a part of a missionary effort (because *of course* the Underworld would have Christian missionaries still attempting to spread the good word from beyond the grave) to uplift humanity through automatic writing.

MIGHTY DEAD

First appearing in an occult context in Gerald Gardner's *Witchcraft Today*, the Mighty Dead is a term that tends to refer to enlightened, ascended, or holy dead, particularly those who died in a state of awareness or enlightenment.[81] Many witches would refer to ancestors of their tradition as the Mighty Dead, who are individuals inclined toward assisting their spiritual descendants.

---

80 Moyra Caldecott, *Ghost of Akhenaten* (Mushroom Publishing, 2003), 1.
81 Gardner, *Witchcraft Today*.

That's the Spirit!
In *The Rebirth of Witchcraft*, Doreen Valiente speaks about being visited over a period of months by a spirit named John Brakespear.[82] Doreen shares many varied things disclosed to them by John, who through that spirit, even learned several ritual techniques which are relayed to us in their telling of the tale.

ATTRACTING AND WORKING WITH SPIRITS

I'm often asked why some people can only see or experience apparitions of the dead in places that are "haunted," but not everywhere like mediums (or someone like myself who just happens to be a little bit dead) can. As the old saying goes, it isn't you, it's me. First things first, it's important that we realize every person is different and we all have unique talents and skills that often take years to hone. When I'm in my kitchen making dinner, I try not to think too hard about Gordon Ramsey, because if I do, I'll feel inadequate. I'm sure as hell not saying I'm the Gordon Ramsey of mediumship or necromancy (though I'm just as ill-tempered), but I have been *doing it for a long time*. My ability to connect effortlessly with the dead comes from working with that skill every single day for thirty-five-plus years. That said, I'm really awful at lots of completely ordinary witchy things. I'm not a psychic, don't understand astrology, and couldn't properly meditate if my life depended on it. So maybe mediumship doesn't come *naturally* to you, but that doesn't mean that you can't spend time with it just like any other skill and eventually be awesome at it. Practice makes perfect, after all.

WHY CAN EVERYONE SEE THINGS IN CERTAIN PLACES?

Manifesting takes work. The dead need particular kinds of energy to manifest in loud or visible ways, and it's certainly easier in some places than others. In my everyday work, I purposefully give up and create energy for the surrounding dead to take advantage of, but

---

82   Doreen Valiente, *The Rebirth of Witchcraft* (London: Robert Hale, 2007), 99–116.

some haunted places are effective simply because they have energy sources inherent to them. You might notice that a haunted location has power lines overhead, is positioned on a ley line, or has a strong magnetic field in the area. These are the sort of things that can help eidōlon manifest their presence in a way that anyone can see.

DEATH IS A GREAT EQUALIZER, SO MEET THEM WHERE THEY ARE.

We're all on the same playing field in death, so try not to let the perspectives of the living color your interactions with the dead. It's important, especially in necromantic magic, to meet the dead without expectation—simply offer yourself up as who you are in your own way and see if they meet you there. The dead are (generally) unwilling or unable to lie or mislead, so consider your own authenticity in the experience. Not everyone is comfortable working with the dead, and because of this, there are legions of dead from all of history that go without veneration. While many cultures have traditions of venerating the dead, it's likely that many of the dead you call upon are not actively remembered/called upon by any other living person, so they may simply be delighted to have your company, your recognition, your gifts, and in turn, be delighted to do work for you.

EXERCISE: CONNECTING WITH THE EIDŌLON IN YOUR OWN SPACE

Time and Place: Midday; Any
Supplies: Offerings; Alcohol swab; Lancet; Lancing device; Bandage; Sharps container
Purpose: Establishing a connection with the dead in spaces familiar to you.

Modern society spends a lot of time on autopilot. So, in terms of experiences with the dead, are people actively looking for those experiences, or are they spending the majority of their time working, or exhausted from work, on the phone, on the internet, and watching television? It's important to take time with the quiet of spaces you spend your time in and simply hear what the space has to say to you. So, in the middle of the day, when everything is perfectly ordinary and the sun is shining, I'd like you to take a moment to connect with the eidōlon present in those familiar spaces. Eliminate as much noise as you can. If applicable (and safe), turn off your cell phone and unplug any electronics that you can.

Try seating yourself in a highly trafficked part of the space. Personally, I prefer kitchens as they're a place where people do a lot of living. Having cleaned and prepared your skin, focus on the energy of the incorporeal being you are interacting with and draw three drops of blood from the left ring finger, allowing them to fall to the floor without interference. Introduce yourself. Say how you came to be in this place and clarify that the energy you have given is a gift for the eidōlon to aid them in manifesting their presence should they so choose. Then, there in the quiet of perfectly ordinary spaces, simply *listen*. I bet you walk away from the experience, surprised by what's around you all the time. Things that simply went unnoticed.

BACK TO BASICS

There is more on the use of blood in spell work in both the Prologue on page xxii, and under Necromantic Instruments and Materials on page 77. For an alternative to blood, see *Granting the Qualities of Blood* on page 157 of the Skills and Attributes section of the Book of Shades. If you'd like to try a divination to determine what facet of the soul you've been communicating with, see *Identifying Parts of the Soul in Contact* on page 170 of the Correspondence and Congruence section.

CLASSIFYING THE INCORPOREAL DEAD

In *The Witches Book of Spirits*, author Devin Hunter alludes to it being a rarity for eidōlon to become lost, or as Hunter puts it, to fail at "reorientation," but I would make the argument that while the truly confused or *cursed* are indeed rare, it's much more common indeed for eidōlon to make informed and intelligent choices to return.[83] So why do the dead come back at all? In *The Return of the Dead: Ghosts, Ancestors, and the Transparent Veil of the Pagan Mind*, Claude Lecouteux says "the reasons for postmortem manifestations and apparitions are rarely put forward, but they can be deduced from context."[84] It usually isn't altogether difficult to sort out. It is often painfully clear whether a spirit is choosing to protect loved ones, haunt someone who's done them wrong, or cling to an ancestral home.

There are many reasons why eidōlon might choose to return or make themselves known to the living in an active way, but we could boil it down into three succinct categories: protection, vengeance, and guidance. Those seeking revenge have clear-cut goals and motivations. To do harm to those who have harmed them or others, the protectors cling to family lines or homes, the guides may attach to a singular person or perhaps a magical lineage. General exceptions to the rule are those who've been cursed, are bound here as punishment for some misdeed, or those who are seeking out a proper disposition/burial—but these won't be the bulk of the eidōlon you encounter. Among these, of course, there could be any combination of incorporeal manifestations of the dead (or living); and the rare (truly) benevolent or the even rarer (truly) malevolent variations on any of these three themes. Their motivations are more likely to be as varied as your own—they are, after all, only human.

PROTECTOR

Among the more common reasons that eidōlon choose to manifest is to protect the living. Be it a small child who's suffered a trauma manifesting a poltergeist to protect themselves, or a murder victim

---

83 Hunter, *Witch's Book of Spirits*, 203.
84 Lecouteux, *The Return of the Dead*, 134.

returning to warn someone away from their killer, the deceased have a vested interest in protecting life.

That's the Spirit!

In *the Aeneid*, we see the shade of Sychaeus, who comes to their spouse Dido in a dream.[85] Murdered by Dido's sibling Pygmalion, Sychaeus warns Dido to flee for their own safety.[86] Virgil tells us that "the ghost of (Sychaeus) appeared [...] amazingly pale and ghastly: (Sychaeus) opened to (Dido's) view the bloody altars, and (their) breast transfixed with the sword, and detected all the hidden villainy of the house."[87] After this vision, Sychaeus begs Dido to leave the country entirely, and to assist, "reveals treasures ancient in the earth, an unknown mass of gold and silver."[88] In this story, Sychaeus fulfills several potential roles, not only as Protector, but as a Guide, by providing Dido with information and the location of an otherwise unknown treasure.

GUIDE

The Guide can take the form of a spirit ally, guide, control spirit, or even a loved one returning to share knowledge with their surviving family. Where was that copy of the will? Where did I leave that stash of family heirlooms? And so forth.[89] The Guide is here to ensure that we have the tools we need to ensure a successful life; so that through you, they might live on.

That's the Spirit!

One example of a guiding spirit might be that of the eidōlon who visited young Ann Nutt, insisting that something was

---

85 Richard F. Thomas and Jan M. Ziolkowski, *"Sychaeus,"* in *The Virgil Encyclopedia* (Chichester, UK: Wiley Blackwell, 2013).

86 Felton, *Haunted Greece and Rome*, 8.

87 Vergilius Maro, *The Works of Virgil* (Bern, Switzerland: University of Bern, 1853).

88 Ibid.

89 Felton, *Haunted Greece and Rome*, 8.

hidden in their home.[90] Eventually able to persuade a worker to pull up a flagstone that had been pointed out by the eidōlon, Ann found a pot containing several hundred valuable antique silver coins, a small Roman coin hoard.[91] What a helpful guide that was indeed!

AVENGER

Many eidōlon return with a goal of protecting their living loved ones/ family (or in some cases, others like them) or seeking vengeance and justice for a wrong perpetrated against them (or others). All over the world, across every culture, the vengeful spirit remains a constant.[92] Those who, in the absence of a just world, haunt the Material Plane seeking to set right grievous wrongs.

THAT'S THE SPIRIT!
Agnes Sampson was a midwife to the Keith Marischal Barony—their indictment stating simply that the Wise Wife of Keith was a widow—with children.[93] Having been accused of Witchcraft by Gillis Duncan, and of participating in raising storms that threatened a ship bearing both King James VI and their new spouse, Anne of Denmark, across the sea. In a series of events that ultimately set the world aflame with accusations of witchcraft, Agnes was tortured and ultimately garroted and

---

90 Joanne Major, "A Helpful Eighteenth-Century Ghost," All Things Georgian, last updated October 27, 2015, https://georgianera.wordpress. com/2015/10/27/a-helpful-eighteenth-century-ghost/.

91 H. Manville, "Additions and Corrections to Thompson's Inventory and Brown and Dolley's Coin Hoards—Part 1," *British Numismatic Journal* 63 (1993): 91–113.

92 Jerrold E. Hogle and Katarzyna Ancuta, *The Cambridge Companion to the Modern Gothic* (Cambridge: Cambridge University Press, 2014), 216.

93 Robert Pitcairn and Bannatyne Club, Edinburgh, Scotland, *Ancient Criminal Trials in Scotland* (Edinburgh: Printed for the Maitland Club, 1833), 230–31.

burnt at the stake. Today, the naked and shaved eidōlon of Agnes, bearing the wounds of torture, roams the halls of Holyroodhouse in Edinburgh—seeking vengeance for the atrocities they, and so many, suffered at the hands of superstition.

DO THE DEAD HAVE ACCESS TO NEW KNOWLEDGE?

Depending on the culture (or the dead in question), the dead might be treated as knowing quite a lot or not knowing very much at all. Helpful, right? In Germanic and Icelandic sorcery, Dickerson tells us in *The Language of the Corpse: The Power of the Cadaver in Germanic and Icelandic Sorcery* that "the dead were seen as so wise, that Oðinn (themself) sought to gain wisdom from them." [94] Oðinn, you may note, is a twice-born, and is considered to be both living and dead, having sacrificed themselves on the Yggdrasil, thus continuing the narrative that those who have died, and lived to tell the tale, have a special connection to death magic. The Greeks had a different view of what knowledge the dead held, believing that this knowledge varied from shade to shade, was quite limited, and varied in levels of usefulness—just like information gleaned from any living person might be, and this is my position as well. [95]

COMMUNICATING WITH THE DEAD

There is always the practical question of how to communicate with the dead, and I encourage you to start by having a good idea of what you are trying to achieve. If you are seeking to work with the dead as some kind of party trick, prank, or otherwise non-serious venture: go no further. This is not for you. Working

---

94 Cody Dickerson, *The Language of the Corpse the Power of the Cadaver in Germanic and Icelandic Sorcery* (Three Hands Press, 2016), 25.

95 Duffy, *Rites Necromantic*, 8.

with the dead is serious business, and not to be taken lightly. It should be done with respect for the agency and consent of the deceased that you are calling upon. While communicating with the dead doesn't always have to be *serious*, it should always be *taken seriously*. You should set out on your task well-informed, well prepared, and with a goal in mind. It's crucial that you have patience and wait before communicating with your recently deceased loved one. Being newly dead is very disorienting—it takes time to settle into this new phase of your existence and settle any business with the Underworld and your gods. It isn't fair to pull them away from this mere moments after death, and there are very few exceptions to this rule.

Additionally, and I can't stress this enough: *not all spirits wish to be summoned, and not all spirits are available to summon.* If you come from a spiritual practice that espouses reincarnation, then you must accept that your loved one may very well have moved on. Nothing breaks my heart more than having someone ask me to commune with their dead, only to discover they simply aren't there to speak to. Oh yes, there is one thing that breaks my heart more. The living loved ones' inevitable rejection of that statement. Nobody wants to accept that sometimes they can't get answers or the closure that they are seeking from a medium or necromancer, but it's important that you accept it as a possibility.

CONSULT YOUR BOOK OF SHADES:
To gain a better understanding of the Underworld, refer to *Pathworking the Underworld* on page 143 of the Book of Shades, which will help you learn to navigate that space in a controlled manner. If you'd like to remain unnoticed by the dead while you explore, the *Invisibility* sigil spell on page 158 of the Skills and Attributes section will help you accomplish just that.

LAST WORDS

Why is it that bad behaviors we might've tolerated from a loved one in life are intolerable, or even evil, when the perpetrator is deceased? Human beings are only human, living or dead. To me, there seems to be a general belief that we have more control over the dead than the living and that the dead can inherently do us more harm. I'm in total disagreement with this and find the living to be far more frightening (and dangerous). Bad behavior shouldn't be tolerated—lay down boundaries for yourself whether the perpetrator is living or deceased. Just remember that the dead *are who they are*. I would hope that throughout, I've encouraged you to have conversations with the dead and to attempt to uncover their motivations, because, more often than not? They're there for *you*, to help, to guide, to protect. The dead don't need saving, and rarely are they ill-intended.

6

NECROMANTIC
INSTRUMENTS
AND MATERIALS

"Necromancy, in many ways, is just confirming ancient truths...
but those truths are horrifying."
—Rebecca McNutt, *Necromancy Cottage, Or, The Black Art of Gnawing on Bones*

Any practitioner will have the general working tools of the art, but the necromancer will likely have a few other things in their arsenal. Certain pieces of magical equipment have always been intrinsic to working with the dead (or death) and so, consider this an introduction to items you might find in that toolbox. Particular to them will be the effects of death, which would be things that belonged to the dead or places associated with death, as well as their counterpoint, the effects of life, which will likely appear in the form of offerings and gifts of Vitality. Using these instruments won't be that different from using any other magical tool (or ingredient/component as the case may be), aside from origins, intent, and the energies they carry.

As is the case with working tools, you're likely to see a lot of similar ingredients and materials in necromantic practice as you would in any other, but there are certainly some unique variations. These materials stand out in many cases because of the extreme need for thoughtful consideration and an ethical approach to acquiring them. It isn't as easy as walking into the local occult shop and picking up many of these items, as it's crucial that you know not only that they are authentic, but that they were acquired without breaking any laws or causing harm to the dead or their living loved ones. There are quite a few historically notable materials unique to necromantic practice, and some (but not all) listed herein are unlikely to be easily accessible unless you are able to purchase them from someone working directly within the deathcare industry. However, owing to their common inclusion in historical practice, these are worthy of specific comment. Certainly, any tool or ingredient common to magical practice generally has application in necromantic ritual; certain instruments and materials have uses particular to death magic, and some of the more common tools may have unusual requirements or usage. There will always be some finicky notes regarding materials and their intention when it comes to working with the dead, and it is crucial that any relevant items mentioned herein come to you with the consent of the deceased—as well as their living families if applicable.

INSTRUMENTS OF THE ART NECROMANTIC

In many ways, your *basic* working tools won't change from what might be ordinarily expected in any Western magical system. Blades (such as a sword, athame, white-handled knife, and so on) have utility here, as do a wand (preferably yew), and other common magical tools—my most trusty sidekick is the bident. A twist on the stang common to Traditional Witchcraft, the bident is a forked piece of wood representative of Hade's bident. Realistically, any tools you utilize in your daily practice will have a home in necromancy, though I do recommend consecrating them for this purpose.

EXERCISE: MAKING A BIDENT

TIME AND PLACE: Any
SUPPLIES: Forked branch; Woodworking tools; Sandpaper; Coffin nail ☠, 1
PURPOSE: To make a bident.

One instrument that will feel much like a familiar crossover will be the bident. A bident is quite like a stang, though its use may be different. When making your own, you may wish to choose a yew branch, though it is unlikely that you have one growing in your neighborhood and will need to seek one out from a vendor that provides exotic woods. Certainly, you can use any material you like, but that is up for consideration if you are choosing to use yew, such as I do. Having made offerings as you feel are appropriate for the wood taken, carefully strip away any bark and sand down the wood. Once it is as smooth as you like, you may finish it in any manner you please, using stain, wood burning, and other techniques. Last, though many stangs are finished with an iron nail driven upward from the bottom, however, here I recommend driving a coffin nail downward into the fork, taking care not to split the wood.[96]

BACK TO BASICS
Any number of items in this chapter may be something you wish to consecrate using the *Consecration of Ritual Instruments for Necromantic Practice* ritual located on page 123 in the Rites and Rituals section of the Book of Shades.

---

96 Kelden, *The Crooked Path*, 47.

SALT

It seems to be the common wisdom that salt is anathema to the dead and should not be used for necromantic ritual (least of all, placed on an altar for the dead), but this is just flatly untrue. It has been noted by authors such as Sebastià Giralt that salt was, in fact, a frequent sacrifice or offering made to the dead as part of medieval necromantic practices.[97] Indeed, as was noted by French alchemist Pierre Borel:

> *"The essential Saltes of Animals may be so prepared and preserved, that an ingenious (person) may have the whole Ark of Noah in (their) own Studie, and raise the fine Shape of an Animal out of its Ashes at (their) Pleasure; and by the lyke Method from the essential Saltes of humane Dust, a Philosopher may, without any criminal Necromancy, call up the Shape of any dead Ancestour from the Dust whereinto (their) Bodie has been incinerated."*[98]

In some historical necromantic practices, the remains of a deceased individual are referred to as "salts," and in fact, some historical necromancers would not consume it at all, considering it a form of cannibalism! I like to think that knowledge is half the work in a magical practice, so I leave you with this: the average human body is comprised of 0.4 percent salt (that's just shy of one full cup, or 240 grams, for the average adult if you're curious). Never forget that you're your own salt ring—if salt banished spirits as a rule, none would ever come near you.

---

97 Sebastià Giralt, "Medieval Necromancy, the Art of Controlling Demons," Sciència.Cat, 2006, https://www.sciencia.cat/temes/medieval-necromancy-art-controlling-demons.

98 Cotton Mather, *Magnalia Christi Americana: Or, the Ecclesiastical History of New-England, from Its First Planting in the Year 1620. Unto the Year of Our Lord, 1698. in Seven Books, vol. II* (London: Thomas Parkhurst, at the Bible and Three Crowns in Cheapside, 1702), 37.

EXERCISE: MAKING GRAVE SALT

Time and Place: New moon; Any
Supplies: Salt used in preparing the dead; Censor ash; Grave dust 💀
Optional Supplies: Ground mistletoe, a pinch; Cremated remains, a pinch
Purpose: To create grave salt for ritual use and spell work.

There is always a selection of my favorite salts (generally Red Alaea, Celtic Sea, and Kala Namak) in my embalming kit which I use when cleaning and preparing the recently deceased for burial/cremation. Any excess, I bring back home at the end of the day, adding graveyard dust, ash from my censor, a pinch of ground mistletoe, and a pinch of cremated remains from a beloved ancestor. This blend of salt that has been used in the preparation of the dead, or grave salt, serves a wide range of purposes, but those most important to my daily practice surround altar use, consecrations, and curse removal. The salts included should have been used in preparing the dead (not the dying) and reserved afterward for this purpose. If you do not have access to such materials either through your own work, volunteerism, or other, it may be that you could acquire these ingredients through a deathcare worker friendly to your beliefs so long as they have received consent from the family to do so.

BLOOD AND OTHER BODILY FLUIDS: THE EFFECTS OF LIFE

While the only bodily fluid I use in my practice is blood, some are of the mind that bodily fluids such as semen are necessary for necromantic magic or provide some added benefit of control over the dead (or others), and I disagree.[99] Yet others still have suggested that by performing lewd acts in graveyards they might cause harm to the living—and even control the dead. Putting aside the very real risk of being charged with

---

99 Cagliastro, *Blood Sorcery Bible*, 80–81.

public indecency, it is important to remember that the dead want what anyone wants: respect, kinship, and most certainly, consent. As such, I would heartily caution against behaving in an unseemly manner toward the dead or in their spaces, and most of all against *taking* from the dead. As to giving gifts of living blood, that's a different story altogether. I do often advocate for blood as a gift of Vitality, symbolic of your own life, to the dead, but it needn't be unsafely done, specific (menstrual blood, blood from certain parts of the body, and so on), or a lot—just a few drops will do.

While blood does not *need* to be specific, I do have a *preference* for blood drawn from the left ring finger. Why? The left ring finger has long had a connection to the heart, but also to resurrection through its mythical association to the *Vena Amoris*, the vein of love. This finger, upon which we place our bonds of marriage; a ring, themselves an endless circle, their open center a doorway to the unknowable.

HEALTH, SAFETY, AND ETHICS

The use of blood in magic is one of those things where anytime I stumble upon it in a book, I'm either left chuckling at how timid the discussion is, or shocked at the lack of concern for the reader's health and wellbeing. No middle ground, really. So, ethics? My very terse thoughts on the topic, generally, are that so long as it's your blood and you consented, there's no ethical concern—*unless you aren't properly disposing of potentially hazardous waste.*

So, let's roll through a little checklist here on the health and safety end. Have you spoken to a trusted healthcare professional for some guidance? Definitely start there. No, you don't have to tell them what it's for, but you could get them to show you how to do a proper finger prick or use a diabetic testing kit (it never hurts to know your glucose levels!), as well as advise you on safety. Additionally, your physician's office (or others in your area) is usually a drop-off location for sharps containers. You'll need one for collecting used lancets as they shouldn't be disposed of in household waste.

Do you have any health concerns such as a bleeding disorder (which could make drawing blood dangerous for you) or communicable illness? These might not mean you cannot use your own blood in magic, but they might mean that you have extra safety and/or disposal concerns.

Do you have the proper equipment on hand (sharps container, alcohol prep pads, bandages, lancing instrument, lancets, or single-use lancets)?

If you've successfully made it out the other end of this checklist, congratulations! You're all good to collect a few drops of blood safely and responsibly.

EXERCISE: DRAWING BLOOD

Time and Place: Any
Supplies: Alcohol swab; Lancet; Lancing device; Bandage; Sharps container
Purpose: To draw blood for ritual use and spell work.

Begin by thoroughly washing and drying your hands before swabbing the chosen area with an alcohol pad. Notably, while many commercials for these devices show the tip of the finger, the *side* of your fingertip has fewer nerve endings and is, therefore, more comfortable. Following the instructions on the lancing device you have chosen (most have a trigger mechanism), lance the area. Blood should rise to the surface immediately, which you can encourage by rubbing the skin of your finger toward the lanced area. Apply to the spell component/area needed. Wipe any excess blood away with an alcohol prep pad, applying a bandage if necessary. Dispose of the lancet and any hazardous materials in an approved container. Remember that blood is not only optional, but a biohazard. Work safely should you choose to work with blood, and clearly label any items to which it has been added.

BACK TO BASICS
For more on the use of blood in spell work refer to page xxii in the Prologue. For an alternative to blood, see *Granting the Qualities of Blood* on page 157 in the Skills and Attributes section of The Book of Shades.

THE EFFECTS OF DEATH

Generally speaking, the "effects of death" are simply items that have been touched by—or have directly interacted with—the dead. These can range from the simple and easily acquired (such as clothing inherited from a deceased relative) to things as seemingly ghoulish and impossible as suture thread that's passed through the flesh of the deceased. As a rule of thumb—though not always—the greater the distance between the material and the deceased, the less powerful its necromantic energies will be. Items that have had intimate interactions with the recently deceased will be the most powerful (such as corpse water) while those items which simply *belonged* to the recently deceased prior to death are less so.

CLOTHES OF THE DEAD

Clothing belonging to the deceased has always had a great deal of application in necromantic magic, particularly in terms of connecting with a particular individual. Other uses include connecting with the energies of death itself through the wearing of such items. Any good necromancer should have a subscription to their local newspaper. Watch the obituary section daily, as this will inform you of the comings and goings of death in your area, but also watch the classifieds. Often, in the days, weeks, and months following a death, you'll find estate sales. These overgrown yard sales tend to be an open door to the home of the recently deceased in which you can not only support a family in a time of grief, but acquire rarer ingredients for your practice, such as the clothes and shoes of the dead. Simply compare estate sale addresses to recent obituary columns to determine which will be appropriate for you.

CORPSE WATER ☠

Corpse water is a commonly used, and often misunderstood, ingredient in necromantic magic. In concept it's quite simple: corpse water is simply water with which the dead have been bathed. It is necessary that the water collected be from the first bathing of the dead prior to any preliminary washing, embalming, or other rites. If this is an act you are unable or unwilling to perform, your deathcare professional can collect this item for you during the course of their work, though it would be sensible to provide consecrated salt, incense, and appropriate containers. Notably, if working with a funeral establishment to collect corpse water during the course of a loved one's burial rites, you should be aware that many items in the preparation room (as well as any medical facilities such as hospice or a hospital room) are flammable. While incense is possible, depending on the area, a candle flame may not be.

EXERCISE: GATHERING CORPSE WATER ☠

To be gathered while preparing the recently deceased for burial/ cremation.

TIME AND PLACE: Any, wherever the recently deceased is located
SUPPLIES: Soap; Spirit calming incense ☠; Censor; Jar; Labels; Pen
OPTIONAL SUPPLIES: Consecration oil ☠
PURPOSE: To gather corpse water for ritual use and spell work.

Begin by lighting a bit of incense, wafting it over the body. Then, rub salt over the body, consecrating as you go. Begin the process of a preliminary washing of the body (without soap), using your prepared containers to collect water as it runs off the skin, and being certain to talk to the dead as you work regarding your purpose. Once you have collected as much or as little water as you are inclined, move on to a full washing of the body, their hair, and so on with soap and water. Though this water is not of use to you, this is a sacred act you perform in service to the dead. As a last step, you may choose to consecrate the body with oils, and, once again, wafting incense over their form. Of course, if the deceased had a communicable illness, they are not ideal for gathering corpse water, and, in any case, heat your gathered water to 212 °F (or 100 °C) to eliminate any pathogens.

CONSULT YOUR BOOK OF SHADES

For a *Consecration Oil* appropriate for dressing the recently deceased, refer to page 194 of the Acts and Devotions section of the Book of Shades.

EXERCISE: CURSE REMOVAL AND CORD CUTTING

TIME AND PLACE: Any
SUPPLIES: Corpse water
PURPOSE: Curse breaking and cord cutting.

Curses, hexes, negativity born from poor magical or psychic hygiene, or unwanted energetic connections, generally have an expiration date: death. This method of curse removal/cord cutting is deceptively straightforward and lacking in pretension. What could be simpler than just…being dead? Corpse water temporarily bestows upon you the qualities of death, dropping away all attachments, and then returns you to a place of life. While you may choose to do your curse removal or cord cutting in ritual space, it does not have to be that formal. In fact, it can be as simple as dampening a cloth with corpse water and wiping down your body—assuring that you're utilizing water that has been properly gathered for safety. For a ritualized form, utilize the *Consecration of Death* on page 121 of the Rites and Rituals section of the Book of Shades, followed by the *Consecration of Life* on page 122.

SUTURES OR SUTURE NEEDLES

If you are fortunate enough to have access to the funerary side of things, either through your own work, or through a friend, an old needle used for suturing—or even some scraps of used suture—is excellent (if biohazardous) materials for your magical practice. These items can be used for any number of things that need *fixing*. Much like coffin nails, these items have the properties of fixing something into place, or even preventing their theft. These should, of course, be suture needles used for stitching the skin during embalming, scrap lengths of suture that have been pulled through the flesh, or needles that have been used to sew the deceased into a shroud or clothing.

I acknowledge that short of having direct access to the dead or having a friend in the deathcare industry, you are unlikely to encounter this material. If, however, it is important to your practice, working to train as a home burial guide, death doula, funeral director, or embalmer, will put you in the position of sewing those shrouds closed, or applying those sutures. There hasn't been a day's work so far that a mountain of used sutures didn't go into the biohazard bin, which is exactly what it is: a biohazard. Any material or (unsterilized) instrument that has passed through human flesh will be a biohazard.

But don't forget that when utilizing sutures and suture needles in your spell work, they should be, according to *The Graveyard Wanderers*, "the same (needle or thread) as was actually used, and no other," to attempt otherwise would be to invite an opposite action.[100]

GRAVE DUST ☠

Graveyard dust can refer to any number of blends, powders, herbs, and other components, but when I say graveyard dust, I mean something specific: dust. From a graveyard. When out doing my magical caretaking of the cemeteries in my local area, I spend some time

---

100 Johnson, *The Graveyard Wanderers*, 26.

with a soft paint brush cleaning the crevices on headstones. As I work, reading out the inscriptions on headstones, speak the names, and chat with the dead. The debossed lettering of names, years, and epitaphs gather dust, moss, and other debris over time, and this is the material I use as graveyard dust in my work. This dust is a symbol of the passage of time there, of nature, and of the work that I do for the dead. It comes to be recognized as a sort of offering of service, and that has been very effective in my work.

Grave dust can be a powerful ingredient in most anything and I add it to most things I create, such as incense, grave salt, and so on. In this application, it is a gesture to the dead with whom you are working, even if they are new to you, that you give of your time and energy to the upkeep of Liminal Spaces. Grave dust is one of few material components that when gathered is not considered *taking* materials from Liminal Spaces in the same way that removing items such as grave dirt might be. Here, you are giving your time and service, and this material is a by-product of that work. As such, it is not necessary to give thanks or leave offerings unless you so choose.

OBOL, OR, CHIRON'S PAYMENT

Few ritual acts for the dead are more universally recognized than that of placing a pair of coins over the eyes. These payments for the "ferryman" (or conductor, as is my preference) are a simple act the living can perform for the dead, a last gesture of assuring they have all that they need for the journey. In *Rites Necromantic*, Martin Duffy notes that "Nearly all necromantic rites demand libation, a tithe to 'pay the ferryman,'" and that is worth keeping in mind as well.[101] Ordinary coins can be used as payment for any conductor of the dead, but also items that have behaved as money, such as buttons, salt, et cetera, and even items that are fictitious currency, such as chocolate coins, or Monopoly money! What matters is the symbol. Personally, I prefer silver Mercury dimes for this purpose.

---

101 Martin Duffy, *Rites Necromantic* (Three Hands Press, 2020), 33.

INSTRUMENTS OF COMMUNICATION AND COMMUNITY

Humanity has always had an obsession with communicating with the dead, so it makes sense that in 1920, Thomas Edison boldly announced plans to create a telephone that would allow mediums and spiritualists to work within the boundaries of science.[102] We'll never know if their invention, the Necrophone, managed to blend science and séance since Edison joined those beyond the veil before revealing it, though there is a takeaway from the story. It seems that we're only of a mind to find ourselves successful if we get an answer, or a specific kind of response from a specific kind of person, and that's just not always how it will be. Sometimes, it will be a one-way message, and sometimes, someone we don't recognize will pick up the phone. Being open to the experience, no matter the outcome, is a magic of its own. After all, Edison never accomplished his goal of capturing recordings of the dead, but the Necrophone still exists in our memory as a symbol of humanity's desire to call out and be heard.

SPIRIT BOARDS

In 1890, Elijah Bond created a game called "Ouija" based on talking boards popularized by the spiritualist movement of the time, and today, it's almost impossible to talk about the dead without addressing them.

Ouija has nearly become the spooky elephant in the room, with entire generations of people out there convinced that a board game is responsible for demonic possessions and hauntings. It must just be hell to work at a Ouija board factory with all those evil spirits and demons running around (Get lost Casper, I'm on my lunch break!).

Prior to the theatrical release of *The Exorcist*, spirit/talking/Ouija boards were seen as so mundane, so domestic, so *wholesome*, that Norman Rockwell painted a couple playing *Ouija* for a May issue of

---

102 Alessandra Serrano, "Edison's Necrophone," Seiðr: University of Tromsø, October 31, 2017.

the *Saturday Evening Post*. May! It was a spring cover! A generation of parents, frightened by a movie, passed all that fear on to us—I vote we give it back.

The precursor of talking boards is, of course, automatic writing, done by planchette. Spirit boards rely on something known as the *ideomotor phenomenon*, in which a thought or mental image causes a motor response. Basically, something pops into your mind, and your hands respond by subtly moving the planchette across the board. Do I think they can be magical and an actual form of communication with spirits? Absolutely. Do I buy into the "you'll get possessed by demons, open doors you don't know how to close, it's not for the inexperienced" bit? Absolutely not. Look at spirit boards like a cell phone. You call who you want to call. You hang up if you're not enjoying the conversation.

EXERCISE: SPIRIT BOARDS IN PRACTICE

TIME AND PLACE: Any
SUPPLIES: Spirit board; Offerings
PURPOSE: To contact the dead.

Before beginning a session with a spirit board, it's important to pick a spokesperson to ask the questions. It's important to have a plan going in, and while other participants can suggest questions, only one person should be addressing the board during a session. Spirit board sessions can be deeply personal, which can make participants feel vulnerable. To that end, don't ask questions that anyone at the table is uncomfortable with or any questions not agreed on by all. Be certain to end the session immediately if any of the participants feel uncomfortable or unwell. Remember that this is a method for contacting the dead broadly and doesn't necessarily infer an ability to contact a *specific* deceased individual.

To begin, each participant should place the tips of their fingers lightly on the planchette, slowly moving it in circles as everyone grounds. Once everyone is grounded and comfortable, cease moving the planchette, and greet the dead warmly, declaring *"Exsurgent*

Mortui Et Ad Me Veniunt"—May the Dead Rise up, and Come to Me," and begin communicating!

Be respectful, giving the dead time to respond, avoid reductive/impolite questions (for example a common question asked is "Are you male/female?" but I think we can all agree that question serves no purpose and may be alienating), as well as trauma-based questions (how did you die, are you in pain, etcetera) and stick to simple yes/no questions until you get a sense of the session. Next, you could move on to questions that require spelling, such as "What is your name?" When ready to close the session, declare, *"Leave ye departed shade, I license thee to depart into thy proper place, and be there peace between us,"* and move the planchette to Goodbye, The End, or other such session-ending phrase, if your board has such a space. This standard (and polite) dismissal may be used any time you wish the deceased to leave your space—not just in a spirit board session. Remember, lore dictates that leaving the planchette laying on your board leaves it "open," though I don't subscribe to that belief.

SPIRIT HOUSES

I often make the argument for grave goods, given that they are regarded as items that the deceased have access to in the Underworld. But if that is true, where might the dead acquire other things? Short of us gifting items to the dead that are dear to us, the options are limited. Spirit houses serve purposes specific to their creator, and have different applications within different practices, but for my purposes, a spirit house serves the purpose of transferring material items to immaterial space as though they had been buried with a deceased person. Creating a spirit box as a particular home for the dead you work with can be a way of providing them with items to make their existence richer, but also to help them help us. Spirit houses are a truly special gift for the dead that you work with often, being not just a vessel within which the dead can live and receive offerings, but where you can provide them gifts, rendering material items incorporeal and accessible beyond the veil.

CONSULT YOUR BOOK OF SHADES
For the process of creating, presenting, and caretaking a spirit house, refer to *Building a Spirit House* on page 199 of the Acts and Devotions section of the Book of Shades.

GRAVEYARD DIRT 💀

I was asked while writing this how I would feel, ethically, about someone using dirt from the grave of one of my loved ones or ancestors without permission. The simple answer to that? I don't have any problems with it at all. Why? I don't dictate who my ancestors chose to work with—choice and agency being key here. I *would*, however, be upset if someone damaged their grave in so doing (disrupting the earth, plants, headstones, and so on), or committed a crime such as trespassing to gain access—but we already talked about that. If you want to use some dirt from my grandparents' grave? Go for it. They're all stubborn as hell, and if they like you enough to work with you, then I would probably like you too.

ETHICAL CONSIDERATIONS

What I don't like, however, is when materials on this topic suggest that your necromantic magic requires graveyard dirt from the graves of specific *types* of deceased individuals. These named sorts of earth often rely on victims of various types of crime, earth from gendered graves (a headstone may not reflect who someone truly was), from Native American burial places (absolutely do not disturb the burial places of cultures/groups that you are not a part of), murder victims, the abused, the "insane"—often reducing them to their cause of death and seeking to inflict it upon a target.

This practice reduces the dead to what they suffered in life, placing value only on their pain. I find this to be both reductive *and* disrespectful to the dead.

Similarly, I stay away from any suggestion that earth from mass graves/death be utilized, those who were lost to suicide, and so on. Let these souls who have suffered so much in life have peace in death. Though I have, on occasion, found that spirits of those victimized by such atrocities are often happy to assist in any sort of working intended to protect or aid someone in a similar situation, or to bring justice in such situations. Consider those aspects of *social justice necromancy* when doing your work.

TYPES AND USES

To the extent that I was comfortable doing so, I've provided a table of *types* of earth for you to consider. But personally, I tend to work with only two varieties: earth from an open or freshly dug grave, and earth from a disinterred grave. Additionally, I like to use earth gathered from several cemeteries/graveyards rather than just one. My reason for this is that the earth from these types of locations is fairly universal and relies on the energies and connections to death without disturbing any particular eidōlon. Personally, I find that it's most important that you gather from spaces with which you have a good relationship—somewhere you are caretaking and taking a vested regular interest in.

- ◉ **Ancestor:** A beloved connection (does not necessarily need to be a blood relation) whom you feel will have an interest in helping. Particularly useful for protection magic.

- ◉ **Creator:** Artists, performers, et cetera, make for excellent sparks of inspiration and are often very responsive and happy to be working as a muse for a creator who is feeling uninspired.

- ◉ **Child:** Innocence, new friendships, open-mindedness, learning, freeing oneself from stress.

☾ **Companion Animal:** Yes! Earth from the grave of a companion animal can be very useful. Consider the loyalty and devotion one receives from a beloved companion animal and make that a component of your magic.

☾ **Death During Childbirth:** Those who died while delivering a child might be protective of children, those pregnant or seeking to become parents, or individuals who are suffering from fertility issues.

☾ **Disinterred Grave:** Earth from an older grave that has been dug up for forensic purposes or to relocate the deceased can be very useful in tapping into the older energies of death. When connecting with the Underworld or the gods of death, this type of earth makes a wonderful connection.

☾ **Elder:** Those who died at the end of a long life could be used to promote wisdom or to guide.

☾ **Healer:** Doctor, nurse, et cetera for healing and health concerns.

☾ **Judge:** Lawyers, judges, and other court workers are often helpful in disputes and in seeking justice.

☾ **Open or Freshly Dug Grave:** Letting go, psychopomps, magic done for the elderly, terminally ill, and so on. There is a newness to this sort of earth, and it can be utilized when connecting with the recently deceased as it is an entrance to the realms in which they are journeying.

☾ **Prosperous:** Earth from the grave of a wealthy or successful person can assist in prosperity and abundance spells

☾ **Soldier:** Soldiers are, at their core, protectors. Here, you might employ one or dozens to provide protection in a situation that calls for it.

⟡ **Witch/Magical Practitioner:** This type of earth is universal in usage and can be quite handy to have!

ALTERNATIVE CHOICES

⟡ **Bank:** To assist in financial matters, prosperity, abundance.

⟡ **Courthouse:** To assist in legal matters, disputes.

⟡ **Crossroad:** To alter the course of events.

⟡ **Cypress Tree, beneath:** To bring comfort to the bereaved.

⟡ **Data Center:** Does your hometown (or one near you) have a big tech data center? Earth from here is very useful when working magic for cyberbullying or other internet-centered issues.

⟡ **Garden:** Fertility.

⟡ **Hospital:** For healing.

⟡ **Playground:** For happiness, protection.

⟡ **School:** To gain knowledge.

⟡ **Witches Home:** This might be your house, and this earth is universal in use! Go you.

⟡ **Workplace:** To settle issues on the job, for promotions, raises, and other employment related issues.

⟡ **Yew Tree, beneath:** Underworld travel, confrontations with death and mortality, protection. (I particularly like using earth from beneath a yew tree growing in an older cemetery in my work.)

EXERCISE: RESPONSIBLY GATHERING GRAVEYARD DIRT

TIME AND PLACE: Any time, though a new moon can be useful; Graveyard or cemetery

SUPPLIES: Potting soil; Bottled water; Spade or bulb planter; Zip-top bags; Labels; Pen

OPTIONAL SUPPLIES: Headlamp; Rum; Tobacco; Coins; Empty bottles; Paintbrush; Backpack

PURPOSE: To gather graveyard dirt for ritual use and spell work.

When moving on to actually removing the earth from a burial place, be certain of a few things. First: ensure that you are not trespassing or breaking any local laws. Developing friendships with your local grave-digging crew is a great way to gain that kind of access without causing any issues or even having to disturb the soil. Second: ensure that you are not causing damage. Take only what you need and no more. When working in cemeteries/graveyards, you might do as I do and keep a little kit for that purpose. I generally carry a canvas backpack daily and in it, a small bottle of dark rum, some tobacco, coins, empty bottles, a paintbrush for cleaning headstones, a hand shovel, a bulb planter tool, a small bag of potting soil, bottled water, a headlamp in case I'm working at night (rarely), a collapsible tote bag for gathering herbs, and other small items such as labels, a pen, zip-top bags, and so on.

You can choose to begin by making offerings and asking for permission from the incorporeal beings associated with the cemetery, the occupant of any particular grave you're working with, and the gods before removing any earth. I like to work specifically within a space with which I have a strong working relationship, and therefore have less need to make supplications for this type of work because I am there every day making offerings. Be open to being told no on any given day, in any place, no matter how familiar you are with the location or its inhabitants. The dead get to withdraw consent as well.

For the actual removal of earth, you might choose to use a spade, but I highly recommend a bulb planting tool with a T-handle. This type of tool does less damage, taking a plug of earth out in one go, while leaving the plug of grass in great shape to be placed back on top. Here's where your bag of potting soil comes into play. Once you've removed the earth you wish to take, replace it with the soil you've brought with you before placing the plug of grass back on top, watering it with a bit of water from your bottle. Repair what you have damaged—replace what was lost. You may, of course, wish to record the location, date/time, if you took the earth from a specific sort of location, names, date of birth/death, et cetera, and clearly label your container.

STORING GRAVEYARD DIRT

After arriving back to your living space, you may choose to leave the earth as is (I do, worms and all) or you may wish to prepare it for storage by drying (which you can accomplish in a warm oven on a low temperature, spread out on a baking tray, or in a dehydrator), removing any particulate matter, and sifting it fine. Frankly, I wish for my graveyard earth to remain alive, and for me, that means keeping it in a planter with something growing in it. Never forget that graveyard dirt is *alive*. It is earth, after all.

COFFIN NAILS 💀

One material fundamental to not only necromantic practice—but to all manner of practices—is coffin nails. It is in Pliny's *Naturalis Historia* that we find one of the earliest known spells to utilize a coffin nail, where you are instructed to "take any (iron) naile out of the coffin or sepulchre wherein (the dead) lieth buried, and to sticke the same fast to the lintle or side-post of a dore, leading either into the house or bed-chamber where any doth lie who is haunted with spirits in the night, (they) shall be (delivered) and secured from such phantasticall illusions."[103]

---

103 Pliny the Elder, Philemon Holland, and Adam Islip, *The Historie of the Vvorld: Commonly Called, the Natvrall Historie of C. Plinivs Secvndvs, vol. 2* (London: Printed by Adam Islip, 1634), 515–16.

WHAT IS A "COFFIN NAIL?"

Coffin nails are not so much made as they are gathered, though many coffin nails available today are simply carpenter's nails that have been consecrated to a purpose and buried in a cemetery to be gathered later. I do believe that necromantic practice is best served with fasteners that have been legitimately used in the construction of not just a coffin, as the name implies, but burial containers in general. Perhaps for your spell work, you find yourself using a casket screw, or even a staple from an urn, and that isn't really any different from a nail from a coffin. I would much rather have a screw that was used to hold together a modern casket than to have a consecrated nail that has touched neither a burial container nor the dead. Is magic about intent or function? We can only answer these questions for ourselves.

CONSULT YOUR BOOK OF SHADES
Refer to pages 185 and 186 of the Arms and Armor section of the Book of Shades for both the *Coffin Nail Protection Charm*, and the *Coffin Nail Protection Bath* spells.

RESPONSIBLE SOURCES

I would like to clear up right away that no, it isn't impossible to acquire authentic coffin nails, and no, the only method available to you is not grave robbing them from some unfortunate soul. So, how might one go about gathering such a thing, you may be wondering? Well, it might surprise you to discover that ship-out caskets, disinterred caskets, and decommissioned viewing caskets, wind up in landfills every day—and most have been occupied by the dead. Connect with local funeral homes, or even search your local buy-and-sell sites for caskets that are no longer needed, and simply salvage them for parts.

This is a wonderful way to connect with death on a practical level, while also recycling items that otherwise go to waste. I don't know about you, but I'd much rather do some necromantic dumpster diving than disturb the burial places of the dead.

When salvaging burial containers, work slowly and meticulously while disassembling—collecting each nail, screw, and other pieces of hardware as you go. Nothing should go to waste, so take care in your work. Preserve the wood, fabrics, and so on for whatever use you determine. I've used salvaged casketing materials for everything from building spirit houses from the reclaimed wood to slicing thin strips to use as candle-wicking!

EXERCISE: MAKING COFFIN NAILS

Time and Place: Between sunset and sunrise, new moon, and over a period of one month; Cemetery or your living space
Supplies: Nails; Earth from a disinterred grave
Purpose: To create necromantically charged nails as a substitute for coffin nails.

If you are interested in the process of making coffin nails, which I cannot express strongly enough is not ideal, here's a method. On the new moon, sometime between sunset and sunrise, bury your nails in grave dirt, leaving them for a period of a full month. They will be ready at the end of this time period, but it is best to keep any excess buried in a box of graveyard dirt until such time they are needed.

While this does suggest burial in a graveyard/cemetery, you might also place your box inside a flowerpot or space in your garden that you have designated as a grave by marking it off and turning graveyard dirt into the soil. For this, I recommend earth from a disinterred grave as the energies will be more potent. Remember that if providing these to others for use, it is important to be clear that they are manufactured, rather than authentic.

WORKING WITH COFFIN NAILS

In addition to their connection to death, part of what makes coffin nails such good magic is iron. Iron, much like coffin nails themselves, can be used for its fixing properties. Just like nailing one board to another, a spell effect might be fixed to a purpose, place, person, or thing by the addition of an iron nail. What is added by its contact with death is energetic properties. A coffin nail's connection with closing death's last door is what makes them so useful for not only closing, but *opening*, Liminal Spaces. Imagine driving a coffin nail into the frame of your front door; just like a coffin, it is now sealed against entry or exit by eidōlon.

Generally, I find coffin nails to be a neutrally inclined material, and benevolent leaning. You could use them for cursing, revenge, or harm, but in my humble opinion, it lacks a bit of imagination when you could instead use them in rituals for closure of all kinds. For protection. As a key. From a practical, necromantic standpoint, coffin nails provide assistance in contacting the dead and asking for their aid in your work. Additionally, they neutralize negative influences, give a power boost to any spell you might be working, and are used to break curses. Like any other material inclined toward death, it is important to consider the eidōlon of those who once occupied that burial container (even if it was just for a little while) and make proper offerings in thanks.

HUMAN REMAINS

In *An American Marriage,* Tayari Jones states, "Only our bodies know the truth, bones don't lie," and a very real and practical truth lives in that statement.[104] There's a reason that those who work with death, work with bones, wet specimens, and cremated remains, and that is because these remains retain an elemental portion of the soul of those who once occupied them.[105] Insomuch as the physical form is a portion of the soul, which we discussed in Chapter 4, *The Nature*

---

104 Tayari Jones, *An American Marriage: A Novel* (Chapel Hill, NC: Algonquin Books of Chapel Hill, 2019).
105 Duffy, *Rites Necromantic,* 13.

of a Soul, this remaining link to who that person once was can be a powerful ally in your necromantic work. Not only through these can you tap into the energies of death, but they act as a foothold on the other side, a key to the Underworld, enabling one to push through the veil and communicate with the Underworld. Must you work with the physical remains of humans? Of course not! But why wouldn't you when they're so easily available? Never forget that you can tap into yourself as a source of necromantic power—you are, after all, haunting an entire body/skeleton as we speak.

LEGALITIES

Necromantic practice often gets discarded as a relic from a bygone era if, for no other reason, the perception of legal and ethical considerations. Working with human remains, for example, is often perceived as being vile and illegal—though, in a great deal of the modern world, one can legally purchase human bones and wet specimens. Variable from state to state, country to country, and so on. It's important that you check your local laws before proceeding with the purchase or acquisition of any remains.

Speaking for things here in the United States, it is legal as of the time of writing to own human remains in all but three states, those being Louisiana, Georgia, and Tennessee. Louisiana prohibits the ownership of all human remains excluding teeth, fingernails, gallstones, or cremated remains—you may not own or possess any human remains if you live in the state of Louisiana. In Georgia and Tennessee, you may own (or purchase, sell, and trade) human remains within the state— that means you cannot import or export them. No bringing them in from outside the state, nor can you send them to someone else.

RESPONSIBLE SOURCES

There are a great deal of locations throughout the world from which you can buy retired medical specimens, and it would be deplorable to even consider sourcing human remains from any source other than osteological specimens used in the medical field. While it has not always been the case historically, modern medical donors (or their next of kin) give legal consent for their bodies (and later, their bones) not only to be used for *science*, as is commonly assumed, but for *any purpose* in perpetuity. It is important to remember that due to the inherent anonymity and privacy standards of medical donor programs, we cannot guarantee the life someone lived, how they died, or where they as individuals came from.

Because ethics can vary depending on one's personal belief structure, as I spoke about early on, the best that can be said is that retired medical specimens are *responsibly* sourced, and that you have adhered to the law in acquiring them. Is it ethical, ultimately? That is up to you as an individual to decide. As someone who has, on more than one occasion, witnessed human osteological specimens deemed unusable (due to being broken, missing pieces, et cetera) being tossed into the garbage bin, I find it far more ethical to purchase them and give them a happy magical home. As for fully ethical sources of bone (or wet specimens) don't forget that anytime you are undergoing surgery (or dental procedures) you are well within your legal rights to ask that items removed from your body be returned to you.

WORKING WITH REMAINS (HUMAN OR ANIMAL)

It is important, however, that each piece be given the time and space to communicate whether they wish to be a part of the work you are doing, and it's important that we always be open to hearing a no from humans or animals alike. As for general handling, use common sense when working with remains, human or otherwise. Handle them carefully over a surface to lessen the risk of drops from a height. Be wary of loose pieces, and if handling a skull, never lift by the zygomatic arch or by the sockets of the eyes. These areas were not meant to support weight and you are likely to break a precious item.

EXERCISE: CRAFTING A BONE FLUTE

Time and Place: Any
Supplies: Bone; Woodworking tools; Dowel rod; Sandpaper; File
Purpose: To create a bone flute for ritual use.

For most magical practices, a noisemaker of some sort will be used to clear the space of unwanted energy or entities, but also might be used to invite spirits to the space. Bone flutes and other instruments as a form of performative necromancy are common to many parts of the world, including (but not limited to) China, Sweden, and even the ancient Aztec Empire had their whistles made to mimic a human scream! I myself have carved a penny whistle out of human bone to use in my own magic and have found it to be a powerful ally when calling out to the dead. Dr. Tom Johnson notes in *The Graveyard Wanderers* that a bone flute is used to "blow the spirit through."[106] These instruments can be used for calling, soothing, and/or commanding the dead. Some of the earliest instruments created were made from bone, and flutes have long been made from any number of materials. Turning bone into a flute or whistle isn't difficult and is a fun skill to learn.

The first step is to find the bone that is right for your project. You'll want a bone that is strong and isn't too thin so that the interior will have a diameter that is similar to a standard flute (or perhaps a penny whistle, if you'd like to make something smaller). After determining the length needed, cut off the ends with a coping saw. Bones are naturally hollow, but you'll need to sand the interior, which can be accomplished by wrapping a small dowel rod in heavy grit sandpaper. Simply move it back and forth until the interior is smooth. Next, using sandpaper, a metal file, or a Dremel tool, shape the end of the bone into a mouthpiece. Be certain to remove any sharp edges that could injure the person playing the instrument.

Lastly, drilling carefully to avoid unnecessary damage, make three holes spaced one inch apart, beginning one inch from the mouth end of the instrument. Create a fourth hole in the end opposite the mouthpiece, one inch in. Using your dowel rod and sandpaper, sand the interior once more to remove any fragments. At this point, you may move on to finishing the flute in any way you prefer. You could leave it plain, give it a protective coating, etch it with patterns, or stain it with inks or other stains.

---

106 Johnson, *The Graveyard Wanderers*, 5.

STORING REMAINS (HUMAN OR ANIMAL)

Bones require a dry, temperature stable environment, and cool is best. Rapid changes in temperature (and humidity) will cause bones (of any type) to swell and shrink, which over time will cause the bone to crumble. Bones should not be stored in direct sunlight as UV radiation destroys the proteins that bones are made up, of and will cause them to become brittle over time. If bones become wet, it is important to air dry them before placing them back into a closed area such as a cabinet, shelf, or cloche. Wet bone will grow mold, and this mold will discolor or damage osteological specimens.

CLEANING REMAINS (HUMAN OR ANIMAL)

Bones do become dirty, and, owing to their porous nature, will absorb oils from your skin which can cause them to become stained over time. To avoid this, ensure your hands are clean when handling remains, and you might choose to wear gloves. Keeping your osteological specimens in a covered container such as a cloche will prevent a lot of issues such as dust or environmental grime. Should they require cleaning, however, this can be simply accomplished with a soft brush (I prefer a soft-bristled toothbrush that has been purchased for this purpose) and warm water with a bit of dish soap—never use bleach to clean or lighten bone. Gently clean as though you were brushing your teeth, ensuring not to wet the bone all the way through. Soaking your bones will cause decomposition to occur at a faster rate, and the bones may crack as they dry.

A NOTE ON WET SPECIMENS (HUMAN OR ANIMAL)

If choosing to work with wet specimens, remember that it isn't enough to simply purchase them and sit them on a shelf. First, they do need to be in a cool, temperature stable environment, just like osteological specimens. Most importantly, the environment should not be *hot*, and that they be stored out of direct sunlight. It's additionally important to remember that wet specimens should be considered toxic, as they are (often) stored in fluids that are harmful for consumption or handling. One of the first things I do when acquiring a wet specimen is to replace the fluid, as often I do not know what fluid is in the container, and solutions such as formalin will degrade the specimen over time. When doing so, be certain to wear gloves, a respirator rated for *organic vapors*, and to do this work outdoors in an area in which you've laid down an absorbent pad for catching any drips (old fluid should be jarred and disposed of at the nearest waste disposal location that takes household chemical waste).

If cleaning up after spilled fluids, *never use bleach*—I cannot emphasize this enough—as this can interact with aldehyde-based preservative solutions to produce a deadly gas. Instead, clean the area several times in a row with plain water, placing all paper towels into a plastic bag to be disposed of with your chemical waste and PPE. Once the old fluid has been contained, gently rinse your specimen with bottled distilled water to remove any particulates and debris. Wash the original container (containers should always be glass) with soap and water, drying *fully* before placing the specimen back inside and filling the container with 70 percent isopropyl alcohol. Be certain to note on the bottom of your container using an acid-free, archival quality label, the date of restoration, as well as noting what solution you've placed inside to ensure you (or the next person) have this information. Going forward, simply look for clouding of the fluid, particles, and debris, or lowering fluid levels to determine when you should repeat this process.

EXERCISE: BONDING WITH YOUR INSTRUMENTS

TIME AND PLACE: Any
SUPPLIES: Newly made or acquired instrument
PURPOSE: Getting to know your necromantic tools and instruments.

In *The Crafting and Use of Ritual Tools: Step-by-Step Instructions for Woodcrafting Religious & Magical Implements*, Eleanor and Phillip Harris note a bond is formed when a magical tool accompanies a practitioner through ritual after ritual.[107] Through repeated magical

---

107 Eleanor Harris and Philip Harris, *The Crafting & Use of Ritual Tools: Step-By-Step Instructions for Woodcrafting Religious & Magical Elements* (St. Paul, MN: Llewellyn Publications, 1998), 195–207.

acts with an item, this bond becomes stronger, but we don't always have the time in our busy modern lives to ensure that will happen in a timely fashion. So, what are we to do aside from being purposeful and intentional about this bond? Set aside time to sit with your new instrument in meditative space, really getting to know that instrument and contemplating the forces of life and death within it. Wood, taken from a living tree; iron from the earth not that dissimilar to the iron in your own blood. Perhaps your instrument contains leather, or is bound with sinew, the fibrous tissue binding bone to bone, a vital part of a living body. All these pieces of life and death, vital to the function of what they once were, and now, what they have become. Through the work of necromancy, you have given new life to these materials—these corporeal remains—truly raising them up from death.

BACK TO BASICS

Any number of items in this chapter may be something you wish to consecrate using the *Consecration of Ritual Instruments for Necromantic Practice* ritual located on page 123 in the Rites and Rituals section of the Book of Shades.

LAST WORDS

As it is noted by Dr. Johnson in *The Graveyard Wanderers: The Wise Ones and the Dead*, their collection of wisdom from the *Black Art Books*, "You must before your own death, return all that you have taken from the dead; lest you have no peace in the grave."[108] Any items that cannot be returned prior to your death should be interred (cremated, et cetera) with your body so that they are returned to the places of the dead.

---

108 Johnson, *The Graveyard Wanderers*, 83.

7

NECROMANCY IN PRACTICE

"Be hole, be dust, be dream, be wind / Be night, be dark, be wish, be mind, / Now slip, now slide, now move unseen, / Above, beneath, betwixt, between."
—Neil Gaiman, *The Graveyard Book*

In *Forbidden Rites: A Necromancer's Manual of the Fifteenth Century*, Richard Kieckhefer writes that "the rites contained in a manual of necromancy are flamboyantly transgressive, even carrying transgression toward its furthest imaginable limits." I thought of that line when sharing a portion of the rituals contained herein, only to be told that they seemed *heretical*.[109] This was particularly funny to me at the time, given that the person saying as much was also (Gardnerian) Wiccan, and the idea that we might have an orthodoxy that one might commit heresy against in the first place is absurd. You see, heresy is to have an opinion *profoundly at odds* with generally accepted orthodoxy (beliefs or practices generally accepted to be correct), and I can't get a dozen witches in my living room to agree on a type of pizza, least of all a dozen covens to agree on what are correct practices for a Wiccan, Gardnerian or otherwise. But where it really falls apart for me is in the idea that necromancy, or rather, my personal take on it, is profoundly at odds with Wicca. *Oh no*, you think to yourself, recalling the prologue in which I insisted this book wasn't going to be fluffy. Yes. The practice I have provided here has a foundationally Wiccan flavor, and I don't intend to be apologetic about that. Am I "Wicca-washing" necromancy? Absolutely not, this is a choice, it is purposeful.

---

109 Kieckhefer, *Forbidden Rites*, 10.

Classically, Wiccan rituals at the least have been led by a pair of individuals with one (ostensibly) representative of life, and the other, death, and somewhere between lies that balance of reincarnation, rebirth, and the story that is creation. So it was that rather than considering what makes a ritual necromantic, I found myself considering instead what makes the ones we are all too familiar with about *life*. The general construct of a magic circle is reasonably straightforward. Declare your intentions, consecrate needed items, cast the circle, call quarters, invoke necessary figures, do any intended work, make offerings, and close the space.[110] On a more metaphorical level, the magic circle could be described as a great clock—midnight set in the east—entrances, beginnings, turning on a pivot point. This circle, with its quarters neatly laid out, represents a build of energy, upward round and round, right hip to the altar as we move clockwise, creating. But why? Life is linear, and as we move forward in our inexorable march toward death, the hands of the clock move ever forward, the right hand in which we hold our athame, positioning the bodies inferior vena cava toward the center, a reminder that, as is nature's way, we are *dying*.

Historically, necromantic rituals have relied upon the concept of invoking death as a return, and therefore, of reversals.[111] So, what then does it mean to turn this life oriented magic circle on its head? Our clock face reoriented. Midnight now lies in the west, and we begin and end our circumambulations there. That cross-quarter compass laid out across its face, now a crossroads, a path by which the dead might travel to and from this space.[112] Athame in the left hand, we move counterclockwise around, now anchored to our magic circle the side of the body upon which lies the descending aorta from which life-giving oxygenated blood flows into our bodies, the left atrium of the heart having revived—nay, *raised from the dead*—lifeless deoxygenated blood within the context of our own body's natural systems.[113]

---

110 Jason Mankey, *Transformative Witchcraft: The Greater Mysteries* (Woodbury, MN: Llewellyn Publications, 2019), 73.

111 Duffy, *Rites Necromantic*, 35.

112 Aaron Oberon, *Southern Cunning: Folkloric Witchcraft in the American South* (Winchester, UK: Moon Books, 2019), 62.

113 Susan Whittemore and Denton Cooley, *The Circulatory System* (Facts on File, Incorporated, 2014), 16.

What then is functionally different about the necromantic ritual? Walking our ritual back in time, we begin with libations, and end with consecrations. Rather than building up a cone of power, our energy, reversed, spirals downward into the cavernous depths of the earth.[114] In many folk practices, one danced anti-clockwise around a grave to summon the dead and commune with them; here, we dance round an altar—a bowl of grave dirt at its center—the shades of the dead spun upward to walk the path that we have laid down for them.[115] A necromantic ritual is, in essence, adjusting your intention and turning your magic on its head. The center of our magic circle now truly a fulcrum point upon which we might declare mastery over both palingenesis, *and* death.

Just because necromantic magic operates on a system of reversals doesn't make it a perversion of anything at all; rather, that to have no elements of death at all is the perversion. We have forgotten that death is a part of the balance, for as Samuel Beckett said in *Waiting for Godot*, we "give birth astride a grave, the light gleams an instant, then it's night once more."[116] Necromancy isn't really about death, it's about birth, for any magic that is about life will always be about decay, and the magic of death cannot help but be about living.

THE NECROMANTIC CIRCLE

A great deal of historical references for necromantic ritual refer to these rituals taking place within a cast circle. While these references often refer to those circles as a tool to protect the practitioner from the dead (or demons as the case may be), historically, circles were seen as a way to strengthen the power of the individuals casting them. The dead need energy to manifest. And circles? Circles are *excellent* for building up and containing energy. In this context, the circle is not just sacred space, but a powerhouse of energy for the dead to tap into as you work collaboratively toward your goals.

---

114 Mankey, *Transformative Witchcraft*, 101, 117.

115 Duffy, *Rites Necromantic*, 35.

116 Samuel Beckett, *Waiting for Godot: A Tragicomedy in Two Acts* (London: Faber and Faber, 1959), 89.

I encourage you to consider the circle within necromantic practice neither boundary nor containment, but rather a Liminal Space—a place betwixt and between—carved out between the Material Plane and the Underworld itself, thereby meeting the dead halfway rather than forcing them to manifest on the Material Plane. Do you always need a circle? Certainly, you could forgo it, but know that the energetic cost for manifestation across the vast distance that lies between life and death is significant. Without creating that liminality, the cost may simply be too high for the eidōlon you are attempting to work with.

LAYING OUT AND PREPARING YOUR CIRCLE

Ordinarily, you might begin preparing for a circle by cleansing the area. This often includes physically cleaning by sweeping the area, burning incense, marking/asperging the area out with salted water, and even ringing bells to dispel energy and remove unwanted incorporeal beings. Obviously, we don't necessarily want to do that, but I'd like to give you a new perspective for asperging, because when I go around the circle sprinkling with salted water and censing? I'm reminded of another action: smoking and preserving meats.

Salt has historically been used for curing, as a preservative, thus its usefulness in mummification. I propose that when we salt and cense the circle that we preserve it, mummify it, and hold it aside. Spaces for necromantic ritual might have been marked out with charcoal, functioning as the cremated remains of a now deceased tree, and you can do the same, or simply draw that intention into your space using the charcoal disks in your censor as you cleanse and prepare the area.[117]

Not unlike many magic circles, a circle for necromantic ritual should be nine feet in diameter. Nine is a number that appears often in death magic, and necromantic circles often include nine candles or stones around the perimeter.[118] In a typical circle casting we see the quarters neatly laid out, with candles at each of the four points—here,

---

117 Aleister Crowley, *Moonchild* (United Kingdom: Red Wheel Weiser, 1975), 202.

118 Ibid.

we have eight, reconnecting again in the west to reach the number nine as we complete our circle. Though it is certainly UPG, I associate each of these points with a portion of the soul identified in Chapter 4, *The Nature of a Soul*, and notably absent is the Sobriquet. Because you yourself, your back to the east—your Carnal form anchored to life—face the ghost of your future. The west. The Ethereal. Death. Here you stand representative of a name, of a moment, of a memory of who you are today and may never be again.

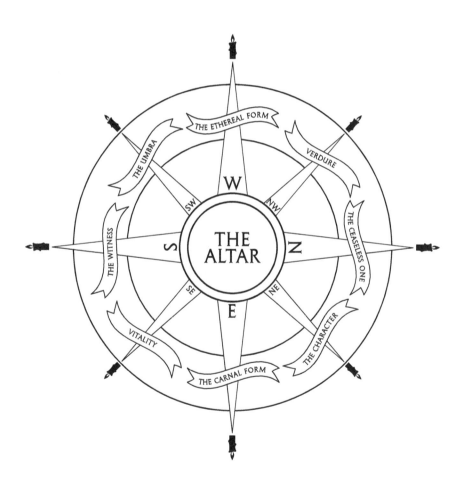

Quarter correspondences and oppositions for
the purpose of laying out ritual space.

THE ALTAR

Altars are a space in magical practice that is inherently liminal. A place where the material is ethereal, where the physical touches the spiritual, a place where we can sit down with those entities and share space. Used the world over by the religious, and irreligious alike, an altar is a space where you alone direct your path. Many would never choose to cast a circle or have a ritual practice but may still wish to build an altar for the dead—if only for their specific ancestors.

HOW TO SET UP YOUR ALTAR

To begin, you'll need to select a piece of furniture appropriate for the task. For ritual proper, I'm very fond of a round table, and enjoy the flow of magic within the space that a round table makes possible. But for a more permanent working structure? I prefer a rectangular piece of furniture that I can place against the wall, preferably something with a small cabinet space underneath.

A lot of the spells you will find herein will suggest that you keep items under your altar, often stored in grave dirt, for a period of time. In this regard, a cabinet works well as it functions as a symbolic burial place, an ossuary, a crypt, a tiny little sarcophagus. As to what direction your altar should face? While many altars (at least in Wiccan traditions) would face north, I orient my ancestral/death/necromancy altars to the west. While ultimately it is up to your personal practice, and there is no wrong way, there are better ways, and for this magic, that way is west.

Next, you'll wish to select items to place into the space. Two small bowls each for salt and water, a censor, a shallow bowl of grave dirt (which would ideally house a small bell jar containing an osteological specimen), two candles, and eight small objects placed around the perimeter, oriented cardinally if it's safe to do so. I have small children (and a dog), so I worry about small items. To cut down on choking hazards, I've simply driven nine coffin nails into the altar completely flush with the surface, marking out the quarters and cross-quarters.

On the wall over this altar, I have a small shadow box hung (available at most large retailers, a shadow box is simply a deep picture

frame that you can place objects inside) where I collect meaningful tokens of the dead such as photographs, toe tags, bits of suture thread, and so on. They're not only enshrined, but protected from wandering toddler hands, and kept free of dust. When it comes to flowers, I like collecting forgotten bouquets when I'm cleaning in the cemetery and bring those home with me to use in my altar. Insomuch as much of our work is about imbuing things with the properties of death, those forgotten flowers are imbued with a family's love for those whom they venerate.

In addition to the above, you might add any number of things important to you. My own altar has a few pieces of broken headstone gifted to me by gravediggers. My altar does have a covering, and it is sewn from bits of satin casket liner that I rescued from a rental casket. Your ritual altar will be arranged similarly, with the addition of your preferred ritual knife and bident.

ENERGY AND THE CONE OF POWER

It's always simultaneously amusing and validating to find that someone else out there shares a bit of UPG with you. Part way through writing, I happened to acquire a copy of *Transformative Witchcraft: The Greater Mysteries* by Jason Mankey, stumbling across an anecdote in the process regarding their spouse's "invention"—the "Inverse Cone of Power."[119] I was delighted, of course, to discover that someone else out in this big, wide world was doing magic in a way similar to myself. Mankey notes that "operationally it's very similar to the traditional cone of power, but instead of sending energy up and out, energy is sent downward, where it's sent directly to whoever or whatever it's being raised for," and this is where our UPG deviates.[120]

In noting that it is a way to send energy directly to whomever it is being raised for, Mankey implies a belief that their ritual space is "above" other individuals in the world. In contrast, it is my belief that my ritual space, though liminal, occupies space right here on

---

119 Mankey, *Transformative Witchcraft*, 117.
120 Ibid.

the Material Plane and not "above" anyone at all. When I'm sending energy to other living beings, I am sending it outward like ripples on a pond. Because we're on the same level playing field, right?

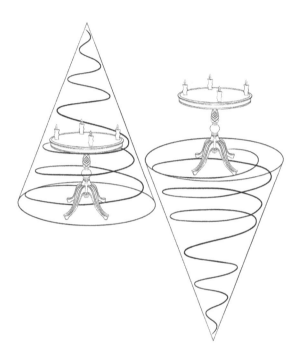

The Inverse Cone of Power

In addition, we should not presume to send energy to the dead in this form, regardless of our altitude in relation to the Underworld. The dead are thought made matter, magic made manifest, a divine spark—the foundation upon which egregore might be built. Dark matter, antimatter, and all sparks in between—the Underworld, a sea of consciousness and energy. What we offer instead is a liminal pathway, an invitation, a place in which we meet the dead halfway. And so it is that rather than building up a cone of power, our energy, reversed, spirals downward into the Underworld. To the Underworld, to the dead, to that zero point of the universe—to a place where all energy must go, and from which it must return.

BANISHING AND INVOKING PENTAGRAMS

An element of ceremonial magic, banishing and invoking pentagrams are often an element of circle casting within certain traditions. Within the basic ritual, I've asked that you utilize only an earth invoking and banishing pentagram, with, contrary to the norm, the banishing pentagram being used to *begin* the ritual and invoking to end.

Why? Our work here is focused on working collaboratively with death, the dead, and the dying. In *banishing* the earth element, we loosen our connection to the physical, to the material. This aids us in our goal of creating a liminal pathway within our ritual space. By closing with the *invoking* earth pentagram, this grounds us back to earth, closing the space to the ethereal.

LIBATION

When it comes to making offerings, it's important that we recognize offerings for the dead as separate and distinct from the act of sharing in libation. These offerings are gifts, left in the course of your work, sustaining the dead in a mundane way. In the context of necromantic (and, in my opinion, all) magic, offerings are gifts of Vitality, of the vital spark, the breath of life. That which the dead need above all else to function, to work, and to keep on being. Offerings for the dead, these gifts of Vitality, will become Verdure—that spark of un-life held by the dead, and some are better (and worse) than others, and those are what I'd like to talk about here.

WHAT SORT OF LIBATIONS SHOULD I CHOOSE?

Unlike a ritual such as cakes and wine which might have a symbolic connection to deity, here your libation (taken at the beginning of your rite rather than the end) is more symbolic of the dead, embodying their qualities, and of the energy that we give to them within the context of this work. For much of modern history it has been a feature of necromantic ritual to consume flat wine, stale bread, or other such tokens as a way of connecting, and that would also be appropriate here.

Drinking unfermented grape juice was meant to symbolize the lifelessness of the dead (you might consider flat water for this reason). Leftover stale wine can be put to use in any number of sauces, in marinades or vinaigrettes, for poaching pears, to make jelly, or even vinegar. Just like consuming flat wine, eating blackened bread was meant to symbolize lifelessness. Stale bread can easily be incorporated into your ritual meal by turning it into French toast, bread pudding, croutons, or even breadcrumbs to utilize in recipes.

Conversely, you might consider eating something rich, leaving that libation as a gift to the dead. If this is the route you are taking, consider making your selections based upon the dead you may be summoning if working with specific named eidōlon, otherwise, follow your instincts. Another difference between this libation, and what might be a more familiar cakes and wine is the language around the act, as we are not dedicating this to any particular deity, but rather, to the gods of death, to the dead, and to death itself.

KITCHEN NECROMANCY

Certain acts of consumption have long been associated with the dead, such as the consumption of foods beloved by particular ancestors, items associated with death (such as in the recipe below), or items generally considered dangerous such as baneful plants. It isn't hard, per se, to incorporate a little death magic—or even a bit of bane—to your kitchen, and therefore, your libations. Tomatoes and eggplants are nightshades, herbs such as basil, thyme, rosemary, and mint have common associations not only with death, but in some cases, are used in embalming not only historically, but even still today. Other methods for incorporating necromantic energies into your food include planting container gardens in graveyard dirt to grow edible herbs and nightshades, and leaving bundles of herbs as bouquets on graves to return and collect once dry.

EXERCISE: BAKING BONE BREAD

TIME AND PLACE: Any

SUPPLIES: Active dry yeast, 1 tbsp (7 gm); Raw Sugar, 1 tbsp (12.6 gm); Salt, 1 tbsp (17.1 gm); Warm water, 2 cups (568 gm), under 110 °F (43.33 °C); All-purpose flour, 5 ¾ cups (624.593 gm); 1 large food safe bone, or 2–4 smaller bones

PURPOSE: To bake bread from bone for use in ritual or offerings.

Making bone bread is not that dissimilar to ordinary bread recipes; what makes this recipe unique is simply, the addition of bone. Bone in bread is not that unique an idea, in fact, in the 1590s, starving Parisians driven desperate from hunger resorted to "Madame de Montpensier's bread."[121] What is "Madame de Montpensier's bread," you ask? Bread made with the disinterred and ground bones of those buried in the Holy Innocents Cemetery.[122] You yourself can create something similar by including food-safe bone sourced from your local grocer with this recipe.

© **Prepare Bones:** Begin by boiling food-safe bone, such as chicken or beef bones, clean and baking at 400–450 °F (200–230 °C) for one hour, or until dry and fragile, then ground to powder. You will need ¼ cup (34 gm) for your recipe—more is not ideal and will cause your bread to rise inconsistently, if at all.

© **Step One:** In a large bowl, combine the yeast, sugar, salt, and water. Allow this to stand until yeast is dissolved and bubbling. Mix flour and bone powder, before adding a bit at a time to the liquid mixture, stirring well after each addition, and stopping when dough begins to form. Reserve any leftover flour for kneading.

---

121 Elizabeth Missing Sewell, *Popular History of France, to the Death of Louis XIV* (n.p.), 1876), 389.

122 Ibid.

© **Step Two:** Turn dough out onto a floured surface and knead five minutes before placing dough into a large, greased bowl, turning it over once to grease the top. Cover with a damp towel and place in a warm spot until the dough doubles in size—approximately one to two hours.

© **Step Three:** Punch down the dough, cut in half, and shape into two loaves. Allow them to rest before slashing the tops to allow air to escape while baking. Place a baking dish with one inch of hot water into the bottom of the oven. Brush loaves lightly with cool water, and place onto a baking stone in a cold oven. Bake at 400 °F (200 °C) until golden brown, and hollow sounding when tapped.

Notes: If you'd like to make this bread without fully incorporating the bone powder, you may choose instead to place a whole bone inside your rising yeast mixture, removing it afterward. If you choose this method, increase flour by ¼ cup (34 gm).

LAST WORDS

In *Honoring Your Ancestors: A Guide to Ancestral Veneration* Mallorie Vaudoise says, "There are reasons we give (Vitality) to (the dead) in addition to expressing love. In many cultures, it is believed that certain things, such as food and incense, are needed to sustain the souls of the dead. Just as the living need food to survive, so too do the [...] dead. Otherwise, they become weak and eventually fade away."[123] Don't feel that fine Vitality, fancy gifts, are only to be given after the dead have done something equally grand; gifts are gifts and should have no strings attached.[124] I encourage you to build relationships with the dead that foster friendly exchange, rather than economic exchange.

---

123 Mallorie Vaudoise, *Honoring Your Ancestors: A Guide to Ancestral Veneration* (Woodbury, MN: Llewellyn Publications, 2019), 64–65.
124 Ibid.

PART TWO
A BOOK OF SHADES

*"We talk about the 'miracle of birth' but what about
the 'miracle of death'? We have the science of death pretty much
figured out, but death's magic and inevitability have been feared
and ignored for a long time now."*

—Neil Gaiman, *Death: The Time of Your Life*

HOW TO USE THIS SECTION

What follows is a spell book, a book of shadows—a *Book of Shades* if you will. I hoped to provide a group of spells, recipes, and rituals, that while certainly not comprehensive, would give you a starting point for incorporating necromantic magic into your own practice. This material contained is divided into a few helpful categories, such as:

ⓒ **Rites and Rituals:** The basic rituals of the necromantic practice outlined within.

ⓒ **Skills and Attributes:** Enhancing your own ability to work with the dead.

ⓒ **Reincarnation, Transmigration, and Healing:** The soul's journey and aid to the living.

ⓒ **Correspondences and Congruences:** Communicating with the dead.

ⓒ **Arms and Armor:** Protection.

ⓒ **Acts and Devotions:** Acts of reverence for Death, and for the dead.

Throughout the Book of Shades, you will find sigils of my own design and creation that are themselves spells that I utilize in my own work. Each is accompanied by a short description, a spoken invocation, and simple instructions that should provide the freedom to utilize them in any number of ways including on your body, worked into objects, or placed with the dead and dying.

Additionally, you will see many items flagged with the Back to Basics symbol, indicating that they are basic items utilized in other workings throughout.

8

RITES AND RITUALS

"When is death not within ourselves? Living and dead are the same, and so are awake and asleep, young and old."
—*Heraclitus, On the Universe*

While rituals do exist beyond this chapter, the rites and rituals included here constitute a basic set of rituals for working practice. In essence, a starting point for your work. A basic ritual outline, consecration of your ritual instruments for necromantic use, a year of necromantic sabbat rituals I use in my own practice, and guided meditations pathworkings—intended to impart necessary skills. As you dig into these rituals for yourself, keep in mind the altar layout from Chapter 7 as well as previous discussions about working tools and instruments, libations/offerings, and, particularly, the energy of the space. All of these things begin to fall into place as you work with these rituals, embracing this path—this bone spiral—that I've laid out before you.

NECROMANTIC RITUAL OUTLINE ☠

Time and Place: Any
Supplies: Your preferred ritual tools and instruments; Offerings; Libations; Corpse water ☠; Fresh water; Grave salt ☠; Clean salt; Taper candles, 2; Tealights, 8
Purpose: Ritual setup and structure.

Setup and Preparation

Begin by setting up your altar as shown in Chapter 7, *Necromancy in Practice*, as well as by preparing your body and ritual space as you ordinarily might by cleaning the space, bathing, and dressing in any ritual attire desired.

Asperging

Move to consecrate the salts, waters, and incense by drawing an earth invoking pentagram into each with the tip of a consecrated blade (such as an athame), saying:

> *In the name of Mors, they of the pallid face—death itself, I cast out from this material all suggestion of influence, that it may be bathed with the unflinching eye of death itself, neutral, unwavering, that in my hand it work only what I will—nothing more or less.*

Mix a bit of grave salt into the corpse water, then move anti-clockwise about the circle with the mixture, asperging the perimeter before returning to light the incense and altar candles.

Calling the Directions

Picking up the bident, move to invoke the eight directions, as you draw an earth banishing pentagram in the air, and saying:

> (West) *To the Ethereal ones my allies, my guides.*

> (Southwest) *To the Umbra, the darkness that exists in the presence of light, the repository of dread memory, and the paths we fear to tread.*

> (South) *To the Witness, I ask that you see me now, and hear my vow to act in service, doing only what is necessary—never more.*

(Southeast) *To the vital spark I carry within me, may I honor this gift of life, and offer up that gift in service to death.*

(East) *To the corporal form, that with which I touch, and hold, and take up arms—a symbol of my ability to give Vitality, and to take it away.*

(Northeast) *To the Character that has been imbued herein, and to all those for which I might do service.*

(Northwest) *To the Verdure which I feed.*

(Returning to the west) *And to all the names I have been and will be, to all those whom I call out to, those that I have yet to know.*

CONSECRATION OF DEATH

Orient yourself, facing north ideally. Turning to the west, pick up the grave salt and corpse water, stirring a bit of each together with the tip of a ritual blade (such as an athame) and drawing a banishing earth pentagram as you stir. Dipping your fingertips into the mixture, say:

I am dissolution,
(Touching the back of the neck)
and by this, am bathed in the unflinching eye of death.
(Touching the brow)
Neutral,
(Touching the left side of the throat)
Unwavering,
(Touching the right side of the throat)
and no influence beyond that of the grave can hold me.
(Touching, and pausing on, the sternum/middle of the chest)
My hands choose this death,
(Running down the interior of your left forearm)
and this death works only my will.
(Running down the interior of your right forearm)

OFFERINGS AND LIBATIONS

Setting aside a portion of the libation you have selected as an offering for the dead, lift your glass to the inhabitants of the Underworld, toasting to:

> *"That undiscovered country, from whose bourn no traveler returns."*[125]

CASTING THE CIRCLE

Taking up the bident, starting in the west, ending in the west, and moving anti-clockwise say:

> *I summon, stir, and invoke thee O' spirits: by salt do I mummify and preserve this place that is not a place, that it may sustain us. Though we gather here as equals, in the name of Mors do I, Death's agent, deign to command this space. So mote it be.*

MAGICAL WORK OR CELEBRATION—SUCH AS A SABBAT

This is the portion of the ritual in which you may perform any work you have set aside to do. You may choose to precede any magical work or sabbat celebration with an energy raising of your choice. This could include dancing, drumming, singing, and more; you are limited only by your imagination.

CONSECRATION OF LIFE

When you're ready, turning to the east, pick up the clean salt and water, stirring a bit of each together with the tip of your athame, and drawing an invoking earth pentagram as you stir. Dipping your fingertips into the mixture, say:

---

125 William Shakespeare, *Henry V. As You like It. Much Ado about Nothing. Hamlet* (P. F. Collier & Sons, 1912), 87.

I am revivified.
(Touching the back of the neck)
and by this, my Vitality is restored.
(Touching the brow)
Neutral,
(Touching the left side of the throat)
Unwavering,
(Touching the right side of the throat)
Cleansed of all that would do harm.
(Touching, and pausing on, the sternum/middle of the chest)
My hands choose this life,
(Running down the interior of your left forearm)
and this life works only my will.
(Running down the interior of your right forearm)

OPENING THE CIRCLE

After retracing your steps with the bident clockwise around three times, return to the altar saying the following as you extinguish the altar candles:

Though the flames of the material world be darkened, they shall ever burn in the worlds beyond.

After the circle has been closed, take the offerings of Vitality and any libations that you have set aside and place them in the space you have selected for the purpose of receiving offerings for the dead.

CONSECRATION OF RITUAL INSTRUMENTS FOR NECROMANTIC PRACTICE ☠

TIME AND PLACE: Between sunset and sunrise, new moon, and over a period of one month; In prepared ritual space
SUPPLIES: Basic necromantic ritual supplies; Newly made or acquired instrument; Graveyard oil ☠
PURPOSE: To consecrate instruments for use in ritual.

SETUP AND PREPARATION

In necromantic practice, it is important that you view your instruments as an extension of not only your magical energy, but your physical body. In any practice, you should, of course, feel confident in doing your magic without your tools as well as with them, but these instruments are amplifiers for what we bring to the table and batteries for the energy we build. Capable of acting as a container for our will, our intentions, and our energy, these instruments become more powerful with each use over time. Take this into consideration when purchasing/creating and consecrating any tool or instrument, that they might one day be either a powerful heirloom to pass to future generations of practitioners upon your death, or perhaps an item to be buried/cremated with you to act as yet another resource for you in your afterlife. If consecrating a blade, consider whether you might like to empower it either before or after the fact.

THE RITUAL

Begin by **asperging, calling the directions, consecration of death, offerings and libations,** and **casting the circle** per the basic *Necromantic Ritual Outline.* When ready, begin by addressing each of the eight points around your circle and introducing the instrument to each piece of the soul, saying:

(West) *To the Ethereal ones my allies, my guides,*

(Southwest) *To the Umbra, the darkness that exists in the presence of light, the repository of dread memory and the paths we fear to tread.*

(South) *To the Witness, I ask that you see me now, and hear my vow to act in service, using this instrument to do what is necessary—never more.*

(Southeast) *To the vital spark I carry within me, may I honor this gift of life, and offer up that gift in service to death.*

(East) *To the corporal form, with which I touch and hold, wielding this instrument and holding it up as a symbol of my strength to give Vitality, and to take it away.*

(Northeast) *To the Character that it has been imbued herein, and to all those for which I might do service.*

(Northwest) *To the Verdure which I feed.*

(Returning to the West) *And to all the names I have been and will be, to all those whom I call out to, those that I have yet to know.*

Returning to the altar, seat yourself in the east, facing west, saying:

Crafted from the materials of life and death, I bring this instrument before you, may those pieces of me honor this instrument in service, may the dead recognize this instrument's authority, may all act in cooperation.

Positioning your altar facing west, sit in the east with your new instrument for a moment, considering how many hours it took to craft. These moments of your life, given in its creation, can never be recovered. You have given life to create power, instruments of change, and creation. Then, placing a pinch of summoning incense on the coals, pass the instrument through the smoke, saying:

I call to the dead and the dead call to me. Ancestors, beloved dead, Mighty Dead, those of blood and bone, those of memory and imagination, nameless ones, and those known.
I hear you and speak for the silence.

Next, dipping the fingertips of your left hand into the salted corpse water, mark the instrument with this mixture, granting it the qualities of death, saying:

In the name of Mors, they of the pallid face, death itself, I cast out from this instrument all suggestion of influence, that this instrument be bathed in the unflinching eye of death itself, neutral, unwavering, that in my hand it work only what I will—nothing more or less.

End your ritual according to the basic *Necromantic Ritual Outline* with the **consecration of life** and **opening the circle**. Make quality offerings of Vitality to the dead before placing your newly consecrated instrument under your altar in a westward area of your home for a period of one month, dark moon to dark moon, in a container with grave earth. Do not remove or touch your new instrument during this time.

CONSULT YOUR BOOK OF SHADES
If you are consecrating a ritual blade of some kind and would like to necromantically empower it (before or after consecrating), refer to *Necromantically Empowering a Blade* on page 179 in the Arms and Armor section of the Book of Shades, which walks you through the process.

THE WHEEL OF THE YEAR

What I've provided you through this book is a picture of what my own necromantic practice looks like. Giving you a full picture of how I am interacting with death—and the dead—throughout the year, means sharing with you what the sabbats look like to me. As a (Gardnerian) Wiccan, I do celebrate the sabbats, but of course, put my own spin on them. Just like in any other practice, you'll want to experiment a bit with what these holidays mean to you, and whether they are something you'd like to incorporate into your own practice. Not everyone has a practice of working with the sabbats, but it may be a meaningful addition to your ritual practice if you choose it.

Never hesitate to incorporate your own meanings, symbolism, and experiences into what you're doing. A necromancer's job is to always be listening to themselves, to the gods, and to the dead—take what you hear and put it to work for you. Most things in necromantic practice, as I've mentioned, operate as a series of reversals. All things being equal, I do think that the same applies to the Wheel of the Year in some ways. I often joke that Hallows here on the Material Plane is Beltane in the Underworld, what some celebrate as a time of spirits, monsters, and darkness—a time that the dead roam—is likely a time of lively celebration and of life in the Underworld.

THE FEAST OF TORCHES

Time and Place: On or about February 2nd (Northern Hemisphere) or August 1st (Southern Hemisphere); In prepared ritual space
Supplies: Basic necromantic ritual supplies; Coins, multiple; Bulbs of garlic for offerings; Skeleton Key talisman ☠; Hurricane style lantern; Yellow candle, 1 (sized appropriately for your chosen lantern)
Purpose: To celebrate the Feast of Torches.

Setup and Preparation

February 2nd has been called many names by many people. The Feast of Torches. Imbolc. Candlemas. Nemoralia. The Ides of Hekate. I for one always get a chuckle out of explaining to places of employment why Groundhog Day is sacred. By any name, it is a center point to the dark half of the year, a time of hope, a time of glass-half-full energy, a time when the other side of winter is finally in sight. The Feast of Torches has energy that surrounds being buried in the earth, seeds, ready to burst forth with new promise. I suggest celebrating it in the name of Hekate, Greek deity of ghosts and necromancy—delving into the earth to light the way for any who are lost on the banks of the river.

Changing roles during this time of year, we see Persephone return to the land of the living, and Osiris, Egyptian god of death, changes roles as well, taking on the qualities of growth and fertility. Death has a unique connection to our seasons, holidays, and sabbats. These are just a few that you might be able to incorporate into your own practice.

☺ **A Little Symbolic Cannibalism?** During Nemoralia (which falls opposite the Feast of Torches for our friends in the Southern Hemisphere), it was common to make representations in clay or bread of body parts that needed healing which were given as offerings.

◉ **Brigid, Deity:** Some suggest that due to the many losses suffered within their myths that Brigid could be the origin of "keening," a type of musical and dramatic mourning cry performed at funerals and wakes.

◉ **Eggs:** We regard eggs as a symbol of life and fertility, but in the form in which we use them, they will never be life. Consider your eggs a death entombed, a sacrifice, life for life.

The Ritual

Place your lantern in the east in front of the bowl of earth. Have the *Skeleton Key* talisman on your person as well as a handful of coins to gift to any dead you find wandering the banks of the river for lack of fare during the pathworking. Begin by **asperging, calling the directions, consecration of death, offerings and libations,** and **casting the circle** per the basic *Necromantic Ritual Outline*, then light your lantern, saying:

> *I call upon Hekate, ancient and wise.*
> *I call upon you to raise your torch—shedding your light upon our path.*
> *With your keys open to me all doors, lending me your protection and wisdom.*
> *You, who looks forward and back, who abhors all evil.*
> *I call upon you to see those who would do harm,*
> *Those who would use their power to act against the will of others,*
> *And to reject their works against those who stand in your light.*
> *I stand at the crossroads and call upon you to see me,*
> *To grant me sanctuary through the long nights, as I grant it to others.*

Begin the *Underworld Pathworking* located at the end of this chapter, visualizing yourself carrying a lantern to light the way for any wandering dead. After the pathworking has ended, place a number of coins equal to those you gave to the dead, along with bulbs of garlic, with any other offerings and libations. End your ritual according to the basic *Necromantic Ritual Outline* with the **consecration of life** and **opening the circle**. Afterward, leave the garlic, coins, and other offerings in a crossroad as a gift to Hekate.

BACK TO BASICS
Refer to page 32 for further instructions regarding the talisman requested. Additionally, *Pathworking the Underworld* can be found on page 143 of this chapter.

THE VERNAL EQUINOX

TIME AND PLACE: On or about March 20th–21st (Northern Hemisphere) or September 20th–23rd (Southern Hemisphere); In prepared ritual space

SUPPLIES: Basic necromantic ritual supplies

PURPOSE: To celebrate the Vernal Equinox.

SETUP AND PREPARATION

During the equinoxes, the sun is positioned such that it sets perfectly due west. The west has been regarded by many cultures throughout the world as symbolic of death, or as a gateway to the Underworld. A time of perfect balance. Equal measures of night and day, light and dark, or perhaps, even life and death. These moments of perfect balance are a time to contemplate the ebbs and flows of life and death, as all the sabbats are. A pattern of predictable movement from times of growth, to times of decay, and round again. Death has a unique connection to our seasons, holidays, and sabbats. These are just a few that you might be able to incorporate into your own practice.

@ **Ohigan:** In Japan, the equinox is a time to celebrate Ohigan, which is a time to return to your hometown and pay respects to your deceased relatives. Those celebrating the holiday will spend it visiting graves, cleaning, and decorating them. These observances are made at both the Autumnal and Spring Equinox.

THE RITUAL

Begin by **asperging, calling the directions, consecration of death, offerings and libations,** and **casting the circle** per the basic *Necromantic Ritual Outline.* When ready, say:

Here we stand at a turning point,
The dying time of winter behind us,
The year again full with Vitality and life.
Our journey toward the light,
Rendered brighter by that darkness—
The winter lurking on the other side.
Today we live and celebrate the fullness of the now,
For tomorrow is not promised,
And death waits at the end of every life.

Play music, raising energy through dancing, drumming, or whatever method you prefer. Your focus should be on life and living for today, as tomorrow is not promised. Spend the rest of this time in ritual, sharing things you would like to accomplish in your life before the literal—or metaphorical—winter catches up to us. End your ritual according to the basic *Necromantic Ritual Outline* with the **consecration of life** and **opening the circle.**

BELTANE

TIME AND PLACE: On or about April 30th–May 1st (Northern Hemisphere) or October 31st–November 1st (Southern Hemisphere); In prepared ritual space

SUPPLIES: Basic necromantic ritual supplies; Gardening tools; Graveyard dirt; Seeds or seedlings, including beans; Bone meal; Blood meal; Coffin nail; Water

OPTIONAL SUPPLIES: Container planting materials

PURPOSE: To celebrate Beltane.

Setup and Preparation

Beltane has an interesting relationship with death. Often regarded as a sabbat associated with life, it is positioned opposite Hallows, though its name implies other roots. One proposed origin for the word *Beltane*, is the word *bael*, and that word? It implies a funeral pyre.[126] If we look at our Beltane fires as purifying, cleansing, but also as a funeral—what are we leaving behind? What has died? Our maypole, an *axis mundi*, reaching upward from this Material Plane—the place of the living—to the celestial places, and downward into the depths of the earth and down into the Underworld? What a better connection between the living and the dead, the living and whatever lies beyond the stars. Death has a unique connection to our seasons, holidays, and sabbats. These are just a few that you might be able to incorporate into your own practice.

- **Do a Little Necrobotany:** This would be an excellent time to plan or plant a necromantic garden with laurel and yew, wormwood, legumes, and so on.

- **Liminal Time:** Beltane is a time when, much like Hallows, the veil is thin. Most sources note that on Hallows this facilitates the dead accessing the Material Plane; while on Beltane, this facilitates entry by the Good Folk/Fae. Why would only one be true in either case? In my humble opinion, that's just bad math. If one is true, they must both be.

- **Mock Sacrifice:** It's possible that some performed a mock sacrifice on Beltane. The Cailleach *Beal-tine*, it has been said, was an individual who was unfortunate enough to receive a piece of bannock marked with charcoal as everyone passed around the oatcake. Individuals present at the rite would have acted out sacrificing this person, and then treated them as though they were dead!

- **Bone and Blood Meal:** You may be wondering what bone and blood meal are, and, simply put, both are fertilizers used

---

126 Anonymous and Poetry Foundation, "Beowulf (Old English Version)," Poetry Foundation, July 4, 2021.

commonly in gardening. Bone meal is precisely what you might imagine: ground bone. Blood meal, on the other hand, is dried blood which is used as a "nitrogen amendment" to help plants grow lush, thick, and healthy. Who knew that gardening was so surrounded by death? You won't need an altar, or even the basic ritual setup, unless you choose to utilize them.

THE RITUAL

Should you choose to utilize them, begin by **asperging, calling the directions, consecration of death, offerings, and libations,** and **casting the circle** per the basic *Necromantic Ritual Outline*. Otherwise, begin by turning the soil. Contemplate as you work the similarity between digging a garden and digging a grave, taking time to consider all the creatures that have, over time, become part of the soil you are turning. As you work, turn into the soil of your garden space bone and blood meals (using caution to add the proper amounts as listed on the packaging), thanking the living beings that are a part of those materials. In addition, turn as much graveyard dirt as you like into the garden space, and somewhere in the center, bury a coffin nail. Take the time to carefully plant your seeds/seedlings, watering them when you're done while saying:

To the unquiet earth, these seeds committed,
And out of darkness born.
In this grave I plant a garden,
That life rise in the morn.

Beauty in life like summer flowers—
Never what it seems.
Gardens that lie fallow,
Flourish in fields of dreams.

If you've chosen to cast a circle space, end your ritual according to the basic *Necromantic Ritual Outline* with the **consecration of life**, and **opening the circle**. Be certain to tend the space carefully throughout the year—whether it grows or not. Remember that the goal of this planting ritual is not necessarily to grow things. If your garden is unsuccessful, it will have been just as worthy for our purposes, and we tend the dead just as tenderly as the living.

THE MIDSUMMER SOLSTICE

TIME AND PLACE: On or about June 20th–22nd (Northern Hemisphere) or December 20th–23rd (Southern Hemisphere); In prepared ritual space.
SUPPLIES: Basic necromantic ritual supplies; Boughs of oak and holly
PURPOSE: To celebrate the Midsummer Solstice.

SETUP AND PREPARATION

Some traditions celebrate dueling aspects of a horned god of death and resurrection. Oak and holly, locked in a never-ending battle, the tides of which turn on the summer and winter solstices. It is here at Midsummer that holly defeats oak, taking their place as sovereign until the Winter Solstice, and from that death marks the beginning of the dying time—winter, as they say, is coming. The Midsummer Solstice is a time that is all about the sun, and therefore, about Vitality. Consider dedicating your activities on this day to a deceased person that you venerate or work with often. Let them receive the benefit of all the solstice sun you are soaking up. Death has a unique connection to our seasons, holidays, and sabbats. These are just a few that you might be able to incorporate into your own practice:

@ **Bone-Fires:** One of the three traditional fires lit on Midsummer would have been a bone-fire, using only clean bones as fuel.

@ **Bees:** Often regarded as psychopomps—able to pass between the worlds of the living and the dead. Bees are in the height of honey production at the Summer Solstice, so consider using some of that psychopomp honey to make some *pan de muerto* ("bread of the dead"). Honey is also a common grave good, and makes an excellent offering.

◉ **The Soul's Journey:** It is believed by some that on the Summer Solstice the soul leaves the body to visit their eventual place of death.

◉ **A Sunlit Path:** At Midsummer the sun aligns between the Osireion Temple at Abydos (located at the rear of the Mortuary Temple of Seti I) and the Hall of the Djed in Seti's Mortuary Temple. This sunlight knife cutting a path across the desert would have represented a path for the dead. Traveled from the pillars, representing a liminal doorway that the dead might cross into the Underworld.

THE RITUAL

Having decorated festively with greenery, begin by **asperging, calling the directions, consecration of death, offerings and libations,** and **casting the circle** per the basic *Necromantic Ritual Outline.*
 When ready, invoke:

Here we gather to acknowledge that the sun, in the height of their power,
today, begins their descent into death.
Nights grow longer—
Days grow colder—
Each moment from this one,
A decline.
May we learn from the sun,
And know that in the height of our power—we too are dying.
These moments shared,
With each turning of the Wheel—
Something is lost.
The seasons will not be long before we join the dead beyond the veil,
And as Holly defeats Oak,
We, too, are now ruled by the coming of death.

End your ritual according to the basic *Necromantic Ritual Outline* with the **consecration of life** and **opening the circle.**

AUGUST EVE

TIME AND PLACE: On or about August 1st (Northern Hemisphere)
or February 2nd (Southern Hemisphere); In prepared ritual space
SUPPLIES: Basic necromantic ritual supplies; Locally harvested produce;
Yellow candle, 1 (placed on your altar in the east)
PURPOSE: To celebrate August Eve.

SETUP AND PREPARATION

The beginning of harvest, when many of the goods grown during the year are meeting their fate at the end of the scythe, a traditional piece of farming equipment. While others celebrate the harvest, we will honor the reaping. This would be a good time to revisit your garden planted at Beltane, and to harvest anything grown. If nothing grew at all, sit in contemplation of the grave you tended. Death has a unique connection to our seasons, holidays, and sabbats. These are just a few that you might be able to incorporate into your own practice:

@ **Honor the Dead:** In celebration of the death of Lugh's parent, this sabbat is an excellent time to venerate the dead. Consider having a picnic of recently harvested foods in a local cemetery, spending time with the dead.

@ **John Barleycorn Is Dead:** A time of harvest is a time of reaping and reaping always means death. As we harvest corn and wheat to make beer and whisky, John Barleycorn must die. Have a beer (or a hops tea if you prefer) and sing along to this old folk song, in consideration of the symbolic sacrifice you are consuming as you drink.

THE RITUAL

Adding to your altar the harvested items, begin by **asperging, calling the directions, consecration of death, offerings and libations,** and **casting the circle** per the basic *Necromantic Ritual Outline.*

Then, seat yourself in the east, in front of your altar. Relax your body and visualize all the steps that led from this moment a year ago to now. Seeds (metaphorical or otherwise) that you have sown, things that you have harvested in your life. What grew, and what did not? What from the year prior sustained you to this new harvest? Did anything lie fallow? When you feel ready, light the yellow candle on the altar, saying:

Through these that have been taken
We are given strength.
Reaping that which we have sown,
From this harvest, we create and sustain life.

End your ritual according to the basic *Necromantic Ritual Outline* with the **consecration of life** and **opening the circle**. Afterward, take your harvested items into a space to create a meal for yourself, your household members (if any), and for the dead.

THE AUTUMNAL EQUINOX

TIME AND PLACE: On or about September 22nd–24th (Northern Hemisphere) or March 20th–23rd (Southern Hemisphere); In prepared ritual space
SUPPLIES: Basic necromantic ritual supplies; Pomegranate; Red wine (or grape juice, if preferred)
PURPOSE: To celebrate the Autumnal Equinox.

SETUP AND PREPARATION

The Autumnal Equinox is the time of year when Persephone begins the descent into the Underworld, to beloved Hades, and to the dead. It is at the equinoxes when I feel most balanced. My own life as a deathcare worker is wrapped up in death, and yet, I am a parent. When I leave my children's smiling faces to enter the spaces of death and do my work, it is a katabasis of a kind; and returning from the realms of the dead at the end of the day to my family, my home? It is my Spring Equinox, a return to fullness and life. This dichotomy of life and death swirls around me daily, an array of experiences, both magical and mundane, that occupy who I am—my arms have given comfort to life and death in equal measure. Death has a unique connection to our seasons, holidays, and sabbats. These are just a few that you might be able to incorporate into your own practice.

● **Ohigan:** In Japan, the equinox is a time to celebrate Ohigan, which is a time to return to your hometown and pay respects to your deceased relatives. Those celebrating the holiday will spend it visiting graves, cleaning and decorating them. These observances are made at both the Autumnal and Spring Equinox.

● **Look Westward:** During the equinoxes, the sun is positioned such that it sets perfectly due west. West has been regarded by many cultures throughout the world as symbolic of death, or as a gateway to the Underworld.

● **Balance:** The equinox is a time of perfect balance. Equal measures of night and day, light and dark—and perhaps even life and death.

● **Apple Season:** The Autumnal Equinox is aligned with the beginning of the apple harvest, commonly regarded as food not only of immortality, but of the dead.

While this is one of few rituals dedicated to a deity in these pages, you could choose to eliminate that from this ritual for yourself, working simply with death as an entity. Have a cup of red wine (or juice), and a bowl of pomegranate seeds on the altar.

THE RITUAL

Begin by **asperging, calling the directions, consecration of death, offerings and libations,** and **casting the circle** per the basic *Necromantic Ritual Outline.* When ready, face west and, grounding your energy, say:

Tonight, I have no finery. No libation to pour. No bloom to brighten my halls. Tonight, I find my solace in the fruits of the vine, for tonight is a time of sacrifice. Tonight—I die. I partake of the food of the dead and prepare for darkness.

Take up the cup and seeds, partaking of six seeds and as much wine as you care for. Circumambulating anti-clockwise, say:

I have before me, as all do, a sacrifice to make. Like Persephone, who gave all that we might be sustained, I must give, that I may reap. A sacrifice of self, of place, of want, of comfort—of things known only to myself—things in me must die, that I might seek the sun.

Returning to your place in the east, declare:

I am prepared to die that I might seek. To sacrifice for knowledge, and to make my walk among the dead.

Kneeling before the altar, take a moment to consider what you are sacrificing. Invoke:

Blessed Numen of Night, I am with you. My feet walk the path into the dark of the year, into the dark of the earth. I give thanks to the deities of the dying light, well-earned is your rest at autumn-tide. Memories of your grace at summer's height will give me strength in the coming winter. Go to the earth, O dying God, the grounds will freeze, and we will grieve, awaiting your return in spring.

End your ritual according to the basic *Necromantic Ritual Outline* with the **consecration of life, opening the circle,** and the addition of making offerings of wine and pomegranate.

HALLOWS EVE

Time and Place: On or about October 31st–November 1st (Northern Hemisphere) or April 30th–May 1st (Southern Hemisphere); In prepared ritual space

Supplies: Basic necromantic ritual supplies; White candle, 1; Black candle, 1; Tissues; Paper; Pen; Framed photograph of yourself; Your preferred burial clothing; Bouquet of your favorite flowers

Purpose: To celebrate Hallows Eve.

Setup and Preparation

On Hallows Eve, I often find myself, rather than contemplating death, considering the "Myth of the Goddess"—and that descent into the Underworld to seek out knowledge.[127] Some things can only be found in the contemplative darkness of the Underworld, and to seek out these effects of life, we too must walk the spaces of the dead—join them at least for a moment. This is why on Hallows (or Samhain, if you prefer), my coven group dies a mock death.

For some years now, in South Korea, it has been a trend to participate in living funerals and imagine what it might be like to be a conscious guest on the sidelines of your own death.[128] Populated largely by corporate-types participating in motivational programs for their employers, participants dress in burial shrouds and lie in the darkness for a time, contemplating their mortality. Many walk away from these living funerals surprised at changes effected in themselves during the process; the suicidal suddenly aware of the beating of their heart, with a new vigor for life. Those estranged from loved ones suddenly find their differences silly. The fearful walk away with newfound courage to pursue their dreams. The elderly walk away, unafraid of the looming twilight, and comforted by a life lived. Death has a unique connection to our seasons, holidays, and sabbats. These are just a few that you might be able to incorporate into your own practice.

℮ **Spider Omen:** Did you spot a spider on Hallows Eve? An ancestor is looking over you.

℮ **It Was All in Good Fun:** This Hallows Eve, don't lie down in a coffin, and at any time of the year, don't allow someone deceased to be placed into a burial container wearing the clothes of a living

---

127 Gardner, *Witchcraft Today*, 41.

128 Daewoung Kim, "Dying for a Better Life: South Koreans Fake Their Funerals for Life Lessons," *Reuters*, November 6, 2019, https://www.reuters.com/article/us-southkorea-livingfunerals/dying-for-a-better-life-south-koreans-fake-their-funerals-for-life-lessons-idUSKBN1XG038.

person. Lie down in a coffin, you invite death. Let someone be placed into their burial container in your clothes? As they decompose, so too will your health.

℮ **Pocket-Sized Poltergeists:** If you walk past a cemetery, graveyard, a place where someone recently died—or presumably a funeral establishment or morgue—turn your pockets inside out. If not? You might carry home an eidōlon in your pocket. I suppose if you're wearing "women's" clothes (which rarely have pockets at all), you'll be fine. Do they fit in those tiny watch pockets? Inquiring minds want to know.

When we eulogize ourselves, we are able to walk away with a broader understanding of who we are, what we have accomplished, who we leave behind—what we regret. With this new knowledge gained in death, we can return from our descent into the darkness made whole again, to life, to the living, and to the newfound knowledge of what we might want to change or accomplish. Make minor changes to your altar suggestive of a memorial table. Arrange flowers next to a framed photograph of yourself along with a box of tissues (it is a funeral, after all). Place candles to either side of the photograph—black candle in the west, white in the east. Rather than ritual robes, dress as you would like to be dressed for burial/cremation should your life end today—or dress how you believe your family would dress you!

THE RITUAL

Begin by **asperging, calling the directions, consecration of death, offerings and libations,** and **casting the circle** per the basic *Necromantic Ritual Outline.* Seating yourself in front of your memorial table/altar and placing salt into water, dip your fingertips into the mixture and touch them to your forehead. Pause for a moment before dipping your fingertips again into the mixture and touching them to the right and then left of your chest, your belly button, and again to the right of your chest, forming a triangle. Light the black candle. For this moment, you are a guest at your own services, and having been tasked with eulogizing the deceased, begin to write a eulogy for yourself. What are your accomplishments? What has your life been? Who mourns you? What do you leave behind? When you've completed this task, turn to face your photograph, and begin reading to yourself what you have written.

After completing the eulogy, lie down in the quiet of the room, allowing yourself to drift beyond the edges of life. Feel the quiet of your body and meditate on the stillness of death. When the natural time has come for your ritual to be complete, rise up from this death, lighting your white candle from the existing candle flame, then snuffing out the black candle.

End your ritual according to the basic *Necromantic Ritual Outline* with the **consecration of life** and **opening the circle**. Follow your ritual with a cleansing bath or shower, and a favorite snack/beverage to ground your energy and bring you comfortably back to yourself.

THE WINTER SOLSTICE

TIME AND PLACE: On or about December 21st–22nd (Northern Hemisphere) or June 20th–23rd (Southern Hemisphere); In prepared ritual space
SUPPLIES: Basic necromantic ritual supplies; Holly; Mistletoe; Red tealights, 8; Red taper candles, 2
PURPOSE: To celebrate the Winter Solstice.

SETUP AND PREPARATION

While we think of it as "the most wonderful time of the year" (allegedly), quite a few bits of folklore pertaining to death surround the many, many winter holidays (Winter Solstice, Sol Invictus, Yule, Christmas, and so on). Death has a unique connection to our seasons, holidays, and sabbats. These are just a few that you might be able to incorporate into your own practice.

@ **Throw Open the Doors!** Superstition holds that midnight on Christmas or New Year's is a time to open the front door of your home and release any unwelcome ghosts, ghouls, and spirits.

@ **Liminal Time:** Much like our traditions surrounding Halloween, Scandinavian folklore states that between sunset on Christmas Eve and sunrise on Christmas morning, the dead roam freely.

@ **Clothes Are Important:** Want someone to die? Easy, just make sure nobody gifts them any new clothes and let the Yule Cat carry them away. According to English tradition, not gifting shoes to someone in need during the course of your life ensures you enter the Underworld barefoot yourself, so save a friend from the Yule Cat—and yourself from blisters in the afterlife—by adding a pair of shoes to your gift-giving plans.

@ **Food-Based Death Omens—Good Holiday Fun:** Making a pile of salt the night before Christmas was a way to predict your own death in the coming year. If it's gone in the morning? Start planning your funeral. At dinner, have everyone cut an apple in half. Seeds creating a five-pointed star? Good news for everyone. Someone wind up with only four points? Someone sitting at the table will become ill, or die, in the coming year. But don't forget: the first person to leave the table after dinner is already doomed to an early grave. So…help yourself to another bowl of bread pudding, or maybe all leave at once! Loopholes.

@ **Death and Holiday Chores:** Be certain to clean up well after your festivities. Every pine needle or leaf left behind could indicate the death of someone you know.

@ **St. Nicholas the…Necromancer?** Lore holds that jolly old St. Nick, having discovered that three young children were murdered (as well as dismembered and pickled for food—yikes), reanimated their corpses and reunited them with their grieving family!

This ritual's focus is on the year as a dying entity, an embodiment of all our joys—and difficulties—over the last few months, and this, a time to both celebrate and mourn them. This ritual has the cheerful addition of holiday greenery such as holly and pine, symbolic of immortality, and mistletoe, which represents a life in un-life, reanimation of a kind, decorating the space. The red candles, symbolic of birth, welcome a new year at the end of the longest night.

The Ritual

Begin by **asperging, calling the directions, consecration of death, offerings and libations,** and **casting the circle** per the basic *Necromantic Ritual Outline.* When ready, invoke:

> *The ghost of the old year is with us yet,*
> *We call them forth to celebrate—*
> *And to mourn—*
> *What these last months have been.*
> *The death of the old year is upon us,*
> *But as we attend to their bedside,*
> *It is known that we must lift up what is good,*
> *As we declare what we do not wish to carry into the next life.*

Play music, raising energy through dancing, drumming, or whatever method you prefer. Remembering that death is a time of celebration, for through death, something new can be born. Spend the rest of this time in ritual vocalizing things worth carrying forward from the last year, and things worth leaving behind. End your ritual according to the basic *Necromantic Ritual Outline* with the **consecration of life** and **opening the circle.**

PATHWORKINGS

These guided meditations are intended to impart critical skills, and as most pathworkings do, involve having a facilitator read out the process to the participant. If you don't have someone to read them to you during your work, you may instead choose to prepare a recording of yourself ahead of time. In any case, be certain to read slowly, deliberately, and don't rush the experience.

PATHWORKING THE UNDERWORLD 💀

Time and Place: Any
Supplies: Nightlight or other safe, stable light source
Purpose: Underworld travel.

Whether it be meeting the shades of the dead in their own realm, interacting with the deities of the Underworld, or even finding the flames of those barely clinging to life that we might build them up, or gently usher them toward a comfortable end, it is here, in the Underworld, that we do an abundance of our work. As someone who survived a near-death experience, I've found it works for me to take a familiar path to the Underworld, and it is that path that I will introduce you to here.

Prepare by placing a small light that will be safe for a long period, such as a nightlight, near your body.

Lie down on the floor, settling your body against it, and taking a few deep breaths. Look all around you, moving nothing but your eyes, truly taking in the world in which you reside. Consider your body, and consciously feel any aches or pains that might be present. Contemplate any healed over scars, the texture of them, the pain that once lived there.

(Long Pause)

You begin to feel quite heavy, and almost tired—your body, heavy, and warm. The floor beneath you will begin to feel softer and softer until, at last, you feel you can simply slip through it. You will float downward across what is a vast distance.

(Long Pause)

It feels as though you are in a lake of dark water, and floating toward the bottom. Above you, the light glimmers on the surface, and yet, you fall further and further away—until there is nothing left but darkness.

(Long Pause)

You will question whether this is water at all as you realize that you have no need to breathe. Though your lungs do not long to be filled with air, your heart does not beat, you feel safe…comforted. You feel held by this space, embraced by it. Nothing breaks the stillness but for the occasional fluttering of wings to interrupt the silence.

(Long Pause)

At long last, when the light above is but a memory, you land softly, drifting like a feather onto what feels like a pile of furs. It is here that you will stay for quite a long time. Feeling no anger, no fear, only love, and peace, and comfort. You are refreshed and at peace, and sleep the kind of sleep that only children can have, healing and dreamless.

(Long Pause)

It is here that you remain until you no longer feel the aches and pains of your body above, until you feel safe, until you begin to wonder to yourself that if you are not breathing, then what is, and whether this is a pile of furs at all—or instead, some magnificent beast of the deeps?

(Long Pause)

You know you cannot remain here. That this place of rest is for the weary at the end of their long days, and you must push yourself forward. Willing yourself onto your feet, you realize you cannot see anything at all. The world is utter darkness, and yet, you know the expanse is vast. Sounds in the distance, though not frightful, are uncanny, and set your teeth on edge. Tentatively, you step off the softness of fur, and startle when the sole of your foot touches cold stone. The sensation vibrates through you, though you feel it in a body worlds above.

(Long Pause)

Stepping forward, you take in the cool damp air, and wonder if you might be inside a castle, a cave, a catacomb, perhaps even a tomb. Robbed of your sight in this great darkness, you feel your way carefully forward, and a few steps in sense something great and looming behind you, stand, shake its substantial body, and shrug off into a direction unknown to you. Was that where you were so comfortably sleeping?

(Long Pause)

After walking so carefully for so long, you see a light in the distance, and as you walk closer still, you realize there are lights all around you in this vast expanse. Some bright and roaring bonfires, some cool blue lights floating like moonlight reflected upon a lonely and forgotten sea—some a flickering candle flame. Each flame seems to call out to you, wordlessly communicating their substance—some demanding your presence before them, some shrinking away.

(Long Pause)

But of these flames, one is irresistible to you, your feet helplessly called to its direction. You stride toward it confidently. No longer afraid of what might be underfoot in the darkness, no longer questioning what lies in store, you stride up to the source of light and face the figure from which it emanates.

(Extended Long Pause)

When you have received the message that was intended for you, I ask that you look up. It is there that you will see your bones, glowing like the moon in darkness, singing a song to you of warm blood, of touch, of taste, of lungs filled with air.

(Long Pause)

Allow yourself to rise. To free yourself of the Underworld's gravity and float. Back up through the open expanse, through the dense air that is water, through the earth's crust, and all those layers of time buried in the darkness. Back up, you are pulled through the young earth of the surface and through it to the floor of this very room, settling against your bones with a sharpness, suddenly aware once more of pain, and ache, and grief. Of hunger and of thirst. Of scars grown silver with time. And in those bones, that anchor to your flesh, live, and love, and breathe. For death is patient, but waiting. Rest there, in your body, on the floor of the room that is filled with the life that you live. Take a few deep breaths to center yourself before rising. The air is thin and high, and you may feel faint.

Incorporating the Underworld Pathworking into Your Practice

Consider taking this pathworking as a guidebook to follow along with stories of descent from mythology. Though this working follows my journey to the Underworld during a near-death experience as recounted in *Do I Have to Wear Black*, you might follow along with any myth of descent.[129]

This is an excellent tool for exploration and getting the feel of moving your Ethereal form to the Underworld quickly and effectively, while also having a quick way back if you feel uncomfortable for any reason.

Connecting with individuals in hospice care by finding their flame and discussing with their Umbra the need to cross over can be a healing exercise for families. You may find an Underworld pathworking useful as a yearly assignment, if not a part of your regular routine. Working through this path on New Year, your birthday, or Hallows can be a good way to mark those occasions by connecting with your own mortality and receiving feedback from those who've moved on before you.

Back to Basics
Consider the *Skeleton Key* talisman located on page 32 in Domains in The Darkness to enhance your ability to move around in the Underworld as well as your ability to locate specific areas or individuals.

PATHWORKING THE PARTS OF THE SOUL

Time and Place: Any
Supplies: Nightlight or other safe, stable light source
Purpose: To acquaint yourself with your soul.

---

129 Mortellus, *Do I Have to Wear Black?* 10–13.

Prepare by laying down in a comfortable area in clothes that are not restrictive. There should not be any distracting scent, noise, or light in the space. Settle your body against the surface upon which you are resting and take in a few deep breaths. Look all around you, moving nothing but your eyes, truly taking in the world in which you reside. Consider your body, and consciously feel any aches or pains that might be present. Contemplate any healed over scars, the texture of them, the pain that once lived there. This Carnal form is an important part of your soul, and you should take time to consider how you fit inside it and how it works for you.

(Long Pause)

You begin to feel quite heavy and almost tired—your body, heavy and warm. The surface beneath you will begin to feel softer and you will feel as though you could simply slip through it. Do not allow yourself, however—hold that piece of you that you feel slipping away, tethered to your mind. This piece of you, heavy like the sounds of the world as heard from the bottom of a bathtub filled with warm water, is your Ethereal form. This, the ghost of you, haunting this Carnal form the world sees as who you are. The Ethereal, borrowing your body's link to Vitality, to touch, to taste—necessary companions.

(Long Pause)

As you focus on this Ethereal form, your heart pumps faster and faster, feeling that essence of you attempting to slip away—listen to those drumbeats. Playing that song of life and fear and fury is the Witness. Your heart, standing by to give testimony to the life you have lived, sits there in your chest, pounding away.

(Long Pause)

Take in a breath, filling your lungs deeply, then stop. Holding it until you cannot comfortably do so any longer. That gasping return of air, filling your body and making you feel light-headed, is a product of your Vitality. This piece of you that separates your living self from your deceased form. The breath of life, the drumbeat of your Witness.

This is what the gods take from offering. This is what the dead needs in tribute—that which they cannot otherwise have. The sweat of your body for acts of rendered service, the air that fills your lungs, drops of blood pushed from fingertips by a throbbing heartbeat, the essence of food and drink and flowers, Vitality.

(Long Pause)

Settling back into your space, take a moment to think about your life. What makes you stand out from others? Your purple hair, your stubborn streak, tattoos, your knowledge of how to hot-wire a car? These are your Character, those things that make you uniquely you, holding your memories, experiences, and clinging to the things you love. Sit with it. Consider who you are and have been, and who you might become.

(Long Pause)

As you ponder your Character, you cannot help but consider choices made and regretted, difficulties from your life, bad habits, and all those things you keep hidden in the depths of you. As it rises before you, greet this shadowy face with compassion, for this is your Umbra. If possible, reach out with love to this figure. It has suffered the worst of you, the worst of the world.

(Long Pause)

When you've comfortably and confidently put your Umbra back to sleep, pause to think of all the names you have had in your life. Every nickname, married name, dead name, childhood name, magical name, and so on. Each of these, a face with its own memories and experiences, known uniquely to all those it crossed paths with—the Sobriquet. How many do you have? How do they differ? Are there any you would not want to meet at the other end of a spirit board? Any you would like to ask questions of? Are any dead, now, as you contemplate them? Already relegated to the Underworld, never again a part of you.

(Long Pause)

Summoning up all the light within you, your magical power, your psychic might, all of you that holds space in ritual—that High Priestex within—this, one day, will be the Ceaseless One. Your powerful magical self, a Mighty Dead to be called upon, free of all the burden of those other parts of you. Who do you wish for them to be? What knowledge do you wish for them to possess?

(Long Pause)

Take a breath. Though you cannot touch the Verdure you are yet to possess, you may pause to consider your sources of it. What grave goods will you leave yourself for your journeys? Who will make offerings to you? Who will remember your Sobriquets, and speak them? Will your afterlife be a poor one, doomed to the well of the forgotten? Or will you be rich in Verdure, able to spare Obol for the wandering dead?

(Long Pause)

Take a few moments now to sit with your body and contemplate these pieces of you and how they have served you and continue to do so. How might you like to change them, and who you are in death? How many Sobriquets are you now? Are any of them now dead? Think of your Umbra, and all the darkness it has carried on your behalf. Are any pieces of you haunting some part of the world right now?

(Extended Long Pause)

As you come back to yourself, take a few moments to rest there, in your body, in the room that is filled with the life that you live. Take a few deep breaths to center yourself before rising.

INCORPORATING THE SOUL PATHWORKING INTO YOUR PRACTICE

Make a list of all the Sobriquets you have had in your lifetime. Nicknames, childhood names, dead names, names that only you called yourself, married names, magical names, and so on. Are they all still in use? Are any of them dead? Take time to consider how each version of you is distinct from the memories that name experienced and the people that knew them. Consider what they have done for you, gifts you received from each. Consider holding a funeral for any you feel need a last rite to put them peacefully to rest. Knowing that physical remains are an important part of the soul, will that affect or change how you approach work with physical remains, human or animal?

Make a list of grave goods you would like to have in the Underworld and on your journey there. What items do you believe would make your journey easy? What items do you believe are the bare minimum? Make a plan to have them buried or cremated with you. Think of someone you know who died. What items were they buried with? Can you think of anything you'd like them to have? Did they have fare for the conductor? Put together a care package of items you'd like to send them, along with a personal token linking the items to that person, then bury or burn it. If burning, ensure all items are safe to burn. If burying, take care to only choose biodegradable items, and it is preferred that you burn them in a fire pit that has been dedicated as a nekromanteion.

How will this newfound knowledge about the soul—and yourself—aid you in your work with the dead? Do you now feel that you can assess an incorporeal being you are working with and determine what portion of their soul you are confronting? Through questions, could you find the limitations between Sobriquets? Could you sense an Umbra? A Ceaseless One? Sit with this meditation as many times as it takes to help you feel confident in this area. Each will have its own feeling, its own fingerprint.

CONSULT YOUR BOOK OF SHADES
Consider utilizing the divination *Identifying Parts of the Soul in Contact* on page 170 of the Correspondence and Congruence section of the Book of Shades—it's an excellent method for determining what sort of entity you might be interacting with.

9

SKILLS AND ATTRIBUTES

"Ghosts are guilt, ghosts are secrets, ghosts are regrets and failings. But most times, most times, a ghost is a wish."
—*Steven Crain, Haunting of Hill House*

It isn't necessary that you walk into a space to work with death possessing a full set of psychic abilities, or even a desire to learn them. Often, I tell anyone willing to listen to what I have to say that I'm not truly a medium, just someone who's been dead before, and that anyone can navigate this kind of space. Skills and attributes are what you make of them. Take on what you need, but not more than you can carry; skills do you no good if they cause you harm to work with. What you'll find in the following pages is a set of rituals, spells, and sigils that will allow you to take on temporary abilities that you can put down if they're too much. Try them on for size and see what really resonates with you before dedicating yourself to acquiring/learning those abilities in a more permanent manner.

SPELL: GRANTING THE SPEECH 💀

TIME AND PLACE: Between midnight and 3 a.m.; In prepared ritual space
SUPPLIES: Basic necromantic ritual supplies; Bay leaf; Food-safe pen
PURPOSE: To grant speech to the silence.

SETUP AND PREPARATION

We often take for granted that the living and the dead might simply be able to speak and hear each other, while not considering differences in language. It's long been my belief (UPG incoming) that the dead speak a common tongue, a language of the dead intended to prevent conversational ease between the living and the dead. If it were as simple as speaking, no one would grieve properly, there would be no mourners—we'd all be in long-distance relationships with the dead.

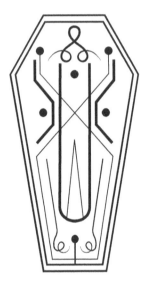

To Grant Speech to the Silence

Martin Duffy notes in *Rites Necromantic,* that "when summoning spirits, sorcerers sometimes use their voice to mimic creatures of night and death, whilst others favor sombre tones, screaming, and wailing" and that the "'low droning' employed by classical necromancers was a kind of 'ghost language' reminiscent of 'shamanic' trance-state speech patterns."[130] It seems to reinforce the idea that there may be a language of the Underworld, a common tongue, a

---

130 Duffy, *Rites Necromantic,* 33.

sort of tower of Babylon situation to overcome when communicating with the dead. The purpose then, of this spell, is to grant the practitioner the ability to communicate in this common tongue, thus overcoming language barriers between themselves and the dead. Bay leaves, while edible, can be very stiff and sharp. You may wish to begin by soaking your leaf prior to attempting this spell, or even grinding it up after creating your sigil and placing it inside a gelatin capsule. As always, you assume risk with these sorts of acts.

THE SPELL

Begin by **asperging, calling the directions, consecration of death, offerings and libations,** and **casting the circle** per the basic *Necromantic Ritual Outline.* Prepare your bay leaf (if you have not done so in advance) by marking the sigil on its surface in food-safe ink. Carefully consume the sigil, saying:

Here in the darkness,
May the night take my tongue.
And singing out a nocturn—
Let the silence speak.

End your ritual according to the basic *Necromantic Ritual Outline* with the **consecration of life** and **opening the circle.**

SPELL: TO GRANT SIGHT 💀

TIME AND PLACE: Between midnight and 3 a.m.; Graveyard or cemetery
SUPPLIES: Offerings; Alcohol swab; Lancet; Lancing device; Bandage; Sharps container
PURPOSE: To assist those with a desire for a short-term connection in perceiving incorporeal entities for a controlled amount of time.

SETUP AND PREPARATION

For those of you who do not possess mediumship abilities, and don't wish to learn them, this will allow you to borrow the ability for a short amount of time. Begin by marking the sigil on your forehead by whatever means you choose—salt water, blood, ashes, and skin-safe ink are all good options.

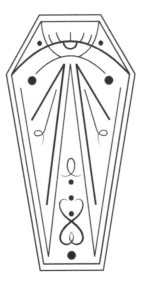

To Grant the Sight

THE SPELL

To be spoken over the grave of an ally, the grave of a known magical practitioner is ideal. Allow three drops of fresh blood to fall to the earth of a grave, saying:

> *I disturb not your sleep,*
> *But borrow your eyes.*
> *That I might see what is hidden—*
> *Perceive paths unknown.*

Thank your ally for allowing you to borrow their eyes and state the amount of time for which you wish to use them. Return at a later time with a gift of thanks.

SPELL: GRANTING THE QUALITIES OF BLOOD 💀

TIME AND PLACE: Full moon; In prepared ritual space
SUPPLIES: Basic necromantic ritual supplies; Sanguine, or red, substance; Storage container; Labels; Pen
OPTIONAL SUPPLIES: Alcohol swab; Lancet; Lancing device; Bandage; Sharps container
PURPOSE: To grant the qualities of blood to any sanguine substance.

SETUP AND PREPARATION

For those who prefer not to give living blood, or don't wish to regularly, this allows you to give the qualities of blood to any sanguine, or red, substance such as wine, ochre, and so on. My preferred substitute is iron oxide-rich Alaea salt, which also has those deep earth qualities of the volcanic clay (called *Alaea*) that it contains. This salt is one that I always use when preparing the dead, and it later becomes an ingredient in the grave salt I use in my magic.

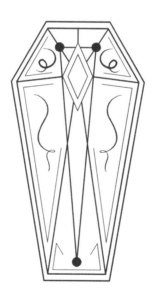

The Sanguine Seal

THE SPELL

Begin by **asperging, calling the directions, consecration of death, offerings and libations,** and **casting the circle** per the basic *Necromantic Ritual Outline.* Begin by marking the accompanying sigil onto the container for your substance, followed by marking an invoking earth pentagram into the chosen substance with the tip of an empowered blade.

@ **Optional:** Having cleaned and prepared your skin, focus on the energy of the task at hand, and using a lancet, draw three drops of blood from the left ring finger, allowing it to fall into the substance before applying the sigil. The purpose of this is to apply the qualities of your blood to the selected substance such that it might be used as a substitute. Marking an invoking earth pentagram (because we are calling on the physical and material) into the chosen substance with the tip of a necromantically empowered blade, say: *This my body, this my blood.* End your ritual according to the basic *Necromantic Ritual Outline* with the **consecration of life** and **opening the circle.**

SPELL: INVISIBILITY

TIME AND PLACE: Any
SUPPLIES: Alcohol swab; Lancet; Lancing device; Bandage; Sharps container
PURPOSE: To travel the Underworld unseen by incorporeal entities—unless you have called them by name, and invited them to know you.

PREPARATION AND SETUP

If you wish to travel the unseen realms unnoticed, this sigil allows you to hide yourself from any beings you have not specifically called by name and revealed yourself to.

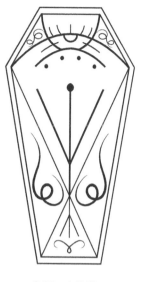

Of Invisibility

THE SPELL

Focusing on the energy of the incorporeal being you are interacting with. Having drawn a few drops of blood from the left ring finger, use it to mark the invisibility sigil upon your brow in blood, saying:

By veil and by night,
I go forth in spirit.
My visage unseen,
My path remains unknown.

Guarded is the bearer of this mark as they traverse the mournful paths.
They shall seek after the dead, but the dead shall not seek them.
Blinded to their light, the dead shall not find paths upon which to seek them,
Lest it be the will of the gods.
And so it remain true, lest the bearer seek them purposefully and by name—
Calling to them in the darkness.

SPELL: ACQUIRING KNOWLEDGE OF THE GRAVE ☠

TIME AND PLACE: Between midnight and 3 a.m.; Graveyard or cemetery
SUPPLIES: Alcohol swab; Lancet; Lancing device; Bandage; Sharps
container
PURPOSE: To gain knowledge of that which is known only to the dead
by taking on the qualities of death.

SETUP AND PREPARATION

Begin by marking the sigil on your body by whatever means you
choose—salt water, blood, ashes, and skin-safe ink are all good options.

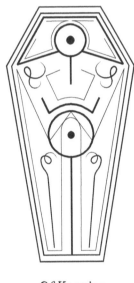

Of Knowing

THE SPELL

To be spoken over the grave of an ally, the grave of a known magical
practitioner is ideal. Allow three drops of fresh blood to fall to the
earth of a grave, saying:

By blood and by earth,
By bonds unseen.

I am one with the dead,
Their knowledge to gain.

Thank your ally for lending you their knowledge, being certain to leave a gift of thanks.

LAST WORDS

Magic has always been about challenging ourselves to step beyond our comfort level (so long as it's safe to do so). Reaching beyond our ideas about what is taboo or off-limits and reclaiming what others have decided is not for us—or anyone. Hopefully, you've been inspired to attempt some skills and practices unfamiliar to you without fear or concern of opening up something that you cannot close if you do not wish to keep it in your practice. And who knows? Perhaps you'll have fallen in love with speaking to the dead, hearing their voices in the night, and wandering the Underworld, a ghost among ghosts.

10

REINCARNATION, TRANSMIGRATION, AND HEALING

"The only reason people die, is because EVERYONE does it. You all just go along with it. It's RUBBISH, death. It's STUPID. I don't want nothing to do with it."
—Neil Gaiman, *Sandman: The Doll's House*

Though healing isn't the first thing we might think of when someone utters the word necromancy, death magic has a long history of being entangled with healing. Even in the mundane world, dying often means life. Whether it be through the generous (donated) hearts of organ donors, through tissue donation, or even whole-body donors contributing to the next generation of healers—the dead give life.

SPELL: RELIEVING CHRONIC PAIN

TIME AND PLACE: Any; Graveyard or cemetery
SUPPLIES: Alcohol swab; Lancet; Lancing device; Bandage; Sharps container
PURPOSE: To cause the dead to heal the living.

PREPARATION AND SETUP

This requires neither a specific grave, nor a specific eidōlon, unless you choose to make it so—this can be a general request for any spirits who are willing. If choosing a general request for any willing to assist, choose a spot in the center of the cemetery for your spell. If you wish to end this relationship, simply return to that same place with a last gift, stating that you no longer require their service.

The Spell

Having cleaned and prepared your skin, focus on the energy of the incorporeal being you are interacting with. Having drawn three drops of blood from the left ring finger, allow them to fall to the grave, saying:

> *You who are beyond pain,*
> *For so long as I offer unto thee.*
> *Take upon you this suffering,*
> *That the living might breathe free.*

At the conclusion of your request, be certain to continue making offerings of Vitality to whichever eidōlon has aided you for so long as they do so.

SPELL: GRANTING TIME TO THE DYING

Time and Place: Any; Preferably in prepared ritual space, but wherever you can make offerings will do.
Supplies: Basic necromantic ritual supplies; Offerings
Purpose: To grant the dying a little extra time.

Setup and Preparation

There may come a time when you wish to grant a few more hours to someone knocking on death's door. Perhaps you wish to ensure that everyone has time to say goodbye, or perhaps there is a chance that, given a little more time, they might heal. In any regard, what better way to ensure that than with a gift to the gods of death, asking that they be denied entrance at the gates of the Underworld for a little longer? It is, however, important not to attempt to prolong death beyond these small requests—beyond an immediate need, the gods of death take what is theirs and will not look favorably on a selfish desire to keep the dying from their rest.

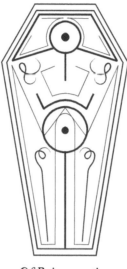

Of Reincarnation

THE SPELL

Begin by **asperging, calling the directions, consecration of death, offerings and libations,** and **casting the circle** per the basic *Necromantic Ritual Outline*. When ready, present your offering to the inhabitants of the Liminal Spaces, and, particularly, to the gods of death and to Death themselves, saying:

> *To those who oversee the liminal lands,*
> *I offer these gifts and entreat you to turn (Name of Individual)*
> *away from your realms.*
> *May these offerings of Vitality keep them strong while they wander,*
> *Until time comes to open the gates to them at last.*

End your ritual according to the basic *Necromantic Ritual Outline* with the **consecration of life** and **opening the circle.** When the time has come to let go, say so to the dying, declaring to them gently that it is okay to leave the land of the living. After the individual has passed on, make further offerings on their behalf.

DIVINATION: DETERMINING THE OUTCOME OF ILLNESS

TIME AND PLACE: Any
SUPPLIES: A twenty-sided polyhedral die
PURPOSE: To determine whether someone will live or die.

The Greek Magical Papyri in Translation PGM LXII. 47–51 notes that a means to learn from a die whether (someone) is alive or has died, for example:

> *"Make the inquirer throw this die in the [above] bowl. Let (them) fill this with water. Add to the [cast of the] die 612, which is [the numerical value of] the name of/god, i.e., 'Zeus,' and subtract from the sum 353, which is [the numerical value of] 'Hermes.' If then the number [remaining] be found divisible by two, he lives; if not, death has [him]."[131]*

While this method could be duplicated as is, I prefer using my trusty consecrated D20.

THE PROCESS

Roll, and should the number be divisible by two, they will live. If not, then death has already claimed them. Remember when rolling that you may only roll once—never attempt to cheat death. Once you have received your answer, thank the gods of death for the information, making offerings of Vitality.

SPELL: INFLICTING STILLNESS

TIME AND PLACE: Any
SUPPLIES: Graveyard dirt from nine graveyards or cemeteries; Storage container; Labels; Pen
PURPOSE: Creation of stilling earth.

---

131 Betz, "PGM LXII. 47–51" in *The Greek Magical Papyri in Translation*, 293.

Setup and Preparation

This spell is deceptively straightforward, but time-consuming, this is one of those spells that might be used for good, for bad, and for anything in between. It communicates the stillness of death to a living being, which might sound bad, but haven't we all had moments where we could use some of the graves' stillness to quell anxiety? To calm a rowdy toddler? To keep an audience at a lecture nice and quiet so that you could focus? For meditation? There are lots of clever uses for a spell such as this one. Just use your imagination!

The Spell

Having gathered the required earth and made the proper offerings for it, simply place it under your altar for a full turn of the Wheel (a year). Once that time has passed, your earth is ready to "inflict stillness." Store in a cool, dark place until needed, at which time, you simply place a bit inside your shoes before walking a circle around the subject that needs to be stilled.

RITUAL: SOUL RELEASE

Time and Place: Any, prior to cremation; In the presence of the deceased
Supplies: Ash—preferably from the censor you commonly use for ritual
Purpose: To prepare the corporeal form to be unmade quickly, in flame, and to banish the spirit from that experience.

Setup and Preparation

Many believe that the soul remains with the body for at least three days after death, but a reality of modern life is that many are cremated before that time has passed. How better to ensure the dead are spared the experience of cremation than by removing their spirit quickly from the body?

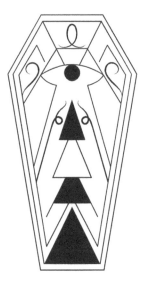

The Cremation Seal

The Ritual

Having marked the accompanying sigil on the body of the deceased in ash, say:

> *Scatter like ashes,*
> *Soul from body.*
> *Seek peace beyond,*
> *Your work here is done.*

End by making appropriate offerings to the gods of death.

LAST WORDS

Think creatively about your necromantic magic. Necromancy always works on a system of reversals, so what might you be able to turn around to the benefit of life?

11

CORRESPONDENCE AND CONGRUENCE

"…No-one is finally dead until the ripples they cause in the world die away…The span of someone's life, they say, is only the core of their actual existence."
— Terry Pratchett, Reaper Man

In *Transcendental Magic: It's Doctrine and Practice*, Lévi notes that "evocations" (summoning the dead) should always have "a motive," because to summon the dead out of "curiosity, to find out whether someone will appear, "whether we shall see anything," is a work of "darkness and folly" that is dangerous for "health and reason."[132]

While I don't necessarily agree with this position (I certainly disagree that it is dangerous), he makes an interesting note in going on to say that there are two primary motives for a necromantic evocation: love, or intelligence, noting that "evocations of love require less apparatus and are in every respect easier," and with this, I do agree.[133] Presumably, evocations motivated by love would be evoking loved ones you have lost, and with such a direct connection to the dead, little is needed as it represents, in Ogden's words, "an opportunity to return briefly to a longed-for life."[134]

---

132 Lévi, *Transcendental Magic*, 284–285.
133 Ibid., 285.
134 Ogden, *Greek and Roman Necromancy*, 265.

DIVINATION: IDENTIFYING PARTS OF THE SOUL IN CONTACT 💀

TIME AND PLACE: Any
SUPPLIES: Ten-sided polyhedral die; Alcohol swab; Lancet; Lancing device; Bandage; Sharps container
PURPOSE: To aid in simply and effectively determining what type of being is responsible for phenomena.

When it comes to communication and divination, I utilize a lot of dice. Sets of modern polyhedral dice like those used in tabletop role-playing games, such as *Pathfinder*, are not only an important part of one of my favorite hobbies, but they also play an important role in my magical practice as well. Polyhedrals don't just belong at the gaming table, however. Many ancient examples of twenty-sided dice are hidden away in museums today, some of which were numbered like modern dice (albeit in Greek or Latin), some corresponded to astragal (knucklebone) throws, and some examples sport the names of Egyptian gods on each face.[135] These archeological finds suggest that dice have long served a role as an accessory to both games and magic. While those you find for gaming are likely going to be plastic (and are just perfect for testing out this and the second method included here), I prefer those made from gems, minerals, wood, or even bone, which I have consecrated specifically for this use like I might any other magical tool or instrument.

SETUP AND PREPARATION

When working with the dead, it is very important to determine what part of the soul one might interact with. A simple solution is to pop down to your local game store and pick up a ten-sided die (or D10 for the RPG players reading).

---

135 The Metropolitan Museum of Art, "Twenty-Sided Die (Icosahedron) with Faces Inscribed with Greek Letters," accessed 2020, https://www.metmuseum.org/art/collection/search/551072.

THE PROCESS

Focus on the energy of the incorporeal being you are interacting with and draw three drops of blood from the left ring finger, allowing it to fall to the floor. Roll your die across the bloodied area, being careful not to interact with the environment in any way that might disturb the fall of the die, or its location after rolling. Read as follows:

0: This activity was caused by an incorporeal being that is neither human nor animal; investigate further.

1: This activity was caused by an Ethereal Form, human or animal (possibly a living being). Intelligent, and may answer questions about any number of things if you share a language.

2: Many incorporeal beings passing through this space over time caused this activity. This space is a liminal pathway.

3: This activity was caused by a Ceaseless One. Intelligent, and may answer questions about any number of things, but powerful, and capable of either great good or great harm. Tread carefully.

4: A Character—human or animal—caused this activity. The Character is unintelligent but may answer narrowly framed questions.

5: A living being, human or animal, caused this activity. Investigate further.

6: This activity was caused by many living beings passing through this space over time.

7: This activity was caused by a living being currently occupying the space. Investigate further.

8. This activity was caused by an Umbra (possibly a living person). The Umbra may answer questions, is intelligent, and can be dangerous. Tread carefully.

9. A Sobriquet, human or animal, caused this activity. Investigate further to determine which name—if you share a language. Low intelligence, but may answer narrowly framed questions as pertains to this name's specific memories and experiences.

RECIPE: NECROMANTIC INK 💀

Time and Place: New moon; Any

Supplies: Red ochre powder; Myrrh; Wormwood; Pine needles; Water; Gum arabic; Salt; Vinegar; Whole clove; Glass bottle; Coffee filter; Storage container; Labels; Pen

Purpose: To create a necromantic ink for sending written communication to the dead.

Setup and Preparation

There are quite a few necromantic spells in the *Greek Magical Papyri in Translation*, but few are as useful in practical application as the ink listed within "Pitys the Thessalian's spell for questioning corpses."[136] For my personal use, I've adapted the recipe heavily, and rely on herbs I've grown in forgotten burial spaces scattered about my very rural community. Notably, aside from the creation of the ink, this spell states, "On a flax leaf write these things: 'AZEL BALEMACHO'" and little else aside from noting that the leaf be placed into the mouth of a corpse (and not even particularly the one you're attempting to speak with).[137]

Having performed that spell as written, I can offer a bit of UPG and state that I much prefer to use a bay leaf for this spell because of its associations with death, but either is effective. If you're hoping to maintain communication with a loved one after their passing, creating an item such as this leaf and having it placed in the mouth

---

136 Hans Dieter Betz, ed., *The Greek Magical Papyri in Translation, Including the Demotic Spells, Volume 1* (University of Chicago Press, 1996), 76.

137 Ibid.

of your loved one by your deathcare worker during their embalming is an excellent way to do so. But if you don't mind a bit of one-way communication? Necromantic ink is a great place to start.

THE RECIPE

Add myrrh, wormwood, pine, and water in roughly equal parts in a small saucepan. Add to this a dash of salt and one teaspoon (5 ml) of vinegar per cup (128 gm) of material in the pot. Heat carefully and slowly for around an hour, preventing the substance from boiling. Remove from heat and add in red ochre until you reach the color you desire. Placing a coffee filter over your glass bottle, carefully pour the mixture through. Within your glass bottle, add one part gum arabic to ten parts ink, mixing well before dropping one whole clove inside as a preservative and closing with a tight-fitting lid.

Besides this necromantic ink, you can follow these basic ratios and instructions to make many different magical inks, and it can be a very satisfying project. Level up the necromantic qualities of this recipe by choosing to use grave salt in place of ordinary kitchen salt, and by turning flat wine into your own vinegar.

SPELL: SENDING MESSAGES TO THE DEAD

Adapted from *Do I Have to Wear Black? Rituals, Customs & Funerary Etiquette for Modern Pagans.*

TIME AND PLACE: Between sunset and sunrise; In Prepared ritual space
SUPPLIES: Basic necromantic ritual supplies; Necromantic ink 💀; Bay leaves; Small cauldron or fireproof bowl; Fire extinguisher; Pen
PURPOSE: To send messages to the dead.

SETUP AND PREPARATION

Writing to the dead is far simpler than you might think, so long as you don't mind that it's a one-way conversation. In my first book, I express my preference for bay leaves rather than the flax suggested in the *Greek Magical Papyri in Translation* because of the many rivers that run through the lands of the dead, and bay laurel's association with Peneus, the Greek god of rivers.[138] I've long thought that when bay is burned for the dead, Peneus carries the scent, the gift, and your messages along with them, to the dead on the currents.[139]

The Spell

Begin by **asperging, calling the directions, consecration of death, offerings and libations,** and **casting the circle** per the basic *Necromantic Ritual Outline.* Place your burning bowl with a candle placed inside above the bowl of grave dirt at the center, and in the west. Utilizing your writing instrument and necromantic ink, write whatever messages are necessary on your bay leaves, burning them as you write them.

End your ritual according to the basic *Necromantic Ritual Outline* with the **consecration of life** and **opening the circle**.

RITUAL: MIRROR SÉANCE

Time and Place: Between sunset and sunrise; In prepared ritual space
Supplies: Basic necromantic ritual supplies; A pair of consecrated mirrors; Link-breaking wash 💀; Summoning incense 💀; Releasing incense 💀
Optional Supplies: Banishing incense 💀
Purpose: To summon the dead.

Setup and Preparation

This, for the brave, is an effective way to communicate with dead that are otherwise unknown to you but attempting to make contact. I say "for the brave" as seeing a face staring back at you where one otherwise should not be, can be startling. The dead do not always have an appearance that we will find familiar or pleasant/comforting, be prepared to meet them where they are—and as they are—free of

---

138 Mortellus, *Do I Have to Wear Black?* 260–61.
139 Ibid.

judgement. Begin with two full-length mirrors (having been previously consecrated utilizing the consecration ritual in Chapter 8) in an open room, facing one another, with the center of your ritual space in between, one in the east and one in the west.

THE RITUAL

Begin by **asperging, calling the directions, consecration of death, offerings and libations,** and **casting the circle** per the basic *Necromantic Ritual Outline.* Using the summoning incense, welcome the dead to the space. Begin by lighting the white candle, representing their life, followed by the black, representing the death in which they now reside. Position yourself in between the two mirrors, facing your reflection in the easterly one, and begin counting your western reflections in the mirror behind you—attempt to get lost in the numbers. One of the many faces staring back at you will be the subject of your summoning, having assumed your place in the pattern of reflections.

Once you have made contact with the dead, release them with some releasing incense and make appropriate offerings. Should they remain stubborn, banishing incense will do the trick. Before closing the space in a way appropriate, clean the mirrors well with link-breaking wash to sever any connections they have with the dead. Remember that when washed in this way, the mirrors will be inactive to this purpose for a moon cycle.

End your ritual according to the basic *Necromantic Ritual Outline* with the **consecration of life** and **opening the circle.**

RECIPE: SUMMONING INCENSE ☠

TIME AND PLACE: New moon; Any

SUPPLIES: Vervain, 1 part; Myrrh, 1 part; Wormwood, 4 parts; Patchouli, 1 part; Copal resin, 1 part; Mullein, 1 part; Tobacco, 1/2 part (I prefer clove cigarettes, broken open); Storage container; Labels; Pen

OPTIONAL SUPPLIES: Graveyard dust, a pinch ☠; Cremated remains of a loved one or ancestor, a pinch; Graveyard dirt, a pinch ☠

PURPOSE: To create an incense that aids in summoning the dead.

Setup and Preparation

Summoning incense serves the purpose of calling the dead to your circle or space. It does not prevent them from leaving of their own volition. Keep in mind that these entities with which we engage magically are intelligent sentient beings. Beginning with simply having a conversation about your needs and theirs is often perfectly sufficient, however, this summoning incense is a good aid in calling to the dead, particularly when making first contact or when working with eidōlon on someone else's behalf, or an eidōlon with which you are personally unfamiliar. This incense makes a good burned offering on an ancestor altar.

The Recipe

Mix your primary ingredients in a mortar, grinding until as fine as you prefer. If you've chosen to use the optional ingredients, add a pinch of each, stirring after the addition. You can store this blend in a jar until needed, and it will keep indefinitely.

SPELL: SUMMONING AND EVOCATION

Time and Place: Between sunset and sunrise; In prepared ritual space
Supplies: Basic necromantic ritual supplies; Black candle, 1; White candle, 1; Tokens of the dead (include offerings of their favorite food and drink); Photograph of the deceased
Purpose: To summon the dead.

Setup and Preparation

If you are simply in need of the company of your dead, this can be accomplished straightforwardly. Excellent uses of this type of summoning are simply spending casual time with your loved one, speaking to them, communing with them. I, for one, have ancestors I call on sabbats/holidays to spend the day with me, and sometimes if there is a special occasion, such as a birth, or even a death, I might call upon those to aid or guide in transition.

THE RITUAL

Begin by **asperging, calling the directions, consecration of death, offerings and libations,** and **casting the circle** per the basic *Necromantic Ritual Outline*. Add to your prepared altar tokens of the individual you wish to summon. A photograph of them, items that belonged to them, the food they enjoyed eating, and other similar objects. Have in the center of your altar two candles: one black, and one white. Begin by lighting the white candle, representing their life, followed by the black, representing the death in which they now reside. While lighting these candles, recite the following incantation:

> *Across the span of time, I call to you.*
> *Across death's great divide, I long for you.*
> *Across the veil of worlds—I summon you.*
> *Come to me.*
> *Come to me.*

It should quickly become apparent if your summoning has been effective as you see signs such as changes in your candle flame, shifts in temperature, or perhaps simply a pervading sense within you that they have arrived. If you have no such signs, don't despair. After you have spent your time as you will, remember to release the dead by placing some releasing incense onto hot coals, and snuffing out the candles. End your ritual according to the basic *Necromantic Ritual Outline* with the **consecration of life** and **opening the circle**.

LAST WORDS

Never forget that speaking to the dead is about them as much as it is about us. I imagine that for many, the Underworld is a lonely place. Particularly in a day and age when we don't venerate our dead. Much like reading to someone in a coma, there's still value in having done it. Healing for them, and healing for us.

12

ARMS AND ARMOR

"We'd stared into the face of Death, and Death blinked first. You'd think that would make us feel brave and invincible. It didn't."
—Rick Yancey, *The 5th Wave*

In the absence of any knowledge that you can be a threat, choosing peace, kindness, or diplomacy has no value. Rather than goodness—it is harmlessness. Make clear, if to only yourself, that peace was a *choice*—and one you may not make next time. In arming ourselves for battle, it does not imply that we have come to fight, *but that we can*; and in arming ourselves against harm, we do not show that we expect slings and arrows—but that we are prepared for them. This has value not only between you and incorporeal beings, but between you and the living. When you choose kindness, demonstrate that it was not your only choice and be fiercely kind. Remember always that a sword on your altar is never a hollow threat. It lies there as a challenge to any who would do harm, a reminder that death is preferable to a heart filled with fear, and that you must be prepared to weld it.

RITUAL: NECROMANTICALLY EMPOWERING A BLADE ☠

TIME AND PLACE: New moon; Graveyard or cemetery
SUPPLIES: Blade; Piece of responsibly acquired headstone; Offerings; Alcohol swab; Lancet; Lancing device; Bandage; Sharps container
PURPOSE: To empower a blade through the creation of a symbiotic relationship with the dead.

Setup and Preparation

To prepare for your spell, contact a local monuments company and ask if they have any broken pieces or replaced/unusable markers that you might purchase pieces of for a "craft" project. You could then carry this piece of a headstone with you to the cemetery to work your magic and keep it for further use. We should be leaving no trace in the places of the dead, and certainly not damaging markers, so do not perform this spell without having first *ethically* and *responsibly* acquired a piece of headstone.

The Ritual

Focus on the energy of the incorporeal being you are interacting with. Draw three drops of blood from the left ring finger, allowing them to fall to the earth near where you are working. To be spoken rhythmically, repetitiously, as you whet your blade on your piece of headstone.

> *Power yours,*
> *And power mine,*
> *Sharpen the blade,*
> *Our bond to keen.*

When finished, thank your ally for their aid, and be certain to return regularly with gifts of thanks.

RECIPE: RELEASING INCENSE 💀

Time and Place: New moon; Any

Supplies: Blessed thistle, 1 part; Vervain, 1 part; Sandalwood, 1 part; Copal resin, 1 part; Wormwood, 3 parts; Oak moss, 1 part; Storage container; Labels; Pen

Optional Supplies: Graveyard dust, a pinch 💀; Cremated remains of a loved one or ancestor, a pinch; Graveyard dirt, a pinch 💀

Purpose: To gently dismiss an incorporeal entity from your space.

SETUP AND PREPARATION

This serves the purpose of gently dismissing an incorporeal entity from your circle or space. It does not prevent their eventual return. Keep in mind that these entities with which we engage magically are intelligent sentient beings—beginning with simply having a conversation about your needs and theirs suffices to solve an issue you might be having.

THE RECIPE

Mix your primary ingredients in equal parts in a mortar, grinding until as fine as you prefer. If you've chosen to use the optional ingredients, add a pinch of each, stirring after the addition.

RECIPE: LINK-BREAKING WASH ☠

TIME AND PLACE: Full moon; Any
SUPPLIES: Water collected from a nearby river, 1 gal (128 oz); Dogwood bark, coarsely ground, 2 ½ tbsp (32 gm); Storage container; Labels; Pen
PURPOSE: To create a wash with temporary banishment properties.

SETUP AND PREPARATION

You may find that you require something to break a link with incorporeal entities and remove them from your space. There are quite a few routes you could take, but this is a simple enough one. As noted by Martin Coleman in *Communing with the Spirits*, dogwood has protective properties, and to that, I have added river water drawing upon the folkloric notion that eidōlon cannot cross certain bodies of water.[140]

Through washing surfaces, your body, and your home, with this solution, a temporary sort of warding is set into place. This is an excellent way to politely remove (or ward away) any unwanted house guests while you plan other approaches and can also be quite useful in breaking spirit bonds with objects such as family heirlooms and

---

140 Coleman, *Communing with the Spirits*, 183.

so on. Talismans carved from dogwood make wonderful tools for warding away any entities that may seek to follow you home should you visit somewhere active.

The Recipe

Place bark in a stockpot, covering with river water and bring to a boil. Turn off heat and cover, allow to steep for ten minutes, and strain to create a concentrate which may then be canned or frozen. For use, mix in a ratio of 1:15, or 8 oz concentrate plus 120 oz water to make one batch. Use this as one might any household cleaner, using it to wash down affected areas, mop the floor, cleanse objects, or even bathe your body.

SPELL: BINDING THE PROBLEMATIC DEAD

Time and Place: Between sunset and sunrise, on the new moon; Any
Supplies: Consecrated thread; Dogwood branches
Purpose: To bind the dead to their place of interment for harms done, until such time that they reach enlightenment, or their victims have lived out their natural lives.

Setup and Preparation

If you find yourself in the unfortunate position of having a person in your life who has caused you harm, and fear that in death they may continue to be an issue, this is an effective tactic. For my purposes, I have used this spell in my work as an *ad litem* for binding the criminally abusive should they pass on before their victims have received justice from the legal system.

For this spell, I recommend a red baker's thread, which has been previously consecrated utilizing the consecration ritual in Chapter 8. Should you be unable to bury (cremate, et cetera) your charm with the dead, you may instead bury it in the location where they have been interred or scattered, or if all else fails, burn it along with an item that belonged to the deceased.

THE SPELL

Having created an "X" out of dogwood branches bound together with consecrated thread, place it upon the chest of the deceased in their burial container prior to disposition, saying:

A domain of no repose,
here now, you'll linger.
For your crimes committed,
A prison of bone.

RECIPE: SPIRIT CALMING INCENSE ☠

TIME AND PLACE: New moon; Any
SUPPLIES: Vervain, 3 parts; Wormwood, 3 parts; Copal resin, 1 part; Mullein, 1 part; Blessed thistle, 1 part; Storage container; Labels; Pen
OPTIONAL SUPPLIES: Graveyard dust, a pinch ☠; Cremated remains of a loved one or ancestor, a pinch; Graveyard dirt, a pinch ☠
PURPOSE: To calm and sooth the dead.

SETUP AND PREPARATION

This is useful for the recently deceased, those who died traumatically, and other similar situations in which the dead might experience some anxieties about their situation. Keep in mind that these entities with which we engage magically are intelligent sentient beings—beginning with simply having a conversation about your needs may suffice to solve an issue you might be having.

THE RECIPE

Mix your primary ingredients in equal parts in a mortar, grinding until as fine as you prefer. If you've chosen to utilize the optional ingredients, add a pinch of each, stirring after the addition. You can store this blend in a jar until needed, and it will keep indefinitely.

RECIPE: BANISHING INCENSE ☠

TIME AND PLACE: Any

SUPPLIES: Mandrake, 1 part; Benzoin, 1 part; Dragon's blood, 1 part; Garden sage, 2 parts; Sandalwood, 1 part; Blessed thistle, 1 part; Copal resin, 1 part; Wormwood, 3 parts; Oak moss, 1 part; Storage container; Labels; Pen

OPTIONAL SUPPLIES: Graveyard dust, a pinch ☠; Cremated remains of a loved one or ancestor, a pinch; Graveyard dirt, a pinch ☠

PURPOSE: To authoritatively dismiss an incorporeal entity from your space.

SETUP AND PREPARATION

Banishing incense serves the purpose of authoritatively dismissing an incorporeal entity from your circle or space. It does not prevent their eventual return, and, certainly, it should not be your first choice. Keep in mind that these entities with which we engage magically are intelligent sentient beings—beginning with simply having a conversation about your needs and theirs is sufficient to solve an issue you might be having. However, if you have reached a point of feeling unsafe, or otherwise uncomfortable with a situation, banishing incense is a quick way to say "get out" like you mean it.

THE RECIPE

Mix your primary ingredients in equal parts in a mortar, grinding until as fine as you prefer. If you've chosen to utilize the optional ingredients, add a pinch of each, stirring after the addition. You can store this blend in a jar until needed, and it will keep indefinitely.

RECIPE: GRAVEYARD OIL ☠

TIME AND PLACE: New moon, and over a period of one month; Any

SUPPLIES: Your preferred carrier oil, 10 parts; Graveyard dirt, 1 part ☠; Mullein, 1 part; Vetiver, 1 part; Patchouli, 1 part; Grave salt, 1 part ☠; Storage container; Labels; Pen

OPTIONAL SUPPLIES: Grave dust, a pinch 💀
PURPOSE: To create a graveyard oil for use in your work.

SETUP AND PREPARATION

Graveyard oil can be used for all sorts of magic, and, like most things, can be used for good or ill. Graveyard oil is all about imbuing the oil with the qualities and protections of a space, so it can be as simple as earth taken from a singular ancestor's grave, as elaborate as earth from twenty-one cemeteries, or as specific as earth only from the graves of those who died of a specific illness. This is the sort of recipe that can bend to your needs. Optionally, you may choose to add a shard of cooperative bone if available to you.

THE RECIPE

Mix all components and bury in graveyard dirt for a full month, from new moon to new moon.

SPELL: COFFIN NAIL PROTECTION CHARM

TIME AND PLACE: Overnight and as the sun rises; Home
SUPPLIES: Coffin nail 💀; Small cloth bag
PURPOSE: To protect yourself from unwanted or malintended, directed, magical effects.

STEPS AND PREPARATION

So long as you keep it on your person, this charm will prevent any unwanted or malintended, directed, magical effects.

THE SPELL

Place a coffin nail in view of the rising sun, as you watch it rise, polish and clean the nail until it is new in appearance. Place this item in a small bag and carry it with you wherever you go.

SPELL: COFFIN NAIL PROTECTION BATH

Time and Place: New moon, and over a period of one month; Any
Supplies: Coffin nail ☠; Your preferred bath salts; Storage container; Labels; Pen
Purpose: To create a protective bath.

Setup and Preparation

Place a coffin nail in your bath salts and when you use them, they'll provide not only protection, but wash away a great deal of preexisting harmful effects.

The Spell

Using a clearly marked container filled with the bath salts of your choosing, placing a coffin nail somewhere in the center. Make quality offerings of Vitality to the dead, thanking them for their protection, before placing your salts under your altar in a westward area of your home for a period of one month, new moon to new moon, in a container with grave earth. Do not remove or touch your protective salts during this time.

RITUAL: PROTECTIVE TALISMAN

Time and Place: Between sunset and sunrise; In prepared ritual space
Supplies: Basic necromantic ritual supplies; Cooperative bone
Purpose: To summon a watchful guardian bound to a protective talisman.

Setup and Preparation

The particular purpose of this item is to create a link between yourself and a cooperative eidōlon who will bond with you as an energetic exchange. The eidōlon gets energy, Vitality, and so on, while you receive the benefit of the eidōlons' watchful eye. This eidōlon may guard you against injury or harm, absorb potential pain on your behalf, deflect curses, hexes, and other negative energy, or provide you with warnings pertaining to relevant things in your life. This should be treated as an intimate working relationship between yourself and your guardian.

Begin by **asperging, calling the directions, consecration of death, offerings and libations,** and **casting the circle** per the basic *Necromantic Ritual Outline.*

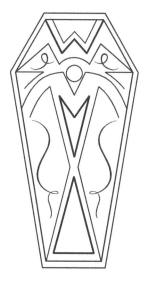

To be marked upon a cooperative bone,
which need not necessarily be human.

THE RITUAL

Having prepared your ritual space as discussed in Chapter 7, mark the bone (which need not necessarily be human) with the accompanying sigil, saying:

From osseous remains I call forth in spirit,
A watchful guardian, Spirit of the bone.
Let none bring harm,
For so long as I offer unto thee.

End your ritual according to the basic *Necromantic Ritual Outline* with the **consecration of life** and **opening the circle**. Thank your new ally for their protection and make offerings of Vitality regularly in thanks.

SPELL: HOME PROTECTION AND WARDING

TIME AND PLACE: Any; Affected space
SUPPLIES: Hammer; Coffin nail ☠
OPTIONAL SUPPLIES: Haint blue paint; Paintbrush; Mirror dust; Herbs
PURPOSE: To protect the home from unwanted or malintended, directed, magical effects.

SETUP AND PREPARATION

I'd like to be very clear in my language that these options will protect a space from directed magical effects that are unwanted or malintended. Meaning: magic that was worked specifically by another living person with you (or members of your household) as the target. These will not protect you from bad magical hygiene, things you bring into the space yourself, your own spells backfiring, or sort of undirected thought-form type hexes (such as someone simply disliking you enough that their thoughts are given form, even though it was not their intention). But for directed magic, and particularly magic that is necromantically inclined, these are very simple while being extremely effective.

THE SPELL

A few steps can be taken to protect your living space. First, simply nail a coffin nail into the frame of your front door. Protection doesn't have to be complicated. A coffin nail closes the door just like it closes a coffin. Things *in* stay *in*, and things *out* stay *out*. Optionally, here in the Appalachian Mountains, it's common to see the ceilings of porches painted "haint blue," a color associated with water and therefore with preventing spirits from crossing it. In my home, the ceilings of sleeping spaces are painted with it. I prefer to add some crushed-up mirror glass, as well as protective herbs and other items to the paint (stirring well) before painting. Why mirror glass? To create a reflective surface that bounces back harm sent your way. This is a tactic you too might employ when warding your space, painting ceilings, or window frames.

RITUAL: GHOST LAYING

TIME AND PLACE: Between sunset and sunrise; Affected space
SUPPLIES: Bay leaf; Necromantic ink; Link-breaking wash; Releasing incense
PURPOSE: To put the dead to rest or move them to another space.

A WORD ON BANISHING

While I'm always careful to avoid the appearance of buying into the dialogue that the dead (or any other incorporeal thing) are evil/bad/dangerous/et cetera, it's worthwhile to acknowledge that insomuch as they are human, there will always be a bad egg or two. At some point, you're going to have to practice ghost laying, which is a primary function of a service-oriented necromancer. The "ghost layers" of ancient Greece, the *Psuchagogoi*, could draw the souls of the dead to themselves or the spaces they maintain, and away from other places. Why not make friends with the troublesome if it allows someone else peace? Perhaps it's a perfectly lovely and useful eidōlon that someone else just simply isn't comfortable around, which is when you move on to ghost laying techniques.

Many include ancestor work as a part of their practices, and it is always disappointing when we must confront the fact that not all of our ancestors are good for us to have around. If you find yourself in the position of dealing with an unwanted spirit that seems stubborn about leaving (or something otherwise troubling), these steps will easily get the job done. I want to be very clear and conscious in my language and say that I think you should always begin by talking with your dead, and, as a last-ditch effort, remove them from your space. This differs greatly from banishing (to authoritatively send away), or an exorcism/depossession (expulsion, or casting out), as these ghost laying techniques should put the dead to rest or remove them to another space that is welcoming to their presence.

SETUP AND PREPARATION

NOTES: I recommend that these acts be performed with all members of the household if possible. If these methods have proven ineffective, consider reaching out to an established necromancer (I'll show up for chai and doughnuts) for a good old-fashioned depossession. Do remember that if burning any materials indoors, you should have something on hand for extinguishing any fire that gets out of hand.

THE RITUAL

Make a reasonable attempt to communicate and find out the needs and wishes of the spirit. They don't hang around for no reason. If communication has not proven effective, move forward with the following steps. First, choose the area for your primary work. It may be a central area of the home such as the family room or kitchen, perhaps you would wish to select an area of particularly high activity, or even an area of note in the home's history (a room in which someone died perhaps). You'll additionally need to prepare a pail of link-breaking wash and a bay leaf upon which you have written in necromantic ink "hail and farewell," and have these items at the ready.

Next, sweep the home, beginning at the front entrance and sweeping all debris out the back door, repeating for each floor of the house. If there is no back door, when you've reached the back, gather any debris into a dustpan and toss them out a back window, or carry them around to the back of the home to be tossed out. As you sweep, politely explain to the dead of the home that they are not welcome to stay, and go over the reasons why they are being asked to leave. We are talking about intelligent human dead, and they have the capacity to learn how to be a better guest in the future.

Moving on to your primary work, set up whatever sacred space you desire and begin burning releasing incense in your censor—this you will carry through all rooms of the house, beginning in the front, ending in the back, just as before. When you've completed this task, return to your primary area, and, placing more of your incense along with your bay leaf onto the burning coals, say, "hail and farewell."

Last, the household members should take part in wiping down the floors, windows, and any reflective surfaces with the link-breaking wash. Be thorough, showing extra care in areas of high activity.

LAST WORDS

Always choose peace, kindness, and diplomacy when you can. Be fiercely kind and never apologize for being willing and able to fight or defend yourself if necessary.

13

ACTS AND DEVOTIONS

"Necromancers, like moths to a flame, destroyed by relentless curiosity! It's such a beautiful thing to have such power, frightening, but beautiful! Through terror, we reach enlightenment!"
—Rebecca McNutt, *Necromancy Cottage, Or, The Black Art of Gnawing on Bones*

Certain acts seem, beyond all other spell or ritual work, devotional—intrinsic to the work of the service-oriented necromancer. Those things that are gifts to the dead and to the living: work with ancestors, work with the dying, things done with nothing to be gained for oneself. This is what we give. These things are the true work of the necromancer. It is up to us to decide with every act who we will be, and what we will serve in this life—and to hope that we have left a mark on the world such that we are still affecting it positively from even beyond the grave. That is why it is here, rather than in *Arms and Armor*, that you find a spell for summoning a piece of my own soul—and why would a witch give that? A link, for any, to a piece of themselves? Because this is what I can give. That eidōlon, made powerful by its separation from my flesh, might do good, serve justice, and bring peace to the aggrieved. One day, long after I am gone, I hope that piece of me is still out there, showing up when they are called.

RECIPE: CONSECRATION OIL ☠

Time and Place: New moon, and over a period of one month; Any
Supplies: Olive oil, or your preferred carrier oil, 10 parts; Graveyard
dirt, a pinch ☠; Grave dust, a pinch ☠; Vanilla bean, 1; Myrrh,
1 part; Vetiver, 1 part; Frankincense, 1 part; Sandalwood, 1 part;
Storage container; Labels; Pen
Purpose: To create an oil for use in consecrating the dead.

Setup and Preparation

This oil is perfect for dressing the recently deceased in preparation for
their disposition rites.

The Recipe

While my personal blend contains a few more ingredients than
this, you'll find this basic formula quite effective—but tailor it to
your own needs. Mix all components in a container, placing your oil
under your altar in a westward area of your home for a period of one
month, new moon to new moon, in a container with grave earth. Do
not remove or touch your oil during this time.

RITUAL: SIN EATING

Time and Place: Any time between the day of death and the two
days following; In the presence of the deceased
Supplies: A piece of bread or cake
Purpose: To absolve the recently deceased of any unfinished business,
or heaviness that might weigh down the various parts of their soul
and lead to restless or unsettled eidōlon.

Setup and Preparation

Sin eating has a troubling history, having been indelibly tied to ideas
of, well, sin, and one's need to be absolved of it to be at rest. Historically, it might have involved eating a simple ritual meal, which
then transferred the sins of the recently deceased to the sin eater to

carry on their behalf, absolving the dead of their sin and rendering their soul pure. While that is an accurate picture of the practice, it isn't an altogether complete one. Early associations with witches and witchcraft are apparent in stories such as that of the Welsh sin eater that was notably inclined toward "witchcraft, incantations, and unholy practices" and was therefore generally avoided by the locals but for in times of death.[141]

There's additional evidence of connections to early Mesoamerican practices, albeit as divine intervention in the form of a deity offering a onetime mercy to the elderly in the form of consuming their "filth," rendering them blameless for their life's misdeeds.[142] It does, however, have application in modern day necromancy. What better way to ensure the troubled are granted peace in death than by taking their concerns onto yourself? This might mean finishing their unfinished business, taking a vested interest in their living family, or even just ensuring that their name is remembered by someone.

The Ritual

Having passed the food over the body of the dead, consume it, stating:

Through this, I offer repose.
Through this, I gift you peace;
and for that peace,
I sacrifice my own—so mote it be.

Be wary that you don't take on more than you yourself can process and bear. Sin eating is, at the end of the day, a form of purposeful psychic damage to oneself. It can be a gift without measure for the dead but ensure that you are leaving space for your own healing.

---

141 Bertram S. Puckle and Tarl Warwick, *Funeral Customs: Their Origin and Development* (Createspace Independent Publishing Platform, 2017), Chapter IV.

142 Patrisia Gonzales, *Red Medicine: Traditional Indigenous Rites of Birthing and Healing* (Tucson: University of Arizona Press, 2012), 98–99.

RECIPE: ALLIES AND ANCESTORS OIL 💀

Time and Place: New moon, and over a period of one month; Any
Supplies: Your preferred carrier oil, 10 parts; Graveyard dirt, 1 part
💀; Grave salt, 1 part 💀; Alcohol swab; Lancet; Lancing device;
Bandage; Sharps container; Storage container; Labels; Pen
Purpose: To create an ancestral oil for use in your work.

Setup and Preparation

This oil is perfect for dressing candles burned on your ancestor altar,
as well as adding to a ritual bath when in need of extra protection and
guidance from your allies and ancestors.

The Recipe

While my personal blend contains a few more ingredients than this,
you'll find this basic formula quite effective, but tailor it to your own
needs. In addition to other items, I add a bit of lapsang souchong tea
as it is personal to me and the ancestors with which I am working.
Similarly, you'll want to make adjustments.

Mix all components in a container and having cleaned and prepared
your skin, focus on the energy of the incorporeal beings you are interacting with and, using a lancet, draw three drops of blood from the
left ring finger, adding it to the mixture. Bury this container over an
ancestor's grave for a full month, from new moon to new moon. If you
cannot do so, place your oil under your altar in a westward area of your
home for a period of one month, new moon to new moon, in a container
with grave earth. Do not remove or touch your oil during this time.

RECIPE: KYPHI INCENSE 💀

Time and Place: New moon, and over a period of one month; Any
Supplies: Raisins, finely minced, 2 parts; Juniper, 1 part; Benzoin, 1 part;
Copal, 1 part; Myrrh, 1 part; Sweet grass, 1 part; Cinnamon, 1 part;
Honey, 2 parts; Red wine, as needed; Storage container; Labels; Pen
Purpose: To create an all-purpose offering for the dead.

SETUP AND PREPARATION

A sacred part of ancient Kemetic practice is incredibly useful when working with the dead. I use it in service to Anubis, and it is at once food, drink, and incense for an all-in-one sort of gift. Though you can burn Kyphi directly on a disk of charcoal like any loose incense, you may have a more pleasant experience with a traditional bakhoor burner.

THE RECIPE

Begin by ensuring that your raisins are minced well, and that your dry ingredients are ground to a reasonably similar size. I like a coarse mix, not quite powdered. Thoroughly mix raisins, juniper, copal, myrrh, sweet grass, and cinnamon, stirring well. Add honey, mixing well. Last, add wine small amounts at a time until the mixture binds and takes on the texture of a rough dough. Roll into small pellets and place on a parchment lined baking sheet to cure and dry, which can take up to six weeks.

If, like me, you'd like to speed things up a bit, you can place them in a food dehydrator which works well, or in your oven set to warm/200 °F (or 93.33 °C) for around two hours, or until dry—which is my personal preference. I find this process goes far better if I've heated the honey to a liquid consistency and warmed the raisins slightly before beginning. You may choose to use figs or dates in place of, or in conjunction with, your raisins. This incense works particularly well as an offering of Vitality since it's food, drink, incense, and energy, all in one.

RITUAL: BUILDING THE NEKROMANTEION

TIME AND PLACE: Ideally Beltane, on or about April 30th–May 1st (Northern Hemisphere) or October 31st–November 1st (Southern Hemisphere); Home

SUPPLIES: Basic necromantic ritual supplies; Alcohol swab; Lancet; Lancing device; Bandage; Sharps Container; Offering of khoé (for our purposes here consisting of equal parts sweet red wine, honey, water, and milk); Barley; Grave dirt ☠; Water (or other fire extinguishing method)

OPTIONAL: Lantern

PURPOSE: To create a pathway to the Underworld on your own property.

SETUP AND PREPARATION

A firepit can be an important part of any magical practitioner's home, and even more so for the practitioner of necromancy. At times in history, a firepit has been dedicated as a path to the Underworld itself, and you too can establish a similar place.[143] Taking a page from Homer's *The Odyssey*, we'll be retracing the steps of Odysseus as they build a "seeing place of the dead," a nekuorion.[144] In *Rites Necromantic*, Martin Duffy notes that a "source of flame (is) a consistent factor in the conjuration of shades," and so if you do not have a space in which you can build a full-sized fire pit (or if fires are a particular risk in your area), you might instead amend this ritual to the purpose of imbuing a lantern with similar properties.[145]

This, of course, can double as a simple place to gather and a feature of your home, but do be certain to mark it around with coffin nails at nine points situated cardinally to protect the area, and keep it from becoming a freely flowing gate. I've mentioned that I've always felt that my magical poles are reversed, and that for me, Beltane has always felt quite like Hallows. That is one reason for suggesting this project at Beltane, the simple liminality of it all, but it falls near the feast of Lemuria, which takes place on the 9th, 11th, and 15th of May.

---

143 Homer, *The Odyssey with an English Translation by A.T. Murray, Ph.D. in Two Volumes* (London, William Heinemann, Ltd.: Cambridge, MA: Harvard University Press, 1919), 22.465.

144 Ibid.

145 Duffy, *Rites Necromantic*, 29.

The Ritual

Begin by digging a pit one and one-half feet in radius, or three feet in diameter, turning grave dirt into the center when you are done. Next, pour your khoé all around the firepit, in as many rotations as needed to pour it all out, followed by sprinkling your barley in a circle around the pit. Having cleaned and prepared your skin, focus on the energy of the incorporeal being you are interacting with and, using a lancet, draw three drops of blood from the left ring finger, allowing those three drops of blood to fall to the freshly dug earth for your firepit without interference.

Now that the space is prepared, you might choose to decorate or finish the space to make it a feature of your home. Like me, you may wish to leave the bottom unfinished so that you can bury a box there to access and add or remove items from. These boxes might act as a spirit house, or as a point of access for both the dead and yourself while traveling in the Underworld, as they exist both there and on the Material Plane.[146]

RITUAL: BUILDING A SPIRIT HOUSE

Building a spirit vessel is not only a ritual in two parts—and two locations—but something that requires perpetual upkeep. In part one, you create the vessel. In part two, you present it to the dead. Once they have accepted your vessel, it will require regular upkeep. Keep all of that in mind when embarking on this process.

Part One

Time and Place: Full moon; In prepared ritual space
Supplies: Basic necromantic ritual supplies; Graveyard dirt ☻; Human bone; Alcohol swab; Lancet; Lancing device; Bandage; Sharps container; Spiritus (a poppet of appropriate form); Vessel, large enough to contain the types of gifts you anticipate giving
Purpose: To build a spirit vessel.

---

146 Coleman, *Communing with the Spirits*, 33.

SETUP AND PREPARATION

Spirit houses are a special gift for a spirit that you work with often, and the instructions laid out here are not just for a vessel within which the dead can live and receive offerings, but where you can provide them gifts, rendering material items incorporeal and accessible beyond the veil.

The Spirit House

THE RITUAL

Begin by **asperging, calling the directions, consecration of death, offerings and libations,** and **casting the circle** per the basic *Necromantic Ritual Outline*. Place the vessel you have chosen and marked with the spirit house sigil in front of your altar, placing graveyard earth in the bottom and laying a human bone of your choosing on top of the earth. Then, sit for a few moments with your poppet, breathing into it and giving it a measure of life, after which it too should be placed onto the dirt at the bottom of your vessel. Having cleaned and prepared your skin, focus on the energy of the incorporeal being you are interacting with and, using a lancet, draw three drops of blood from the left ring finger, allowing it to fall to the spiritus in the bottom. Next, perform the *Consecration of Ritual Instruments for Necromantic Practice* and end your ritual according to the basic *Necromantic Ritual Outline* with the **consecration of life** and **opening the circle**.

PART TWO: PRESENTING THE SPIRIT HOUSE TO THE DEAD

TIME AND PLACE: During the new moon, at dawn; Cemetery or dirt crossroad—best yet, a crossing of two dirt paths within a cemetery
SUPPLIES: Offerings; Spade; Coins, 3; Pins, 3; Prepared spirit house
PURPOSE: To present the spirit house to the dead.

THE RITUAL

Having prepared a vessel as stated above, head to the cemetery (or crossroads) a bit before dawn to wait for the turning of the light. Using your spade, bury the three coins, and three pins in the center of the space, saying:

> *Up and meet me, in the place of my choosing.*
> *Up and greet me, and into my service.*
> *Up and meet me, where two roads meet and part—*
> *Up and greet me, in the rising of the light.*

LASTLY, THE CARETAKING AND USE OF YOUR SPIRIT HOUSE

I prefer to keep my spirit house under my nekromanteion, once per new moon digging up the spirit house, and adding three drops of my blood to feed the spiritus. Any items that I wish to give to the spirit in question, I add to this vessel. If you cannot bury your spirit house, placing it under your altar in a westward area of your space is also acceptable. Notably, I keep a similar box buried that is for my own use when doing Underworld travel, placing within it objects I feel I might need such as coins, weapons, ritual tools, and matches.

RITUAL: SUMMONING THE SPEAKER FOR THE SILENCE

TIME AND PLACE: Between sunset and sunrise; In prepared ritual space

SUPPLIES: Basic necromantic ritual supplies; A bowl, carved from yew; Crow feather; Rose thorns, 3; *Digitalis* blossom, 1; *Solanum carolinense* blossom, 1; *Cirsium vulgare* blossom, 1; A steel wartime penny, dated 1943; Dust swept from three different "X's" carved into a headstone—each from a different cemetery; Whiskey tincture (Lapsang souchong, 1 ¼ tbsp [18 gm]; Irish whiskey, 3 cups [750ml]); A piece of natural chalk; Alcohol swab; Lancet; Lancing device; Bandage; Sharps container

PURPOSE: To summon the avenging Umbra of Mortellus in a time of need. This living eidōlon, separated from Mortellus in a moment of trauma, finds peace in acts of protection, justice, and sometimes—vengeance. This ritual was crafted to allow this sliver of a soul to be called upon by any in need. And one day, when the author is simply a ghost haunting these pages, this ritual will serve to summon them wholly.

A COMMENT ON CONSENT

When I was making the decision to include this ritual, quite a few people expressed concern about allowing even a piece of my soul to be used in such a way. And so it is, for their comfort, that I add the following: I alone have the authority to consent to this use—and I emphatically do. Performing such a spell with the intent to summon a person other than myself would not work, as the method would be deeply individual. In addressing vulnerabilities, remember that they—I—can simply *decline to appear*. Most of all, keep in mind that should the ritual be attempted for nefarious purposes, as the old saying goes, I won't be trapped in there with *you*—you'll be trapped in there with *me*.

SETUP AND PREPARATION

Prior to the ritual, you will need to have prepared your whiskey tincture by adding 1 ¼ tbsp (18 gm) of loose-leaf lapsang souchong tea to 3 cups (750 ml) of Irish whiskey (preferably Slaine)—best blended in a 32 oz jar. Steep for 45 minutes, then strain out the tea leaves, returning the whiskey to its original container. Be certain to amend the label to note the alteration. In addition to being useful for this ritual, it's *delicious*.

THE RITUAL

Begin by **asperging, calling the directions, consecration of death, offerings and libations,** and **casting the circle** per the basic *Necromantic Ritual Outline*. Moving into the rite itself, just inside the edge of your circle, in the west, mark out a triangle pointed westward with natural chalk with the point directed westward. Place inside this triangle the bowl made of yew, adding to it the feather, blossoms, penny, rose thorns, and dust. Pouring a small amount of tincture over top (please use caution when alcohol is near an open flame), light a match to it, declaring:

I seek the sword of the broken—the speaker for the silence.

Focus on the energy of the Speaker as you pour a small amount of whiskey into a libation cup, drawing three drops of blood from the left ring finger, allowing them to fall into the beverage. After imbibing it, declare the nature of your request. If the Speaker has accepted, some sign will be made.

End your ritual according to the basic *Necromantic Ritual Outline* with the **consecration of life** and **opening the circle**. Regardless of whether the Speaker appeared or accepted, the contents of the bowl are to be buried—split as evenly as possible between the three graves from which your dust was taken and leaving a libation of tincture at each. When the work is done, an offering of a handwritten letter is to be mailed to the author.

PLEASE NOTE: North American crows are a protected species under the Migratory Bird Act in the United States, and therefore their remains—including feathers—are illegal to possess in any form. Be certain to check your local laws. Additionally, do not, *under any circumstances,* allow any rose blossoms, rose oil, rose water, or uncovered mirrors, into the room where this ritual is being performed.

RITUAL: DRAWING DOWN GRIEF

Time and Place: New moon; In prepared ritual space
Supplies: Basic necromantic ritual supplies
Purpose: To draw grief into oneself on behalf of the forgotten or unmourned dead.

Often, I am struck by something in fiction that informs me magically; perhaps that's a failing on my part, but it was an ordinary day of enjoying the Twitter feed of the *Welcome to Night Vale* podcast with friends that I was caught in just such a moment. "When a person dies and no one will miss them, the mourning is assigned to a random human. This is why you sometimes just feel sad."[147] Huh. I found myself feeling a way down in my bones, about all the moments of inexplicable melancholy, and of the *Indeplorati,* those for whom no one has wept—wandering the earth for lack of mourners. So it was that I found myself alone in ritual space a few days later, attempting to draw down grief.

A Drawing Down

Classically, a drawing down would be, well, the moon, and has meant taking into oneself a deity, allowing them to act out their will through you. It tends to be a ritual done with a partner, where after preparing the ritual space, one participant calls to a deity, asking them to inhabit the other, allowing the deity to deliver messages and interact with those present. Drawing down grief, however, is not at all the same sort of experience.

Here, you are challenged to draw into yourself the grief and mourning of someone overburdened with mourning, or to take upon yourself the task of grieving those for whom no one has wept. To grieve the Insepulti, the Indeplorati, to give peace to the wandering, to the unclaimed, to the unidentified—to all those whose funerary rites were attended only by the deathcare workers assigned to the

---

147 Welcome to Night Vale. 2012 "When a person dies and no one will miss them, the mourning is assigned to a random human. This is why you sometimes just feel sad." Twitter, November 12, 2012, 9:33 a.m., https://twitter.com/nightvaleradio/status/268013658825703424?lang=en.

lonely task. Drawing grief into oneself is one of the greatest gifts a practitioner of necromancy can give, a true test of empathy and compassion, offering up your tears as a consecration for the dead. Whereas drawing down the moon is, as Jason Mankey puts it in *Transformative Witchcraft: The Greater Mysteries*, "a willful surrendering of consciousness in order to become one with deity so that others around you may experience that deity," this is giving one's body over to an emotion that was absent for someone, giving your body over to pain, to tears, and to loss.[148]

Here, instead of calling out to deity, we will instead call on the dead who would find peace and the ability to continue on their soul's journey in having been mourned. Just like any invocation, there is certainly the opportunity for the dead to decline your call on any given day, and this shouldn't feel like a disappointment. You'll get better at calling to the dead, and even still they will come when and if they please, so don't let it feel like a failure if you are unsuccessful in any given attempt. It is, however, an important distinction from a drawing down that though you are calling the dead to be mourned to your space, you are not calling them into yourself. Instead, you are calling into yourself the sense of grief and loss that would have been felt by their loved ones at the time of their death. This too can be used in a circumstance such as during the COVID-19 pandemic when so many died while alone in hospital rooms and received funerary services that could not be attended by family. Here, you fulfill the role of a mourner as though you attended those rites, and so we might then consider this more of an evocation as we "bring a feeling to the conscious mind."[149]

Interestingly, Mankey goes on to note in *Transformative Witchcraft: The Greater Mysteries*, that "one of the closest parallels to drawing down the moon is the Christian practice of speaking in tongues."[150] You may be wondering about the relevance of that detail here, but it might surprise you to learn that some of our earliest recorded instances of "speaking in tongues" are necromantic; using the voice to mimic the spirits of death and darkness, a sort of ghost-language

148 Mankey, *Transformative Witchcraft*, 228.
149 Ibid., 234.
150 Mankey, *Transformative Witchcraft*, 241.

emitted through trance.[151] While speaking in tongues in the Christian sense, one is channeling the "Holy Spirit" and speaking in an "angelic" language, when speaking in the necromantic tongue, you channel the spirit of death itself, speaking in the language known to the dead, and it is only the dead that might comprehend your words.[152]

HOW TO ACCOMPLISH IT

The most important part of a drawing down is, simply put, letting go. Though you're not opening yourself up to a deity, or even the dead, you are allowing yourself to be given over to an emotion, to pain, and you must be willing.[153] For the evoked emotion to overtake you fully and sincerely, you must embrace it, but don't fool yourself into believing that just because deity does not inhabit you that this is not a powerful or even dangerous experience—or that deity isn't involved. These are good reasons why this can (and perhaps should) still be a rite performed with a partner, someone to keep you safe and assure that you are able to ground properly afterward. I also think it goes without saying that if you are not in control of your own emotions, struggle with empathy boundaries or mental health issues like depression—this ritual might not be for you. It can be easy to get lost in this much grief.

Like most necromantic rituals, preparation begins long before the ritual itself. Assure, first of all, that you are prepared for it mentally, emotionally, physically, and that you have a good grasp of your intention; what you are evoking, and for what purpose. This is not, in my opinion, the sort of ritual that you want to work in an altered state of consciousness. Whether or not that sort of thing is useful in ritual aside, I don't think it's necessary, and certainly not in this instance. On the day or days leading up to the rite, do not forget that like attracts like. Behave like the dead and utilize the effects of the dead for the space.

---

151 Duffy, *Rites Necromantic*, 33.
152 Ibid.
153 Mankey, *Transformative Witchcraft*, 260.

The Ritual

Begin by **asperging, calling the directions, consecration of death, offerings and libations,** and **casting the circle** per the basic *Necromantic Ritual Outline*. When ready, invoke:

> *I call to you, those for whom none have wept,*
> *Join me—descend upon thy servant,*
> *who seeks to descend into deep-eddying Eridanos,*
> *and consecrate thee with tears.*
> *Though Lethe has claimed you,*
> *I claim you as ancestor,*
> *By blood, and by bone—*
> *through the sacred connectedness that is all of creation.*
> *Blessed are we who mourn—*
> *and the grief that dwells within us.*
> *Blessed are these eyes,*
> *Which weep sacred tears.*

Aftercare

This ritual should be allowed to proceed from the invocation as determined by the mourner, but if that moment does not come? We might dismiss the dead as such:

> *Leave ye departed shade—*
> *I license thee to depart into thy proper place and be there peace between us.*

End your ritual according to the basic *Necromantic Ritual Outline* with the **consecration of life** and **opening the circle**. Be certain to follow up your ritual by grounding, by whatever means you prefer. As for me, I always enjoy a good shower and a not-insignificant portion of carbs.

RITUAL: BONE SPIRAL DEVOTION

TIME AND PLACE: Between sunset and sunrise; Outdoors
SUPPLIES: Large collection of small bones, found in nature; Long black fabric, ribbon, or scarf; Paper; Pen
OPTIONAL SUPPLIES: Bay leaves; Necromantic ink 💀
PURPOSE: A devotion to the gods of death for daily/regular practice.

SETUP AND PREPARATION

Adapted from the *Inner Sea Gods* devotion to the (fictional) death deity "Pharasma," this devotion should always be in the back of your mind.[154] Carry a pouch for the collection of small animal bones and make searching for them a part of your daily practice as you will need a great many to complete the ritual. In service to the death gods whom you serve, this devotion should be performed when you have gathered the needed items. It's important to note that you should not rush this process, nor should you purchase bones for this purpose. Ideally, they should be gathered slowly in the natural world, or from your own table. Death is patient, and so, too, should you be.

THE RITUAL

Begin by laying out the bones you have gathered in a spiral pattern. At the outside end of the spiral, place a slip of paper, or a bay leaf, upon which you have written the name of a newly born child. At the inside end of the spiral, place a slip of paper or bay leaf upon which you have written the name of someone who is newly deceased—you may choose to utilize necromantic ink for the deceased. From beginning to end, walk the spiral slowly, trailing the length of cloth behind you as you reflect on the short path from birth to death. You may be inspired to dance, sing, chant, or walk the spiral multiple times in reflection—all of these actions are appropriate. When your ritual has come to a natural end, just like the lives that we reflect upon here,

---

154 Sean K. Reynolds, *Pathfinder Campaign Setting: Inner Sea Gods*, ed. Paizo Staff (Paizo Inc., 2014), 123.

gather up any items that may be unsafe or are not biodegradable to dispose of safely, burying the bones that you used for the rite.

LAST WORDS

These acts and devotions, these pieces of ourselves that we give to the world, these acts of raising ourselves from the dead. We who stand as a watchful guardian at the doorways of the Liminal Spaces to act as a speaker for the silence—this is the purpose of the necromancer. *Mortui Vivos Docent*, from the dead, we learn. But the lessons? Those are up to us.

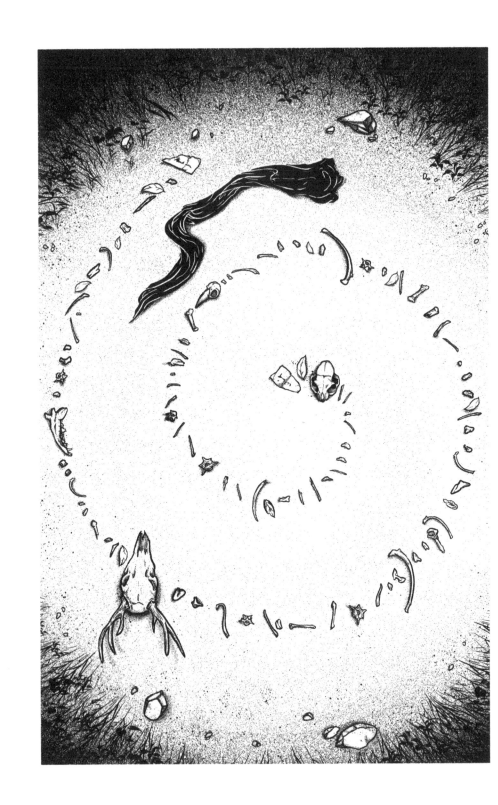

EPILOGUE

At night, my gaze often drifts to the twinkling memory of long dead stars as they glitter above me. Those stars that humanity wishes upon, hangs its hopes and dreams upon—that brings joy to our darknesses. I gaze outward at this memory written in light, as it tells me the story of a past that I have never been a part of. There is beauty in Death. The stars are ghosts, the night sky, a cemetery of light.

It is with this in mind that I encourage you to have no fear of Death, for Death is patient. It is kind. It is…inevitable.

Death has no need to fight against you, and more often than not will fight *for* you, knowing it will gather you home eventually, and Death loves and treasures those who rail against it most of all. The healers and defenders and survivalists and necromancers and mad scientists and immortal gods. They pour everything they are into fighting it, denying it, and Death adores every desperate scrap of strength and will and brilliance and raw determination poured out against it. And when your strength is done, and all your will and brilliance run out? Death gathers you close beneath a warm, dark cloak, and whispers—you were magnificent, well done.

Death does not seek to hasten an inevitable end, and chastises those who seek to hasten it for others in Death's stead; those who would slowly and patiently plot and sow and siphon away from others. Because who are they to hasten Death's domain, who are they to deny Death its time and its place, who are they to cut short these vital glories that illuminate it so? Who are they to presume upon Death's will, one that is so much larger and so much longer than theirs? Who are they to call, and presume that Death, of all beings, should obey?

Death is not a hunter, but a gatherer. Death is always, and eternal, and loves you—and can afford to wait. Death will fight for you and defend you, and will place its hand upon those who would speed you to its embrace. Death has no need to rush, only to greet you when you call.

Death is kind, and patient, and before all and above all, *inevitable*.

"It is at the guarding of thy death that I am; and I shall be."

GLOSSARY

While this glossary communicates many known and established meanings for words and phrases, some rely upon my own unverified personal gnosis, personal practice, and opinion, which have been identified by italicizing. I advise reading with a critical eye toward outside definitions.

AFTERLIFE: One's life after death. Colloquially used to imply the location of one's life after death, such as "Heaven," Valhalla, or other such places.

AKH: The living intellect of the dead, which might be reanimated through offerings and proper funerary rites which reunited the Ba and Ka. The portion of one's soul which might interact with an afterlife, or reincarnate, the Akh represents your spiritual body. This ceaseless part of the soul might also stay behind as an avenging spirit seeking to right a wrong. See also, *Ba, Ka.*

AMULET/CHARM/TALISMAN: An object imbued with special magical qualities or properties by its maker.

ANCESTOR: Someone from whom a person is descended. May be used colloquially to refer to spiritual ancestors (such as founders of a faith group of which they are a part) or deceased with whom they share some commonality.

ANIMATE: Alive or possessing movement. See also, *Inanimate.*

APPARITION: The appearance of something unexpected, often used to refer to a ghostly image.

ASPERGING: To sprinkle, particularly with a "holy" water.

ASTRAL BODY: An intelligent projection of one's consciousness, which is tethered to the mind, visualization, and thought form. See also, *Ethereal Body.*

AUTONOMOUS: Having the ability/freedom to self-govern.

BA: This portion of the soul represents the unique qualities that make up one's personality and all the things that make an individual unique. In this way, an inanimate object might have a Ba—or Character—if it were one of a kind. This vital portion of the soul might be reunited with the Ka to reanimate the Akh with proper offerings and rituals.

BANISH/EXORCISM/SPIRIT RELEASEMENT: To authoritatively expel or banish an incorporeal possessing entity from a particular person or place.

BENEVOLENT: Good, kind, well-meaning/intentioned. See also, *Malevolent*.

BIDENT: A two-pronged implement, not unlike a pitchfork, wielded by Hades in classical mythology.

BONE CONJURER: Originating in the Christian Bible, Bone Conjurer is one of many terms for a practitioner of necromancy.

BOTTLE TREE: A bottle tree is one hung with colorful glass bottles, often blue cobalt bottles, with the belief that spirits are tempted to enter them, and being trapped, burn up in the morning sun. Blue bottles are often chosen due to the colors associated with healing as well as with spirits.

CATAFALQUE: A wooden framework, typically decorative, that supports the burial container of an individual lying in state.

CEMETERY: A cemetery is a burial ground, often available for public use; by contrast, a graveyard is a burial ground connected to and owned by a place of worship. See also, *Graveyard*.

CENOTAPH: An empty tomb or marker placed to honor someone whose remains lie elsewhere.

CHTHONIC: From the Greek *khthónios*, referring to something in, under, or beneath the earth. The modern term is translated as subterranean, and in this context, chthonic refers to anything relating to the Underworld, particularly deities or spirits, and particularly in Ancient Greece or in Hellenic Reconstructionist practices.

COFFIN BIRTH: A postmortem fetal extrusion, a coffin birth is a non-viable fetus expelled from the uterus of a deceased parent after burial. Generally caused by the building pressures of abdominal gases during decomposition.

COFFIN NAIL: Coffin nails are, as the name might suggest, nails from a coffin. Though these can be "made" through a process by which one ritually imbues a common nail with the qualities of a coffin nail, typically, necromantic work is best done with an authentic fastener (nails, screws, brads) from a used burial container.

CONDUCTOR: A psychopomp who not only guides the dead but gives them transport.

CONGRUENCE: Congruence defines communication in which the message between two participants is coherent. Though it tends to imply a situation in which the message is agreeable to both parties, in necromantic magic, the emphasis is on coherence and consistency.

CONJURE/CONJURER: To make something, or someone, appear. Often implies calling upon an incorporeal being and commanding their presence. One who conjures.

CONSENT: Consent is synonymous with permission, agreement, or approval.

CONTROL (SPIRIT): The opposite side of the coin to a medium, a control spirit acts as the medium's partner in the realms of the dead. Fully autonomous and acting independently of the medium with whom they work, controls often operate by displacing portions of the medium's essence to some other location.

CORPSE CANDLE: Appearing as a death omen, corpse candles are lights similar in behavior to corpse lights, though appearing distinctly as candle flames.

CORPSE LIGHT: Typically, phosphorescent lights seen at night floating in the distance or along the ground and considered to be an omen of death.

CREMAINS: A portmanteau of "cremated" and "remains," cremains are the remains of a human body after cremation. Composed of ash and bone fragments, and is largely calcium carbonate.

CREMATION: A process by which remains (human or animal) are reduced to ash and bone by flame.

CROSS CORRESPONDENCE: Describing matching or similar information on a same topic from two or more mediums as received through spirits. Occurring in three types: "ideal," in which the messages combine to create complete messages, "complex," in which the information must be deciphered, and "simple," in which words or phrases are the same or connected in some way.

CROSSROAD: An intersecting pair of roads or pathways, crossroads have always been associated with incorporeal entities. The spirits of the dead can be conjured or summoned there and are said to appear on Hallows Eve as a rule.

DASH, THE: A common phrase among deathcare workers, the "dash" represents all the life that an individual lived and is symbolized by the typographical character between the dates of birth and death on one's headstone. References the poem of the same name, written by Linda Ellis.

DEAD NAME: The birth or other former name of a transgender or nonbinary person that is dead—or no longer of use—to them. See also, *Necronym*.

DEATH DAY: The counterpoint to a "birthday," one's death day is the day upon which they die.

DECLARATION 127: A denunciation of discrimination and groups that promote it.

DEITY: A being revered as divine.

DEOSIL: Clockwise. See also, *Widdershins*.

DICE: A group of die.

DIE: In addition to the usual meaning, a die is a small object with marked sides typically representative of groupings of numbers. The singular of *dice*.

DISINCARNATE: Disembodied or freed from the physical body. See also, *Incarnate*.

DRAUGR: A Scandinavian term for an undead creature, typically corporeal. See also, *Revenant*.

DREAMING, THE: A place somewhere between the living and the dead, the Dreaming is where one goes when they dream. The realm of Morpheus, the god of dreams, consists of symbols, imagination, and ever-changing landscapes.

DUMB SUPPER: A meal held in silence in honor of the dead.

EARTHBOUND SPIRIT: Incorporeal dead, bound to the Material Plane, unable to cross over to any afterlife or underworld.

ECTOPLASM: A supernatural substance produced by some types of incorporeal entities, or exteriorized by mediums, historically.

EGREGORE: Arising from a group consciousness or thought-form, egregore have a distinct incorporeal presence.

EIDŌLON: An ethereal apparition of a being, living or dead.

ETHEREAL: Lacking material substance. See also, *Incorporeal*.

ETHEREAL BODY: Though it holds other meaning, particularly in Neo-Theosophy, the author uses "Ethereal body" to simply mean the ghost of you haunting your physical form. This part of you is best suited to pathworking the Underworld and other such activities and is bound to the physical, to the body, and to sensation. See also, *Astral Body*.

ETHICALLY SOURCED (BONE): To ensure that a given item is obtained (or made) through methods that are responsible and sustainable. In osteological specimens, this often includes an awareness that the living being in question was not intentionally killed.

ETHICS: A system of principles observed within a given group, culture, et cetera.

EVOCATION/EVOCOTOR: The act of calling or summoning incorporeal entities, one who calls or summons incorporeal entities. One who evokes, or a caller of spirits. See also, *Conjure/Conjurer*.

FIREPIT: A pit or vessel for building an outdoor fire, often used as a passage to the Underworld. See also, *Nekromanteion, Underworld*.

FLUFFY: A pejorative colloquial expression denoting something unserious or light, immature, uninformed, or superficial. Particularly as pertains to occultism, magical practice or study, reading materials on such topics, and so on.

FLUFFY BUNNY: A pejorative colloquial expression denoting a person whose magical practice is fluffy.

FREE WRITING/DRAWING: A technique in which an individual holds a writing/drawing instrument over paper and writes/draws whatever comes to mind without any thought or concern toward controlling the outcome.

FULCRUM: The point upon which something, such as a lever, rests or pivots; something that plays a vital role in an activity, situation, event, or similar.

GEAS: A taboo or prohibition put in place as part of a vow or oath to a deity. A geas could be described as a dual self-inflicted curse and blessing. To violate the geas could bring punishment as severe as death but observing the geas often has powerful benefits.

GENIUS LOCI: The distinctive or beloved characteristics and atmosphere of a place or location, and/or the deities and entities that preside over it. Also: *Spirits of Place*.

GHOST LAYING: To put the dead to rest through ritual or mundane acts.

GHOST: Used colloquially to mean any incorporeal being, "ghost" primarily refers to the presence of an incorporeal manifestation of the eidōlon of a deceased human or animal and does not tend to be inclusive of the disembodied living.

GOETE: A practitioner who works with necromantic magic.

GOOS: The mourning wail of the dead, or an incantation used by a practitioner of necromancy.

GRAVE: A place for burying the dead, particularly underground. See also, *Cenotaph, Tomb.*

GRAVEYARD: A cemetery is a burial ground, often available for public use. By contrast, a graveyard is a burial space connected to, and owned by, a place of worship. See also, *Cemetery.*

HAINT: A restless variety of ghost or spirit, regional to the Southern United States, particularly the Carolina Low Country and the Appalachian Mountains.

HAINT BLUE: A shade of blue with the specific purpose of protecting against or warding away incorporeal entities, particularly ghosts or haints. This has the intention of confusion, having some basis in the idea that incorporeal entities cannot cross water. Typically, the ceilings of wraparound porches and window frames in the Southern United States would be painted this shade of blue to prevent entry to the space by haints.

HAUNT: To visit a person, place, or thing, regularly or habitually.

HAUNTED: A person, place, or thing frequented by individuals—living or dead. See also, *Haunt.*

HEXICOLOGY: An obsolete word synonymous with ecology, it deals with organisms' relationships to one another and their surroundings.

HOMEBREW: A tabletop game world that might follow a set of pre-established rules, but includes new places, names, and designations that might not exist in any sourcebook.

IMMATURATA: Referring to someone killed "before their time," the *immaturata* haunt the Material Plane until the day of what was their intended death day. These are typically victims of tragedies such as murder.

INANIMATE: Lacking animation, unmoving. See also, *Animate.*

INCARNATE: Having a physical form, body, flesh. See also, *Disincarnate.*

INCLUSIVE: Welcoming to all kinds of people.

INCORPOREAL: Not having a physical presence, lacking matter. See also, *Corporeal*.

INDEPLORATI: Dead for whom no one has wept, those unlamented, or one who was denied funerary rites/rituals.

INSTRUMENT: While "instrument" is commonly used to describe a device made for producing sound—a particular use of this term is a tool used for delicate (scientific) work. A scalpel, for example, is an instrument.

INSEPULTI: The unburied, particularly victims of drowning or those lost at sea; those without graves or memorial places.

JB: An individual's heart muscle/organ, acting as a sometimes-hostile witness to one's life, and able to give testimony for or against them before the gods.

KA: The vital essence, or Vitality, which distinguishes the living from the dead. Through offerings and funerary rituals, the Ka might be reunited with the Ba to reanimate the Akh.

KATABASIS: A descent, often into the Underworld, but sometimes in theme. See also, *Underworld*.

KHET: An individual's physical body, or Carnal form, which is a vital part of one's afterlife and the soul's connection to the Physical Plane in life.

KHOÉ: An offering of libation used specifically for chthonic gods and denizens of the Underworld. This type of libation is a blend of items, typically equal parts of honey, water, and milk. Rarely, but occasionally, dark red wine is included. Seen in Hellenism, and the worship of chthonic Greek gods.

LARES: Lares are typically the shades of benevolent, incorporeal, entities.

LAZARUS EFFECT: The Lazarus Effect is characterized by having been declared dead after lifesaving measures have failed, and later spontaneously reviving. Also: *Lazarus Phenomenon*.

LEMURE: Lemure are the shades of malevolent, incorporeal, entities. Vengeful and wandering, these entities can be those who did not receive proper funerary rites or were otherwise unsatisfied in death. See also *Immaturata, Indeplorati, Insepulti*.

LEMURIA: Celebrations intended to placate lemure.

LIFTING/REANIMATION: To raise the corporeal/incarnate but inanimate dead to a state of animation. See also, *Resurrection*.

Liminal: A quality of ambiguity that occurs in a boundary or threshold. This can refer to things such as the veil, the Dreaming, or the state of being in a rite of passage when it has begun, but not yet been completed.

Ma'at, upholding of: To uphold certain laws/principles, and to subject yourself to them.

Malevolent: Bad, cruel, ill-intentioned. See also, *Benevolent*.

Material/Mortal/Physical Plane: The physical place of existence in which the living reside.

Medium: An individual possessing a set of psychic abilities that allows them to directly communicate with incorporeal entities, acting as an intermediary.

Mighty Dead: Shades of enlightened, ascended, or holy dead. Refers primarily to those who died in a state of awareness or enlightenment.

Near-Death Experience/NDE: Used to refer to the experiences of someone who has come close to death. Often accompanied by visions of an afterlife, deceased individuals, or other beings. See also, *Lazarus Effect, Revenant, Twice-Born*.

Necrocracy: A government ruled by, or operating under the rules of, a deceased leader.

Necrognosis: Spiritual knowledge or insight regarding the divine spark of death. Also: *Necrosophy*.

Necromancer: A practitioner of necromancy.

Necromancy: Necromancy has a root of *necro*, from the Greek *nekros*, meaning "dead body," and a suffix of *-mancy*, meaning "divination," and is defined as divination, though it may imply simply communication with the dead. The author utilizes the term to refer to a specialized magical practice surrounding work with the dead, either through physical remains, or their incorporeal forms, to gain insight or accomplish magical goals.

Necronym: A name or reference to someone who has died. See also, *Dead Name*.

Necrophagous: Anything that eats dead or decaying flesh. (Omnivorous) humans are, by their very nature, necrophagous—dead things are dead things, even if we've dressed them up as a ham sandwich.

Nekromanteion: A "seeing place of the dead," also referred to as "nekuor(i)on." See also, *Firepit, Underworld*.

NEKUIA: A rite during which the dead were summoned to speak with. Synonymous, in many ways, with *necromancy*.

NEKUOMANTEION/PSUCHOMANTEION: A "prophecy place of the dead."

OBOL: A coin placed under the tongue or over the eyes as fare for the conductor.

ORB: Common photographic anomalies associated with high ISO photography, orbs are typically dust, pollen, or other foreign matter passing over the camera lens at the time a photograph or video was taken. Sometimes mistaken for incorporeal beings.

OSSUARY: A container utilized for the storage of bones.

OSTEOLOGY: The study of bones.

OSTEOLOGICAL SPECIMEN: Articulated skeletons or individual bones of any type.

OUIJA: A game by Hasbro consisting of a planchette and spirit board. Designed by Elijah Bond in 1890, capitalizing on the popularity of talking boards enjoyed at the time. See also, *Planchette*, *Spirit Board*.

PALINGENESIS: Rebirth, reincarnation, the repetitious recreation of the universe. See also, *Reincarnation*.

PATHWORKING: A journey taken through the projection of one's Ethereal or Astral body to a particular location (or the visualization thereof) for the purpose of interacting with entities, and gaining knowledge.

PHANTOM: An apparition or specter without substance, an illusion.

PHASM: An extraordinary appearance; an apparition or specter without substance, an illusion.

PLANCHETTE: A heart or tear-shaped object which may contain an opening for viewing, or an opening for the placement of a pencil. Planchette are often used in conjunction with spirit boards, but not exclusively.

POLTERGEIST: From the German for "noisy ghost," a poltergeist is an incorporeal entity that makes its presence known by manipulating the physical environment through sounds such as knocking, or by moving objects. There is some anecdotal evidence that poltergeists can be a form of telekinetic energy manipulated or manifested by a living person who is unaware of their role in the activity, often a child.

POLYHEDRALS: While all dice are technically polyhedral (a 3D object with multiple sides), colloquially, "polyhedrals" refers to a set of dice used in tabletop role-playing games. These sets typically include a four-sided, (or D4), a six-sided (or D6), an eight-sided (or D8), two ten-sided (or D10)—one of which is typically a "percentile"—a twelve-sided (or D12), and a twenty-sided (or D20) die.

Possession: A state of being under the control or influence of an incorporeal entity, idea, or emotion.

Priestex: A gender-neutral term equivalent to Priestess or Priest.

Prohibition: To forbid something.

Psuchagogion: A "drawing place of ghosts."

Psuchagogoi: Known as "soul-drawers," those with the ability to evoke the dead for ghost laying, exorcism, or other such work.

Psuchopompeion: A "sending place of ghosts."

Psychopomp: An entity charged with accompanying the newly deceased to their afterlife.

Rebirth: The manual facilitation of the spirit of a deceased person being born into a newborn child; often to a particular family, geographical area, or other specificity.

Rehabitation: To return the spirit of an individual to their recently deceased body.

Reincarnation: The rebirth of an individual spirit or soul into a new Corporeal form. See also, *Palingenesis*.

Release: Less forceful than banishing, to release is simply to let go of any hold on an incorporeal entity.

Reliquary: A container for the storage of holy relics. See also, *Ossuary*.

Ren: An important part of the soul, your Ren is your name, or Sobriquet. The Ren constitutes your life's worth of memories, identity, and experiences. One might have as many Ren as they have had names in their lifetime.

Repose: To place at rest.

Requiem: A ritual for the repose of the dead.

Responsibly Sourced (Bone): An osteological specimen obtained through methods that are in keeping with the law. In human bone, this often includes an awareness that the remains in question are retired medical specimens, and were not acquired through grave robbing, archeological finds, catacombs, and so on. This does not imply knowledge of sustainability, nor of any given specimen's means of death. Many individuals are donated to medical donor programs by their next of kin, and this may include individuals who lost their lives tragically.

RESURRECTION: The act of being risen from the dead. Distinct from lifting in that you are being restored to your former state of life. See also, *Lifting*.

REVENANT: Once a common term for any ghost, a revenant tends today to refer to those returned from the grave. In this way, you might consider creatures such as vampires, or even someone who, like the author, survived medical death, a revenant. See also, *Draugr*.

RULE OF THREE: A tenet stating that whatever one puts into the world, good or bad, is returned to them threefold.

SAH: An individual's spiritual body as preserved through proper funerary rites that might go on to an afterlife, reincarnation, or to work as Mighty Dead. Otherwise, this Ethereal form might go on to become an avenging spirit.

SCIOMANCY: Sciomancy has a root of *scio*, from the Greek *skia*, meaning "shade," and is defined as divination through ghosts or shades.

SEAL: Unlike a sigil, which is a symbol representative of a desired outcome, a seal is additionally a signature of either its creator or some other entity who is involved in either the creation or outcome of the magic being done.

SEKHEM: The spark of un-life, or Verdure, one possesses in the Underworld.

SHADE: From the Latin *umbra*, shades are those who dwell in shadow. Distinct from the shut/Umbra discussed throughout, the shade is the spirit or ghost of a deceased human being that now resides in the Underworld.

SHADOW: Exiled or repressed portions of the deep unconscious that might be explored and integrated with the conscious self. The shadow as referred to within the construct of shadow work is distinct from the shut/Umbra, which is a vital piece of the soul. See also, *Shut*.

SHADOW WORK: A concept made popular by psychiatrist and psychoanalyst Carl Jung which refers to exploring repressed parts of the self that have been exiled from the conscious mind. Typically facilitated by an objective third-party professional (such as a therapist) who can hold up a mirror to parts of ourselves we are unable to accept or even see. Shadow Work is not synonymous with the shut/Umbra.

Shut: Always by your side, your shadow—or Umbra—holds something of the self and is, therefore, a part of one's soul. See also, *Shadow, Soul*.

Sigil: A symbol that is regarded as having magical powers or abilities ascribed to it by its creator.

Sinew: Fibrous tissue that connects bone to bone.

Soul: Colloquially used to define the animating force within a living thing, the spirit, Ka, or vital force. The author would define it as any number of parts of the soul. See also, *Spirit*.

Spirit/Talking Board: A board marked with letters, numbers, symbols, or phrases, navigated with a planchette for the purpose of communicating with incorporeal entities. See also, *Ouija*.

Spirit: Colloquially used to define the animating force within a living thing, the soul, Ka, or vital force. The author would define a "spirit" as being any one of the many parts of the soul. See also, *Soul*.

Summon: To authoritatively call upon an entity to present themselves to you.

Tomb: A place for burying the dead, particularly underground, or enclosed within a structure. See also, *Cenotaph, Grave*.

Twice-Born: An individual who has been revived after experiencing physical death, or one who has experienced a near-death experience or the Lazarus Effect. This term holds additional meaning outside of this usage. See also, *Lazarus Effect, Near-Death Experience*.

Undead: See *Revenant*.

Underworld: A colloquial term for the plane of existence in which the dead, and other beings, including some chthonic deities, reside. See also, *Chthonic*.

Unverified Personal Gnosis/UPG: Spiritual beliefs or experiences unique to an individual or based upon personal experience. Generally, these will be missing from, or contrary to, archaeological evidence, folklore, and myth.

Veil, the: In many Pagan traditions, there is a belief in a "veil between worlds," a liminal boundary separating (for example) the living and the dead.

Ward: A magical protection.

Whatevermancy/Whatevermancer: A media trope that borrows the naming convention of the Greek word for the thing, followed by *-mancy*. Examples include, but are not limited to, pyromancy/pyromancer, hydromancy/hydromancer, and so on. Also: *Somethingmancy/Somethingmancer.*

WICCAN REDE: A common piece of advice, typically given as "an it harm none, do what ye will."

WIDDERSHINS: Counter (or anti) clockwise. See also, *Deosil.*

XENOGLOSSY: A paranormal phenomenon that involves a speaker utilizing a language they are unfamiliar with to write or speak, particularly when it could not have been acquired by natural means.

ZOMBIE: See *Revenant.*

BIBLIOGRAPHY

It is important that I communicate clearly that there was necessity during my research on this topic to read (and in some instances, cite) materials (and authors) which I find problematic, as well as materials which are ostensibly outdated, poorly cited, reliant upon unverified personal gnosis without clarifying that fact, and materials as well as authors promoting senselessly dangerous or illegal practices. As such, I advise treading carefully in these waters, and as one always should, read with a critical eye.

Abel, Ernest L. *Death Gods: An Encyclopedia of the Rulers, Evil Spirits, and Geographies of the Dead.* Westport, Conn.: Greenwood Press, 2009.

Ady, Thomas. *A Candle in the Dark.* London: Printed for Robert Ibbitson Dwelling in Smithfield Neer Hosier Lane End, 1655.

Agrippa, Cornelius. *Three Books of Occult Philosophy.* London: Printed by R.W. for Gregory Moule, 1651.

———. *The Vanity of Arts and Sciences.* London: Printed by J.C. for Samuel Speed, 1676.

Allaun, Chris. *Deeper into the Underworld: Death, Ancestors and Magical Rites.* Oxford, UK: Mandrake, 2018.

———. *Guide of Spirits: A Psychopomp's Manual for Transitioning the Dead to the Afterlife.* S.L.: Moon Books, 2021.

———. *Otherworld.* Winchester: Moon Books, 2020.

———. *Underworld: Shamanism, Myth & Magick.* Oxford, UK: Mandrake, 2017.

Allen, James P. *Middle Egyptian: An Introduction to the Language and Culture of Hieroglyphs.* New York: Cambridge University Press, 2000.

Ankarloo, Bengt, and Stuart Clark. *Witchcraft and Magic in Europe: Ancient Greece and Rome.* Vol. 2. Philadelphia: University of Pennsylvania Press, 1999.

———. *Witchcraft and Magic in Europe: The Period of the Witch Trials.* London: Athlone Press, 2002.

Anonymous, and Poetry Foundation. "Beowulf (Old English Version)." Poetry Foundation. Accessed July 4, 2021. https://www.poetryfoundation.org/poems/43521/beowulf-old-english-version.

Apollonius, of Tyana, Cyprian Leowitz, Robert Turner, Frederick Hockley, Alan Thorogood, and Robin E Cousins. *Ars Notoria: The Notory Art of Solomon.* York Beach, ME: The Teitan Press, 2015.

Appel, Jacob M. *Who Says You're Dead? Medical & Ethical Dilemmas for the Curious & Concerned.* Chapel Hill, NC: Algonquin Books of Chapel Hill, 2019.

Appel, Kristoffer, Gordon Pipa, and Martin Dresler. "Investigating Consciousness in the Sleep Laboratory – An Interdisciplinary Perspective on Lucid Dreaming." *Interdisciplinary Science Reviews* 43, no. 2 (November 12, 2017): 192–207. https://doi.org/10.1080/03080188.2017.1380468.

Araignee, Baron, and Baronessa Araignee. *The Gospel of the Ghouls.* The Arcane Press, 2016.

American Legal Publishing Corporation. "Article 17.1: Regulations for Fortunetelling; Permit and License Provisions." American Legal Publishing Corporation, 2020. https://codelibrary.amlegal.com/codes/san_francisco/latest/sf_police/0-0-0-5579.

Attrell, Dan, and David Porreca, eds. *Picatrix: A Medieval Treatise on Astral Magic.* University Park, PA: Penn State University Press, 2019.

Aubrey, John. *Miscellanies.* London: Printed for Edward Castle, 1696.

Auerbach, Loyd. *ESP, Hauntings, and Poltergeists: A Parapsychologist's Handbook.* United States: Loyd Auerbach, 2016.

Badone, Ellen. "Death Omens in a Breton Memorate." *Folklore* 98, no. 1 (January 1987): 99–104. https://doi.org/10.1080/0015587x.1987.9716401.

Barrett, Francis. *The Magus: A Complete System of Occult Philosophy.* White-fish, MT: Kessinger Publishing, 2012.

Barrett, Francis, and Harry Price. *The Magus.* Vol. 2. London: Printed for Lackington, Allen, and Co, 1801.

Beckett, Samuel. *Waiting for Godot: A Tragicomedy in Two Acts.* London: Faber and Faber, 1959.

Belanger, Jeff. *Communicating with the Dead: Reach Beyond the Grave.* Franklin Lakes, NJ: New Page Books, 2005.

———. *The World's Most Haunted Places: From the Secret Files of Ghostvillage.com.* Pompton Plains, NJ: New Page Books, 2011.

Belanger, Michelle A. *Walking the Twilight Path: A Gothic Book of the Dead.* Woodbury, MN: Llewellyn Publications, 2008.

Betz, Hans Dieter. *The Greek Magical Papyri in Translation, Including the Demotic Spells, Volume 1.* Chicago: University of Chicago Press, 1996.

Blanke, Olaf, Polona Pozeg, Masayuki Hara, Lukas Heydrich, Andrea Serino, Akio Yamamoto, Toshiro Higuchi, et al. "Neurological and Robot-Controlled Induction of an Apparition." *Current Biology 24, no. 22 (November 2014): 2681–86. https://doi.org/10.1016/j.cub.2014.09.049.*

Blount, Thomas. *Glossographia.* London: Printed by The. Newcomb, and Are to Be Sold by Humphrey Moseley, at the Princes Arms in St Paul's Church-Yard, and George Sawbridge at the Bible in Ludgate-Hill, 1661.

Boudet, Jean-Patrice. *"Entre Science et 'Nigromance.'" Astrologie, Divination et Magie Dans L'Occident Médiéval (XIIe-XVe Siècle).* Paris: Publ. de la Sorbonne, 2007.

Bracelin, Jack. *Gerald Gardner: Witch.* Octavo, 1960.

Bremmer, Jan. *The Early Greek Concept of the Soul.* Princeton, NJ: Princeton University. Press, 1993.

Brennos, Var Von. *Gravelording.* 1st ed. Black Court Reliquary, 2015.

Brom. *Lost Gods.* New York: Harper Voyager, 2016.

Bulkeley, Kelly. *Dreaming in the World's Religions: A Comparative History.* New York: New York University Press, 2008.

Cagliastro, Sorceress. *Blood Sorcery Bible. Volume One: Rituals in Necromancy: A Treatment on the Science of Blood & Magnetics as They Pertain to Blood Sorcery and Necromancy.* Tempe, AZ: The Original Falcon Press, 2011.

Caldecott, Moyra. *Ghost of Akhenaten.* Bath, UK: Mushroom Publishing, 2003.

Cavendish, Richard. *The Black Arts.* New York: TarcherPerigee, 1983.

Chambers, Robert. *The Popular Rhymes of Scotland, with Illustrations, Collected from Tradition.* Edinburgh: James Duncan; London: William Hunter, C. Smith & Co, 1826.

Coleman, Graham, and Thupten Jinpa, eds. *The Tibetan Book of the Dead: First Complete Translation*. New York: Penguin Classics, 2007.

Coleman, Martin. *Communing with the Spirits: The Magical Practice of Necromancy Simply and Lucidly Explained, with Full Instructions for the Practice of That Ancient Art*. Philadelphia, PA: Xlibris, 2005.

Corcos, Christine. *Law and Magic: A Collection of Essays*. Durham, N.C: Carolina Academic Press, 2010.

Crowley, Aleister. *Magick in Theory and Practice*. Oxfordshire, UK 1929.

———. *Moonchild*. United Kingdom: Red Wheel Weiser, 1975.

Crowley, Aleister, and Hymenaeus Beta, eds. *The Goetia: The Lesser Key of Solomon the King: Lemegeton, Book I--Clavicula Salomonis Regis*. Translated by Samuel Liddell and MacGregor Mathers. York Beach, ME: Samuel Weiser, 1997.

Crowley, Aleister, Mary Desti, Leila Waddell, and Hymenaeus Beta, eds. *Magick: Liber ABA, Book Four, Parts I-IV*. York Beach, ME: Samuel Weiser, Inc., 1994.

Culpeper, Nicholas. *The English Physitian*. London: Printed by Peter Cole, 1652.

———. *Mr. Culpeper's Ghost, Giving Seasonable Advice to the Lovers of His Writings*. London, 1656.

David, Rosalie A. *Religion and Magic in Ancient Egypt*. London; New York: Penguin Books, 2002.

Davies, Douglas. *Death, Ritual and Belief: The Rhetoric of Funerary Rites*. New York: Bloomsbury Publishing Place, 2017.

Davies, Owen. *Grimoires: A History of Magic Books*. Oxford: Oxford University Press, 2010.

———. *The Haunted: A Social History of Ghosts*. New York: Palgrave Macmillan, 2009.

———. *Popular Magic: Cunning Folk in English History*. London: Hambledon Continuum, 2007.

Desjardins, Georges. *Le Dragon Rouge*. Montréal: Messager Canadien, 1948.

Dickerson, Cody. *The Language of the Corpse: The Power of the Cadaver in Germanic and Icelandic Sorcery*. Richmond Vista, CA: Three Hands Press, 2016.

Dionne, Danielle. *Magickal Mediumship: Partnering with the Ancestors for Healing and Spiritual Development*. Woodbury, MN: Llewellyn Publishing, 2020.

Dods, Marcus. *The City of God. Vol. 1*. Edinburgh: T & T Clark, 1888.

———. *The Works of Aurelius Augustine, Bishop, the City of God, 2 Vols.* Edinburgh: T & T Clark, 1872.

Duffy, Martin. *Rites Necromantic*. Richmond, CA: Three Hands Press, 2020.

Erasmus, Desiderius. *Twenty-Two Select Colloquies*. London, 1689.

Eriksen, Marianne Hem. "Doors to the Dead. The Power of Doorways and Thresholds in Viking Age Scandinavia." *Archaeological Dialogues* 20, no. 2 (November 8, 2013): 187–214. https://doi.org/10.1017/s1380203813000238.

Fanger, Claire. *Conjuring Spirits: Texts and Traditions of Late Medieval Ritual Magic*. Stroud, Gloucestershire: Sutton Publishing Limited, 1999.

———. *Conjuring Spirits: Texts and Traditions of Medieval Ritual Magic*. Stroud, Gloucestershire: Sutton Publishing Limited, 1998.

———. *Invoking Angels: Theurgic Ideas and Practices, Thirteenth to Sixteenth Centuries*. University Park, PA: Pennsylvania State Press, 2012.

Feilberg, H. F. "The Corpse-Door: A Danish Survival." *Folklore* 18, no. 4 (December 31, 1907): 364–75. https://doi.org/10.1080/0015587x.1907.9719792.

Felton, Debbie. *Haunted Greece and Rome: Ghost Stories from Classical Antiquity*. 1st ed. Austin, TX: University of Texas Press, 1999.

Feraro, Shai, and Ethan Doyle White, eds. *Magic and Witchery in the Modern West: Celebrating the Twentieth Anniversary of "The Triumph of The Moon."* Cham, Switzerland: Palgrave Macmillan, 2019.

Flowers, Stephen E. *Icelandic Magic: The Mystery and Power of the Galdrabók Grimoire*. Rochester, NY: Inner Traditions, 2016.

Fortune, Dion. *Dion Fortune's Book of the Dead*. York Beach, ME: Weiser, 2005.

Gardner, Chelsea A. M. "The 'Oracle of the Dead' at Ancient Tainaron: Reconsidering the Literary and Archaeological Evidence." *Hesperia: The Journal of the American School of Classical Studies at Athens* 90, no. 2 (2021): 339. https://doi.org/10.2972/hesperia.90.2.0339.

Gardner, Gerald Brosseau. *Witchcraft Today*. Secaucus, N.J: Citadel Press, 1954.

———. *Witchcraft Today*. Secaucus, N.J: Citadel Press, 2004.

Georges Desjardins. *Le Dragon Rouge*. Montréal: Messager Canadien, 1948.

Giambattista Della Porta. *Natural Magick: (Transcribed from 1658 English Edition) (Magiae Naturalis) by John Baptista Porta (Giambattista Della Porta) (1535-1615): A Neapolitane: In Twenty Books*

(1584 A.D.): Wherein Are Set Fourth All the Riches and Delights of the Natural Sciences. Nuvision Publications, 2005.

Ginzburg, Carlo. *The Night Battles: Witchcraft & Agrarian Cults in the Sixteenth & Seventeenth Centuries.* Baltimore, MD: Johns Hopkins University Press, 1983.

Giralt, Sebastià. "The Manuscript of a Medieval Necromancer: Magic in Occitan and Latin in Ms. Vaticano, BAV, Barb. Lat. 3589." *Revue d'Histoire Des Textes* 9 (January 2014): 221–72. https://doi.org/10.1484/j.rht.1.103640.

———. "Medieval Necromancy, the Art of Controlling Demons | Sciència.cat." www.sciencia.cat, 2006. https://www.sciencia.cat/temes/medieval-necromancy-art-controlling-demons.

Goad, John. *Astrometeorologica.* London, 1686.

Gordon, Stephen. "Necromancy for the Masses? A Printed Version of the Compendium Magiae Innaturalis Nigrae." *Magic, Ritual, and Witchcraft* 13, no. 3 (2018): 340–80. https://doi.org/10.1353/mrw.2018.0045.

Griffith, Peter. *A True Relation of the Horrid Ghost of a Woman, Which Hath Frequently Been Seen in Various Habits, in the House of Nicholas Broaday, at the Three Mariners in Depthford, upon the Third, Fourth and Sixth of This Instant April, 1673.* London, 1673.

Guiley, Rosemary. *The Encyclopedia of Magic and Alchemy.* New York, NY: Facts on File, 2006.

———. *The Encyclopedia of Ghosts and Spirits.* New York, NY: Facts On File, 2009.

Hales, Andrew. "Death as a Metaphor for Ostracism: Social Invincibility, Autopsy, Necromancy, and Resurrection." *Mortality* 23, no. 4 (October 6, 2017): 366–80. https://doi.org/10.1080/13576275.2017.1382462.

Hall, Trevor H. *Old Conjuring Books: A Bibliographical and Historical Study with a Supplementary Check-List.* New York: St. Martin's Press, 1973.

Harris, Eleanor, and Philip Harris. *The Crafting & Use of Ritual Tools: Step-By-Step Instructions for Woodcrafting Religious & Magical Elements.* St. Paul, MN: Llewellyn Publications, 1998.

Headlam, Walter. "Ghost-Raising, Magic, and the Underworld." *The Classical Review* 16, no. 1 (February 1902): 52–61. https://doi.org/10.1017/s0009840x00205362.

Hermes, Trismegistus, and André-Jean Festugière. *Corpus Hermeticum.* Edited by Arthur Darnock. Paris: Les Belles Lettres, 2011.

Homer. *The Iliad*. Translated by A.T. Murray, Ph.D. London: Harvard University Press, 1924.

———. *The Odyssey with an English Translation by A.T. Murray, PH.D. In Two Volumes*. London: William Heinemann, Ltd.; Cambridge, MA: Harvard University Press, 1919.

Honorius, Pope. *The Great Grimoire of Pope Honorius*. Seattle, WA: Trident Books, I. E.,1998.

Hornung, Erik. *Akhenaten and the Religion of Light*. Ithaca, NY: Cornell University Press, 1999.

Hunter, Devin. *The Witch's Book of Spirits*. Woodbury, MN: Llewellyn Publications, 2017.

James VI and I. *Daemonologie*. Edinburgh, 1597.

Johnson, Brian. *Necromancy in the Medici Library: An Edition and Translation of Excerpts from Biblioteca Medicea Laurenziana, MS Plut. 89 Sup. 38*. Hadean Press Limited, 2021.

Johnson, Ph.D., Thomas. *The Graveyard Wanderers: The Wise Ones + the Dead in Sweden*. 1st ed. Society of Esoteric Endeavour, 2013.

———. *Svartkonstböcker: A Compendium of the Swedish Black Art Book Tradition*. Revelore Press, 2019.

Johnston, Sarah Iles. *Restless Dead: Encounters between the Living and the Dead in Ancient Greece*. Berkeley, CA: University of California Press, 2013.

Jones, David, Jason M Wirth, and Michael Schwartz. *The Gift of Logos: Essays in Continental Philosophy*. Newcastle: Cambridge Scholars, 2010.

Jones, Tayari. *An American Marriage: A Novel*. Chapel Hill, NC: Algonquin Books of Chapel Hill, 2019.

Jung, C. G. Edited by Roderick Main. *On Synchronicity and the Paranormal*. Edited by Roderick Main. Princeton, N.J: Princeton University Press, 1997.

Jung, C. G., Herbert Read, Michael Scott, and Gerhard Adler. *The Collected Works of C.G. Jung*. Princeton, NJ: Princeton University Press, 1973.

Keppler, Joachim. "The Role of the Brain in Conscious Processes: A New Way of Looking at the Neural Correlates of Consciousness." *Frontiers in Psychology* 9 (August 3, 2018). https://doi.org/10.3389/fpsyg.2018.01346.

Kieckhefer, Richard. *Forbidden Rites: A Necromancer's Manual of the Fifteenth Century /*. Stroud: Sutton, 1997.

———. *Magic in the Middle Ages*. Cambridge: Cambridge University Press, 2014.

Kiesel, William F. *Magic Circles in the Grimoire Tradition*. Richmond, CA: Three Hands Press, 2012.

Kim, Daewoung. "Dying for a Better Life: South Koreans Fake Their Funerals for Life Lessons." www.reuters.com. Reuters, November 6, 2019. https://www.reuters.com/article/us-southkorea-living-funerals/dying-for-a-better-life-south-koreans-fake-their-funer-als-for-life-lessons-iduskbn1xg038.

Klaassen, Frank F., and Sharon Hubbs Wright. *The Transformations of Magic: Illicit Learned Magic in the Later Middle Ages and Renaissance*. University Park, PA: Pennsylvania State University Press, 2013.

Klaassen, Frank, and Sharon Hubbs Wright. *The Magic of Rogues: Necromancers in Early Tudor England*. University Park, PA: The Pennsylvania State University Press, 2021.

Koetting, E. A. *Works of Darkness*. Edited by Timothy Donaghue. Independently Published, 2018.

Lang, Benedek. *Unlocked Books: Manuscripts of Learned Magic in the Medieval Libraries of Central Europe*. University Park, PA: Penn State University Press, 2010.

Leahy, Arthur Herbert. *Heroic Romances of Ireland: In Two Volumes. 2.* Vol. 2. London: Nutt, 1906.

Lecouteux, Claude. *The Pagan Book of the Dead: Ancestral Visions of the Afterlife and Other Worlds*. Rochester, VT: Inner Traditions, 2020.

———. *The Return of the Dead*. Rochester, VT: Inner Traditions, 2009.

Lehnert, Bo. "Zero Point Energy as Origin of Dark Energy and Dark Matter." *Joint ITER-IAEA-ICTP Advanced Workshop on Fusion and Plasma Physics: AIP Conference Proceedings* 1445 (2012). https://doi.org/10.1063/1.3701891.

Lévi, Éliphas. *The Doctrine and Ritual of High Magic: A New Translation*. Translated by John Michael Greer and Mark Anthony Mikituk. New York, NY: TarcherPerigee, 2017.

———. *Transcendental Magic*. Newburyport, MA: Red Wheel/Weiser, 1968.

LifeSource. "Honor Walk Resources." LifeSource, n.d. https://www.life-source.org/partners/hospitals/honor-walk-resources/.

Lovitt, Sean. "The Book, the Mirror, and the Living Dead: Necromancy and the Early Modern Period." Unpublished Masters Thesis, 2009.

Macdonald, Michael. *Mystical Bedlam: Madness, Anxiety, and Healing in Seventeenth-Century England.* Cambridge: Cambridge University Press, 1981.

Macdonald, Michael, and Terence R Murphy. *Sleepless Souls: Suicide in Early Modern England.* Oxford: Clarendon Press, 1990.

Macfarlane, Alan. *Death and the Demographic Transition: A Note on English Evidence on Death 1500-1750' in S.C. Humphreys & H. King (Eds.), Mortality and Immortality: The Anthropology and Archaeology of Death.* London: Penguin, 1981.

Mackin Roberts, Ellie. *Underworld Gods in Ancient Greek Religion: Death and Reciprocity.* Abingdon, Oxon; New York, NY: Routledge, 2020.

Major, Joanne. "A Helpful Eighteenth-Century Ghost." All Things Georgian. Last Updated October 27, 2015. https://georgianera. wordpress.com/2015/10/27/a-helpful-eighteenth-century-ghost/.

Mankey, Jason. *Transformative Witchcraft: The Greater Mysteries.* Woodbury, MN: Llewellyn Publications, 2019.

Manniche, Lise. *The Akhenaten Colossi of Karnak.* American University in Cairo Press -05-01, 2010.

Manville, H. "Additions and Corrections to Thompson's Inventory and Brown and Dolley's Coin Hoards - Part 1." *British Numismatic Journal* 63 (1993): 91–113. https://www.britnumsoc.org/ publications/Digital%20BNJ/pdfs/1993_BNJ_63_9.pdf.

Mather, Cotton. *Magnalia Christi Americana: Or, the Ecclesiastical History of New-England, from Its First Planting in the Year 1620. Unto the Year of Our Lord, 1698. In Seven Books.* Vol. II. London: Thomas Parkhurst, at the Bible and Three Crowns in Cheapside, 1702.

Mortellus. *Do I Have to Wear Black? Rituals, Customs & Funerary Etiquette for Modern Pagans.* Woodbury, MN: Llewellyn Publications, 2021.

Moss, Robert. *The Dreamer's Book of the Dead: A Soul Traveler's Guide to Death, Dying, and the Other Side.* Rochester, VT: Destiny Books, 2005.

Nardo, Don. *Living in Ancient Egypt.* San Diego, CA: Greenhaven Press, 2004.

Novak, Peter. *The Lost Secret of Death: Our Divided Souls and the Afterlife.* Charlottesville, VA: Hampton Roads Pub, 2003.

Oberon, Aaron. *Southern Cunning: Folkloric Witchcraft in the American South.* Winchester England; Washington: Moon Books, 2019.

Ogden, Daniel. *Greek and Roman Necromancy.* Princeton, N.J: Princeton University Press, 2005.

———. *Magic, Witchcraft, and Ghosts in the Greek and Roman Worlds: A Sourcebook*. Oxford; New York: Oxford University Press, 2009.

———. *Night's Black Agents: Witches, Wizards and the Dead in the Ancient World*. London: Hambledon Continuum, 2008.

Owens, Susan. *The Ghost: A Cultural History*. London: Tate Publishing, 2019.

Oxford. "Bodleian Library MS. Rawl. D. 252." digital.bodleian.ox.ac. uk. Accessed April 28, 2021. https://digital.bodleian.ox.ac.uk/ objects/3d223534-59cf-4af6-ad3a-5be422a31e83/.

Page, Sophie, and Catherine Rider. *The Routledge History of Medieval Magic*. London; New York: Routledge, Taylor & Francis Group, 2019.

Paget, R. F. *In the Footsteps of Orpheus the Discovery of the Ancient Greek Underworld*. R. Hale, 1967.

Pennick, Nigel. *Secrets of East Anglian Magic*. London: Robert Hale, 1995.

Peterson, Joseph H. *Arbatel. Concerning the Magic of the Ancients: Original Sourcebook of Angel Magic*. Newburyport, MA: Ibis Press, 2009.

———. *Grimorium Verum: A Handbook of Black Magic*. Scotts Valley, CA: CreateSpace, 2007.

Pitcairn, Robert, and Bannatyne Club. *Ancient Criminal Trials in Scotland*. Edinburgh: Printed for the Maitland Club, 1833.

Plato and R. Hackforth. *Plato's Phaedrus: A Dialogue*. Cambridge, UK: Cambridge University Press, 1952.

Pliny, the Elder, Philemon Holland, and Adam Islip. *The Historie of the Vvorld: Commonly Called, the Natvrall Historie of C. Plinivs Secvndvs*. Vol. 2. London: Printed by Adam Islip, 1634.

Pócs, Éva. *Between the Living and the Dead: A Perspective on Witches and Seers in the Early Modern Age*. Budapest: Central European University Press, 2000.

———. *Body, Soul, Spirits, and Supernatural Communication*. Newcastle Upon Tyne: Cambridge Scholars Publishing, 2019.

Pócs, Éva, and Gábor Klaniczay, eds. *Communicating with the Spirits*. Budapest; New York: Central European University Press, 2005.

Porta, Giambattista della. *Natural Magick: (Transcribed from 1658 English Edition) (Magiae Naturalis) by John Baptista Porta (Giambattista Della Porta) (1535-1615): A Neapolitane: In Twenty Books (1584 A.D.): Wherein Are Set Fourth All the Riches and Delights of the Natural Sciences*. Nuvision Publications, 2005.

Pu, Muzhou. *Rethinking Ghosts in World Religions*. Leiden, Netherlands: Brill, 2009.

Puckle, Bertram S., and Tarl Warwick. *Funeral Customs: Their Origin and Development*. United States: Createspace Independent Publishing Platform, 2017.

Reynolds, Sean K. *Pathfinder Campaign Setting: Inner Sea Gods*. Edited by Paizo Staff. Paizo Inc., 2014.

Rivera-Garza, Cristina. *The Restless Dead: Necrowriting and Disappropriation*. Translated by Robin Myers. Nashville, Tennessee: Vanderbilt University Press, 2020.

Robben, Antonius C. G. M. *Death, Mourning, and Burial: A Cross-Cultural Reader*. Malden, MA: Blackwell Pub, 2004.

Rohde, Erwin, and W. B. Hillis. *Psyche: The Cult of Souls and Belief in Immortality among the Greeks*. Eugene, OR: Wipf & Stock, 2006.

Rohr, Richard. *Everything Belongs: The Gift of Contemplative Prayer*. New York: Crossroad Publishing, 2003.

Ruickbie, Leo. *Witchcraft out of the Shadows: A Complete History*. London: Robert Hale, 2011.

Sanchez, Claudio, and Chondra Echert. *The Amory Wars Series*. Los Angeles, CA: BOOM! Studios, 2012.

Schmidt, Brian B. "Israel's Beneficent Dead: Ancestor Cult and Necromancy in Ancient Israelite Religion and Tradition." *The Jewish Quarterly Review* 88, no. 1/2 (July 1997): 91. https://doi.org/10.2307/1455071.

Schulke, Daniel A. *Veneficium: Magic, Witchcraft and the Poison Path*. Richmond, CA: Three Hands Press, 2017.

———. *Viridarium Umbris: The Pleasure Garden of Shadow*. Xoanon, 2005.

Scot, Reginald. *The Discovery of Witchcraft*. London: Printed for Andrew Clark and Are to Be Sold at Mris. Cotes's near the Golden-Ball in Aldersgatestreet, 1665.

Serrano, Alessandra. "Edison's Necrophone." Seiðr: University of Tromsø, October 31, 2017. http://www.radio-science.net/2017/10/edisons-necrophone.html.

Sewell, Elizabeth Missing. *Popular History of France, to the Death of Louis XIV*. (n.p.), 1876.

Shakespeare, William. *Henry V. As You Like It, Much Ado about Nothing. Hamlet*. P. F. Collier & Sons, 1912.

Siculus, Diodorus, Immanel Bekker, and Ludwig Dindorf. *Diodori Bibliotheca Historica, Vol 1-2*. Leipzig: In Aedibus B. G. Teubneri, 1888.

Skinner, Stephen. *Grimoire of St. Cyprian: Clavis Inferni*. Woodbury, MN: Llewellyn Publications, 2018.

Strongman, Luke. "Conscious States of Dreaming." *The Journal of Mind and Behavior* 35, no. 4 (2014): 189–200.

Suster, Gerald, ed. *John Dee: Essential Readings*. Berkeley, CA: North Atlantic Books, 2003.

Switek, Brian. *Skeleton Keys: The Secret Life of Bone*. New York: Riverhead Books, 2020.

Taunton, Gwendolyn. *The Path of Shadows: Chthonic Gods, Oneiromancy & Necromancy in Ancient Greece*. Colac, Victoria: Manticore Press, 2018.

Taylor, John H. *Ancient Egyptian Book of the Dead: Journey through the Afterlife; [Exhibition at the British Museum from 4 November 2010 to 6 March 2011]*. London: British Museum Press, 2010.

———. *Death and the Afterlife in Ancient Egypt*. Chicago: University of Chicago Press, 2001.

The Metropolitan Museum of Art. "Twenty-Sided Die (Icosahedron) with Faces Inscribed with Greek Letters." Metmuseum.org, 2020. https://www.metmuseum.org/art/collection/search/551072.

Thomas, Keith. *Religion and the Decline of Magic: Studies in Popular Beliefs in Sixteenth and Seventeenth-Century England*. London: Penguin, 1991.

Thomas, Richard F., and Jan M. Ziolkowski. "Sychaeus." In *The Virgil Encyclopedia*. Chichester, UK: Wiley Blackwell, 2013.

Thorndike, Lynn. *A History of Magic and Experimental Science*. Vol. 1–8. New York; London: Columbia University Press, 1923.

tvtropes.org. "Necromancer." TV Tropes, 2021. https://tvtropes.org/pmwiki/pmwiki.php/Main/Necromancer.

Vaidyanath Shastri. *The Atharva Veda*. New Delhi: Sarvadeshik Arya Pratinidhi Sabha, 1984.

Valiente, Doreen. *The Rebirth of Witchcraft*. London: Robert Hale, 2007.

Vaudoise, Mallorie. *Honoring Your Ancestors: A Guide to Ancestral Veneration*. Woodbury, MN: Llewellyn Publications, 2019.

Vergilius Maro. *The Works of Virgil*. United Kingdom: University of Bern, 1853.

Virgil. *Virgil: Eclogues. Georgics. Aeneid I–VI Vol 1*. Translated by H. Rushton Fairclough. Vol. 1. William Heinemann. G.P. Putnam's Sons, 1916.

Waite, Arthur Edward. *The Book of Black Magic and Ceremonial Magic*. San Diego, CA.: Book Tree, 2006.

————. *The Book of Black Magic and of Pacts: Including the Rites and Mysteries of Goëtic Theurgy, Sorcery, and Infernal Necromancy.* San Francisco, CA: Weiser Books, 2008.

————. *The Book of Ceremonial Magic, Or, the Book of Black Magic and of Pacts.* Calgary, Alberta: Theophania Publishing, 2011.

Walter, Thomas. *The Work of the Dead: A Cultural History of Mortal Remains.* Princeton, NJ: Princeton University Press, 2018.

Welcome to Night Vale. 2012 "Twitter Post." "When a person dies and no one will miss them, the mourning is assigned to a random human. This is why you sometimes just feel sad." Twitter, November 12, 2012 9:33 a.m. https://twitter.com/NightValeRadio/status/268013658825703424.

Whittemore, Susan, and Denton Cooley. *The Circulatory System.* Facts On File, Incorporated, 2014.

Wilson, Stephen. *The Magical Universe: Everyday Ritual and Magic in Pre-Modern Europe.* New York: Hambledon and London, 2004.

Zawacki, Neil, and James Dignan. *How to Be a Villain: Evil Laughs, Secret Lairs, Master Plans, and More!!!* San Francisco, CA: Chronicle Books, 2003.

INDEX

C

Y

Z

MORE BY CROSSED CROW BOOKS

Learn more at
www.CrossedCrowBooks.com